TODDLER TWINS

Practical Parenting During the Toddler Years

Complied by the Editors of **TWINS** Magazine

Publisher: Donald E.L. Johnson
Editor-in-Chief: Susan J. Alt
Managing Editor: Sharon Withers
Assistant Editor: Jennifer Luzum
Art Director: Michelle Eberle
Proofreader: Eric Brian

TWINS® Magazine

The Business Word, Inc.
5350 S. Roslyn Street, Suite 400,
Englewood, Colorado 80111-2125

COVER PHOTOS (clockwise)

Zachary and Nicholas Menning
Submitted by Lori Menning, Germantown, Tennessee

Gunnar and Raelyn Schnappauf
Submitted by Laura Schnappauf, Pt. Pleasant, New Jersey

Alyssa and Erikka Arno
Submitted by Sandy Arno, East Amherst, New York

Table of Contents

CHAPTER 7 Language Development

CHAPTER 8 Emotional Development

CHAPTER 9 Play and Creativity

CHAPTER 10 Parenting Guidelines

CHAPTER 11 Growing Stages—Practical Parenting Tips

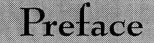

Having twins requires special qualities in every parent—more patience, more endurance, more energy, more organization, more time management. When your twins hit the toddler years, be prepared to move even faster than when they were babies. And be prepared for interesting challenges that arise simply because you have two children eager to move, eager to learn, and eager to engage each other creatively.

Toddler twins provide clear evidence that 1+1 equals more than 2. Twins do, indeed, equal three or more. They play off each other, often acquiring new skills very rapidly because of their interaction. They engage in mischief that is beyond belief. Toddlers will climb up and onto everything in sight—they can scale proverbial mountains just by helping each other figure out how to do it.

Hence, Rule #1 for parents of toddler twins: Nail down, screw down, and firmly attach every piece of furniture, every television set, every stereo set, every cabinet in the house to the floor with brackets, and to the walls with brackets or cables. Two babies will be climbing up them before you know it.

Reconcile yourself to having your twins' "creative" energy displayed on your floors, your walls and other strange places—on bedsheets, furniture, mirrors, on the twins' bodies—almost any place other than where you normally would expect to find scribbles, drawings and paintings.

Hence, Rule #2: Make sure walls and carpets are washable. You can always paper the walls with extra wide shelf paper perfect for drawings and paintings. And change the paper periodically.

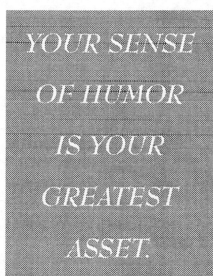

YOUR SENSE OF HUMOR IS YOUR GREATEST ASSET.

Your sense of humor is your greatest asset. Instead of pulling out your hair and screaming, sit down and laugh with your kids, and have conversations with them about what's fun and funny versus what might hurt them and is cause for scoldings or punishments.

You will glory in watching the speed with which your twins teach each other new things. Children's minds are wondrous when they are young—your twins are doubly wondrous because of the learning-synergy they create. Sometimes you will be amazed at what they can learn—and teach each other—in only one day.

Grown twins almost universally look back at their childhoods and recall that the best thing about having a twin is having a built-in playmate who is always nearby. As a parent, you can encourage their creative interplay by having various "props" at the ready that will encourage them to make up games, tell each other stories, and use their imaginations.

Parents are always looking for developmental benchmarks to guide them with their twins. In this volume of the Twinship Sourcebook, called Toddler Twins, we have compiled many of the best articles from 15 years of TWINS Magazine to help you understand the milestones to watch for and the opportunities to seize as your children grow physically, learn to use language, and develop their emotional capabilities.

Some parents find it's essential to have two of many toys; others say "Never!" You'll find what's right for you and your twins, but we want you to have guideposts along the way when dealing with playtime issues. You are not alone, and this collection presents you with the opportunity to learn from the lessons many other parents of twins generously shared about their own experiences.

All children go through phases when they bite, when they fight, when they compete ferociously with other children, and when they're difficult to discipline. Twins can magnify these situations and phases. They can present you with a particularly thorny set of issues related to helping each child develop a healthy sense of self-identity. Just about the time you've begun to figure out what works, their developing identities will flip-flop and you'll find yourself totally confused. But even that is a good thing, and as a parent, you will find yourself encouraging the flip-flopping of traits and behaviors in your young twins.

Above all, you'll find help in the sections at the back of this Sourcebook, Volume 2, that present useful, practical parenting guidelines and tips on everything from nap times to keeping shoes in pairs and saving baby teeth.

Enjoy your toddler twins!

And visit us at **www.TWINSmagazine.com** for even more useful information that you'll put into practice right away. Post your questions and get answers from other parents of twins. Find helpful solutions to some of the really tough parenting questions in Family Talk. And use the Multi-Poll to share your answers, adventures, and even doubts and worries; it has new questions every week.

We'll be waiting to hear from you.

Susan J. Alt
The Editor
TWINS Magazine

Chapter 1

BITING AND FIGHTING

Setting Limits—No Biting Please!

By Alice M. Vollmar

I was watching my twins in the mirror and could tell they were getting frustrated riding in the car. Then each twin lifted up her forearm and at precisely the same moment bit her own arm!"

That's when she knew it was frustration that caused her twins to bite, recalls Barb Clark, mother of identical twins, Kristin and Katie, now 8 years old. That incident occurred when Clark's twins were about a year old, during a one-year span when they also bit each other. "There were many biting incidents between the ages of 1 and 2. I tried lots of things, but a strategy recommended by our doctor worked best. He told us to watch them and if we saw them becoming frustrated, to redirect them," Clark says. To her relief, Kristin and Katie eventually began working things out on their own—without biting.

WHY CHILDREN BITE

"The reason a child bites varies with age," says Lynn Galle, director of the Shirley G. Moore Laboratory School at the University of Minnesota, and coordinator of the Early Childhood Teacher Training Program. "An infant bites because her gums hurt and biting gives relief. Sometimes infants bite as a way of exploring the world. For example, it can be an attempt to get another child out of the way, much as the toddler would push or shove something. Or it might be a misguided social overture, with the intention of being friendly to another child.

"Usually, biting abates with the advent of language skills. However, if a 4- or 5-year-old child is still biting, it's a different problem," Galle continues. "If it is a chronic problem, parents need to get information about situations when the child is biting, state in a calm but firm voice that he can't bite people, then tell him what he can do in such situations. A good solution is to tell the child, 'When you feel like biting, scream as loud as you can and I'll get over there and help you.'"

The goal is to "give a child a dramatic way to impact the environment without biting," Galle instructs, noting that the most effective substitute carries an element of instant drama similar to that of a bite. "The parent communicates that I, the adult, will help you, the child, to gain control of the situation and learn a different way to deal with your feelings so that you don't need to bite."

PREVENTING BITING

Parents can monitor their multiples and note the circumstances that provoke biting. Separate the children when they are getting tired, saying, "It's getting crowded. Let's move over here so you have more room to play," and other strategies. Your multiples will gradually learn to evaluate a situation and initiate changes themselves.

The success of this approach depends upon positive parental involvement.

That's the strategy MaryBeth Funder is adopting with her 1 1/2-year-old identical twins, Jacob and Justin. Funder's twins like to wrestle and, sometimes when wrestling, biting occurs. The first biting episodes happened when the boys were about 8 or 9 months old.

"It was as though Jacob thought he was kissing, but instead he'd bite Justin on the back or the cheeks," Funder recalls. "The biting had stopped by 9 1/2 months, but Jacob has recently started biting again. Now, I try to keep them from wrestling with one another and get them involved with books or a video, or I give them a snack and something to drink."

Taking action

• When biting occurs:

• Take a deep breath; stay calm.

• Attend to the bitten child first.

• Tell the biter in a firm but calm voice, "You cannot bite people. I will help you learn not to bite."

To prevent recurrent biting:

• Monitor and redirect activities

• Intervene before biting occurs.

A few suggestions

To ovoid aggressive behavior, follow these suggestions offered by Arlene Eisenberg, Heide E. Murkoff and Sondee E. Hodhoway, B.S.N., in their book, What To Expect: The Toddler Years:

• Communicate clearly that aggressive behavior is not acceptable.

• Model nonaggressive behavior. Redirect activities and intervene calmly rather than spanking, slapping, pinching, jerking or yelling at a child.

• Set behavior limits and supply structure for activities.

• Notice and comment on desirable behavior.

• Stop undesirable behavior with a minimum of fuss.

• Encourage your multiples to use words to express their feelings.

• Offer alternative ways to vent frustration and anger, such as drumming tools, running games, riding toys or playground outings.

• Initiate new activities and a change of pace before boredom sets in.

• Help your multiples learn social and life skills to lessen frustration.

• Include soothing activities daily, such as singing, reading and rocking.

• Intervene when your multiples' social or verbal skills are inadequate to handle their frustrations.

• Supervise play activities.

YOUR RESPONSE MATTERS

Parents need to be calm in responding to biting—but that's not easy, says Linda Hallquist, mother of fraternal twins, Jessica and Amanda. "I didn't handle it well at first. In fact, I overreacted and that made things worse. I've learned to keep my reaction under control. I know it's not the end of the world, but it is a frustration not knowing what to do."

Most parents agree it's wise to reassure the bitten child first, before dealing with the biter. This helps the parent cool off a bit and not react so forcefully. Child development expert T. Berry Brazelton, M.D., notes in his book, *Touchpoints*, that "apparently aggressive behaviors (including hair pulling and biting) do not start out as aggressive. They occur at times when the child is overwhelmed and loses control. After it happens, the aggressor is as horrified as the recipient."

Dr. Brazelton discourages parents from biting a child back. "The issue is to teach her calmly about the unacceptability of this behavior and to try to give her an acceptable substitute, such as a toy to bang—a way to work it out." Similarly, Galle does not recommend spanking or punitive measures. "Then you are teaching them to counteract negative behavior with negative behavior."

FOCUSING ON HELP

Few things get such a strong reaction as biting," Galle says, "and because of that, a child can learn that this strategy works." It's up to us as adults to be vigilant until the biting ends and to help the child control his bad behavior.

Galle insists punishment is not always an appropriate solution and that the redirection of daily activities, avoiding situations in which biting has occurred in the past and helping your multiples come up with substitutes for biting are more effective than physical punishment, blaming or lectures. ♥

Taking the Ouch out of Biting Battles

By Janet Gonzalez-Mena

Because toddlers do not yet have sufficient command of their language skills to be able to express themselves verbally, they often use their mouths in a very direct way—by biting—to get their point across. The different feelings that they try to express through biting include:

- **Love.** Because they are at an egocentric stage in which they can't perceive the feelings of others, "sinking their teeth" into a beloved person makes sense to them because it feels so good.
- **Curiosity.** Toddlers may be wondering, for example, what their co-twins' arm tastes like or what would happen if they did bite their co-twin.
- **Anger or frustration.** According to Stacee Harrell of San Jose, California, mother of 3-year-old twin boys, "The worst period of biting happened right before Cody and Chase started talking—between 12 and 18 months of age. I noticed that they bit most when they couldn't communicate their feelings and frustrations."

Because they spend so much time together and are both the same age, co-twins may exhibit this behavior more frequently than singleton siblings.

- **Power.** A toddler quickly learns that by biting an older child, she can cause him to suddenly stop his teasing or by biting her co-twin, he will give up the toy with which he was playing.

In addition, she realizes that biting used to express power often elicits some sort of response from her parents. Once a toddler learns this lesson, it's difficult for her parents to get her to cease her biting behavior.

WHAT'S A PARENT TO DO?

In light of the "allure" that biting holds, it seems apparent that the best method for stopping biting is to prevent it from occurring. Because biting is rewarding for many toddlers, the best way to remove the reward is to intercede before the behavior occurs. Nothing that a parent can do afterward is nearly as effective as putting out her hand and physically arresting the intended bite. By doing so, a parent provides the control her toddlers lack, which is comforting to both the biter and his potential victim. In addition, a parent is providing a sense of security through her action that implies, "I won't let you hurt each other."

Other useful techniques to prevent your twins from biting each other include:

- Give your biter an alternative, inanimate object to bite, such as a washcloth, teething ring or plastic toy to satisfy his curiosity about the way things taste and feel.
- Stop biting, nibbling and playfully chewing on your twins if it seems to result in their biting each other.

Sometimes parents of multiples unknowingly model biting behavior when they gently and playfully nibble their twins' fingers and toes, or when they "gobble up" their children's tummies. However, this can result in biting on the part of toddlers that is less than pleasant and fun; they don't know the damage their sharp little teeth can do!

- Model and teach expression of feelings. For example, show your twins how to take out their aggression and frustration in ways other than biting, such as hitting pillows. Also, teach them the language that they need to express their feelings, such as: "I don't like it when you bite me. It makes me angry."
- Find ways to help your multiples assert themselves without biting. In addition, protect your toddler twins from older children and siblings who dominate, tease or hurt them; doing so will help them be less likely to bite as a form of self-defense.
- Be nearby when you sense that your co-twins may be prone to biting each other. Harrell remarked, "I can tell when Cody and Chase are having problems. I just separate them until they can talk to each other. They hate to be separated, so this method is quite effective. I have always told them that it's OK to be angry, but that biting is not allowed. It did take them

awhile to learn the words to express their anger."

- Separate your twins regularly, even when biting doesn't appear to be imminent. "They need opportunities to play alone so they're not always in each other's space," noted Ann Dutson, of Sonoma, California, mother of fraternal toddler twins, Devin and Dianne.

- Give your children feedback about the effects of their actions by explaining that biting hurts the person being bitten. In addition, model gentle behavior and appropriate expressions of affection.

- Refrain from giving your child who bites the attention he is trying to gain from his actions; attention only reinforces his biting behavior. It's also important not to turn all your attention to the child who has been bitten, either, because it can promote victim behavior. It's best to handle the situation calmly, without making a fuss over either of them. However, give them both attention when they are not biting so that they will not feel the need to misbehave to get attention. 💗

Why Your Twins Bite . . . Each Other

By Adam P. Matheny, Jr., Ph.D.

There is no doubt about the fact that an infant's teeth can be used aggressively, a fact that is justifiably unsettling to the parents of the "biters" and the parents of the "bitten." The relationship between having teeth and using teeth to bite others should not imply that the infant is aggressive, however. Nor does it mean that an infant who bites will be more likely to bite at later ages.

In fact, it is natural for a teething infant to sometimes bite others. Gnawing or chewing on objects is part of the teething process, and an infant cannot easily discriminate between another person's ear, cheek or finger and a teething ring, toy or other inanimate object. Moreover, some infants like to have their gums firmly pressed on or vigorously rubbed to relieve pressure caused by teething. It is therefore difficult for an infant to learn that the finger or knuckle offered for chewing is not to be used some other time for biting.

Some infants pick up their biting habit from their parents, who may take little pretend, funloving "nibbles" from their infants' fingers, toes, ears or cheeks! In these instances, the imitative infant is provided with a seemingly innocent model for doing the wrong thing.

Biting may also be fostered by the drama that takes place when the infant takes a nip at an unsuspecting parent or child. Imagine the sense of discovery when the infant learns that by biting someone, he has gained power and control. When co-twins start to bite each other, for example, there is a commotion often more dramatic than knocking blocks down, throwing toys or creating the usual chaos. Even if the consequences are unpleasant, the potential message to the infant is that he can "make the world move" by biting.

Some infants also learn to use their teeth as tools—to take things apart and to change the

When Do Teeth Emerge?

The eruption of an infant's first tooth and the growth of teeth thereafter seem to follow a pattern dictated by that infant's physical endowments. The plan may be guided by genetic heritage, as evidenced by the similarity of teething patterns of identical twins.

With due regard for individual teething patterns, there is a universal "plan" for teething. The usual order of eruption begins with the lower central incisors which usually appear between 5 and 10 months of age for 67% of infants. The upper central incisors are likely to emerge next at about 9 to 10 months of age, and are followed by the upper and lower lateral incisors at about 1 year of age.

Because an infant obtains a complement of 20 teeth by 3 years of age, it is easy to see why teething, especially if it is a difficult process, is a preoccupation of many parents.

shape of objects. When the infant takes a bite from a piece of cracker, he has embarked on a modest path to creative discoveries. But again, the infant is a poor discriminator between objects and flesh as creative media.

There may be infants who bite to gain someone's attention. In this instance, biting serves the same purpose as whining or crying, except that biting is a more powerful attention-getter. While this negativistic manner of gaining others' attention is more typical of older children, we cannot rule out the possibility that some infants learn that if they bite, others pay attention.

Finally, it is possible that some infants are just more likely to bite. Since, statistically, male children are more likely to be biters, perhaps the biting behavior is just one aspect of the prevailing picture, one in which more aggressive patterns of activities are noted for boys.

Dr. Judith Garrard, of the University of Minnesota, recently reported that male children in a day care center were also more likely to be bitten. One suspects that more boys engage in bouts of biting each other than girls, verified by some of the University of Louisville Twin Study mothers' reports that it is the boy twin pairs who engage in these alarming encounters.

Studies of infants have not established a connection between biting during infancy and biting at later ages. As a consequence, it is not known whether boy toddlers or preschoolers were infants prone to bite or, for that matter, were infants who teethed early.

Nevertheless, if the infant bites, his parents should not over react. There is nothing to be gained from biting the infant "to show that it hurts." Shouting or spanking are not effective, either, in controlling the problem.

Any of these reactions potentially teaches the infant how he can control attention and events by biting someone, no matter how unpleasant the consequences of that behavior. A perceptive infant may even learn that even an infant can produce pain in others. The best solution, if the infant looks like he is going to bite, is simply to move the opportunity away.

If co-twins start to bite each other, they should be separated and diverted with another activity. Should the twins start the habit of frequent biting, temporary separation to different areas of the house may be called for so that the copycat biting pattern is prevented. By all means, try not to leave the twins alone with each other for extended periods.

Modeling appropriate ways to interact with people (without biting!) provides the right example for babies to imitate. Be specific in praising the infant(s) who is refraining from biting, as well. ♥

Squabbling: Should Parents Intervene?

By Janet Gonzalez-Mena

hile squabbling over possession of a toy or a position on their parent's lap, for example, twins can learn important social skills, such as negotiation and compromise. They can acquire these skills by being left alone to work out their problems, as well as through parental intervention.

How does a parent know when to intervene? When do toddler twins need help in ironing out their differences, and when can squabblers be left to resolve their own squabbles? Sometimes wrestling and arguing the way puppies roll around with each other is pleasurable! These "play fights" usually need no adult intervention.

Other squabbles are real, but short-lived quarrels, if they are ignored by adults. For example, children in the toddler age group feel strongly about possessing something for a few seconds, but once one child has it, he may abandon the contested object without even playing with it. These kinds of struggles are not worth parental interference unless damage is imminent.

Terry Duncan, the mother of 3-year-old twin girls said, "I often let my girls fight it out and I don't interfere. I used to have to intervene a lot when they were younger because they got more physical. They would really get going over who got to sit next to Mommy or who had what toy. I had to be careful that they didn't hurt each other. Now I don't have to watch them so closely because they do more talking—teasing and arguing—than they do physical fighting." Terry's rule of thumb is to intervene when one of the twins is in danger of being hurt.

Sometimes squabbling has less to do with the twins' relationship than it has to do with getting attention. If this is the case, one approach may be to ignore the arguing by turning one's back and walking way from the children.

Sometimes the squabbling gets worse when one tries to ignore it. Duncan commented, "When others are around, the arguing begins. It often happens when my husband and I finally get a chance to sit down and talk about our day."

If ignoring the squabble doesn't make it stop, and it is continuing to be too irritating for parents to ignore, they should quickly stop the fight while not giving their children much attention, to avoid teaching them that squabbling is the way to get their parents to focus on them. For example, Duncan simply takes dinner away if her girls begin bickering at the dinner table. She says her girls know that their arguing is one behavior that their mother will not tolerate.

If you are looking for ways to constructively intervene in your children's squabbles, try these suggestions:

1) Help your children "talk through their problems" while you provide the matter-of-fact, firm control they may need to keep them from hurting each other. Allow them to express their feelings to you even if their emotions are strong.

2) Don't get caught up in your children's feelings. Remain detached, calm, and slightly apart from the situation when you intervene.

3) Try to help your twins feel safe—both physically and psychologically. It is easy to see why parents should stop physical hurts—they don't want their children hurt.

Saying angry and hurtful things to one another can cause psychological harm. Twins have a "lifetime relationship" and early fights can leave permanent scars; parents need to intervene when their children's anger becomes harmful.

4) Help children learn to express strong emotions in ways that communicate their feelings without causing physical or psychological damage. For example, teach them to say, "I'm so mad at you right now that I feel like hitting!" instead of actually hitting, or, "I'm mad because you took my toy" instead of, "You're mean and ugly and selfish."

Of course, toddlers don't use words like these very much—they most often use physical actions and simple name calling. But they will soon pick up their parents' habits, so it is a good idea for you, too, to use the above non-damaging ways of expressing your anger as a model for them to follow.

5) Don't intervene if the squabble is playful, even if it looks serious, unless, of course, someone is about to get hurt.

6) Don't intervene when the purpose of the squabble is to get your attention (unless the fighting bothers you greatly, or if physical or psychological harm is likely).

7) Look at the causes of squabbling and deal with them when possible. Squabbling is often caused by rivalry which, in turn, may be caused by the scarcity of individual attention. If you believe that competition like this is the underlying cause of your twins' fighting, find ways of giving each twin the attention he needs rather than focusing on the squabbling itself.

Knowing what to do about squabbling won't make it go away, nor will growing out of the toddler phase. As long as two people share daily life together, they are bound to have disagreements. Instead of trying to rid your home of all squabbling, teach your twins how to fight fairly and avoid damaging each other. ♥

Chapter 2

COMPETITION AND RIVALRY

Curbing Co-Twin Competition

By Janet Gonzalez-Mena

Sometimes in my parenting classes I hand out apples and ask students to "get to know" the one they receive. This ice-breaker stimulates powers of observation and gets students to focus carefully. When they have gotten thoroughly acquainted, I ask them to "Introduce" their apples to two other people in the room, sharing with them the unique characteristics of their own.

Finally, I have the students put their apples into a basket, and at the end of class I pass it around. The directions are, "Find your apple." They always can, even when there are 40 other apples in the basket.

Lots of wonderful insights come out of this exercise, but the one that sticks with me is the one that came to me when I first experienced the exercise as a participant. I had trouble getting to know my apple without comparing it to another one. This became clear when I started "introducing" my apple to someone else. Immediately I noticed that my apple was bigger and more red. Its color and size were hard for me to define until I had something to measure it against.

I also noticed that when I wasn't comparing, I was focusing on blemishes. My apple's defects were what made it distinctive in my mind—the dent on one side, the bruise near the stem end, etc. When I realized that to find uniqueness I was focusing on imperfection, I felt uncomfortable.

That experience made me realize how limited I am in the way I see things. Imagine what it does to children to be raised by a parent who distinguishes her children mostly by comparing them and by their deficiencies.

Until this exercise, I thought I had done an outstanding job as a parent raising my children in a competition-free environment. I was careful never to compare them to each other because of my own childhood experience: The favorite game in my family had been to compare my sister and me. Since I always came out ahead, you'd wonder why I have such negative feelings about comparisons. Why would the one who was "prettier," "smarter" and "better behaved" complain? I saw what "not measuring up" did to my sister. As the younger one, she couldn't compete with me in any area except virtue, and she refused to do that. She made an early decision to distinguish herself by being the opposite of me in that department.

She became the "bad" one to my "good" girl. We were both trapped by our labels, just because our family insisted on comparing us and holding me up as a model to her. My sister spent her whole childhood getting in trouble. Luckily, she finally outgrew the need to get her attention through inappropriate behavior. Unfortunately, some children never outgrow that need.

Comparisons and labels affected the relationship between my sister and me. We fought a lot—and no wonder! We were entered in a competition not of our choosing.

Even if parents of toddler twins believe competition is healthy, they won't produce good "competitors" by promoting rivalry at home in the early years. The toddler stage is the time to avoid all competition, if children are to build the self-esteem necessary to make it in this dog-eat-dog world.

The job of twins at this age is to come to see themselves as unique individuals, each with special areas of strengths. Promoting competition between them doesn't accomplish this purpose, but rather hooks them into "besting" each other without regard to their own talents and interests. Worse, competition produces winners and losers. Toddlers are hurt when they incorporate "loser" into their self-image.

When my children were toddlers, I was very careful to downplay any natural competition. My cautious approach was the result of reflecting on my own childhood experiences with my sister. I never labeled my children, and I certainly never said, "Why can't you be more like your sister?—a statement my sister heard frequently from family, friends and teachers.

But though on a conscious level I am very careful to avoid comparisons, after the apple exercise I began to wonder how I operate on a subconscious level. I know now how stuck I am in the ways I see the world. But I'm also aware that there are other ways.

I've studied enough anthropology to realize that some cultures never compare individuals to each other—or to a standard or ideal. They don't analyze people in terms of characteristics; instead, they value existence just for itself, without any qualifiers or judgments.

Although I don't know how to do that yet, I'm working on it. I'm committed to broadening my view and eliminating unhealthy competition from my life—for the benefit of my children, as well as myself. ❦

The Don'ts of Comparing Apples and Oranges

So what can parents of toddler twins do to minimize negative effects of the natural tendencies for competition that may arise in their children? Here are some suggestions:

Avoid all contests. It's tempting to talk about milestones reached, and who gets there first. But don't do it! What difference does it make whether Blake or Dallas walked first? If you make an issue of milestones, you can set a competitive tone that may not go away. Don't compare your children!

Don't hold one child up as a model for her co-twin, no matter how tempting it is. "Look how good Ashley is being," sounds innocent enough, but it can cause problems even if it's not followed by,

"Why can't you be good too, Brianna?"

Don't use competition as a motivator. "Let's see who can get dressed faster," may seem a useful device at the time, but that device will backfire on you.

Don't play games that have winners and losers. Any game that involves competition can be adapted for toddlers to a win-win conclusion. The game's over when everyone finishes, or even when anyone tires of it.

Don't give prizes for performance. Kids have a whole life ahead of them to compete for various kinds of honors. Keep toddlerhood free from those kinds of pressures.

Guiding Behavior

By Janet Gonzalez-Mena

Has this ever happened in your house? Michael and Brianna, age 2, are struggling over a stuffed bear. Each has a firm grip on a leg, and the two are engaged in a fierce tug-of-war. Finally Brianna pulls the toy out of Michael's hands. He sits back hard on his padded bottom and begins to screech at the top of his lungs. This is the time you arrive on the scene. What do you do?

TACTIC ONE: "THE JUDGE APPROACH"

The parent arrives as a judge to settle the argument. But this is no trial, so instead of examining evidence he or she makes a quick decision based on what was seen or what was imagined. "Michael had it first, Brianna. Give it back to him." Brianna runs the other way holding the bear against her tightly. "Make me," she seems to be saying by her actions.

Michael screams louder.

The parent gets mad now. "Young lady, you get back here right now." Brianna disappears down the hall.

The parent tries to comfort Michael, then storms down the hall to remove the bear, pry it out of Brianna's hands if necessary. The parent returns, hands Michael the bear, and Brianna can be heard screaming in the distance. Michael holds the bear for a fraction of a second, drops it and then is off to find something more interesting with which to play. End of scene.

Michael didn't want the bear after he finally got it. He's happy now to go play. On the other hand, Brianna is furious. You can be certain that she'll be back to hassle Michael. This scene probably won't end until nap time.

TACTIC TWO: "THE QUICK SOLUTION APPROACH"

The mother gets up from the desk, pulled to the scene by Michael's screams. She's busy paying bills, and in a hurry to settle this. She takes the bear from Brianna, puts it on a high shelf and says in a firm voice, "If you two can't share the bear, neither of you can play with it." As she goes back to paying the bills, she notices that Michael has pulled a chair over to the bookcase. She removes the chair, puts the bear in a locked cupboard and sits back down to the bills. Five minutes later the two are tussling over a toy telephone.

What's a parent to do?

TACTIC THREE: "THE PROBLEM-SOLVING APPROACH"

Consider this third tactic: the problem-solving approach.

The mother moves over to be close to her squabbling twins before the screaming starts. She comes not as a judge or referee but as sports announcer. She crouches at their eye level and says calmly, "You both want that bear very much!" There is no hint of judgment in her voice.

Michael gives way, lands on his seat and begins to scream. He's not hurt, just unhappy.

Still calm, the mother says, "Brianna has the bear now. You don't like that!" She doesn't do anything. She stays close by knowing that Michael might get up off the floor and hit Brianna. She won't let that happen. She'll use words backed up by action to prevent any violence. He doesn't get up, but sits crying. His screams subside to sobs. Brianna stands watching him.

The mother says, to Brianna, "Michael is unhappy because he doesn't have the bear." She waits. She has presented the problem, acknowledged the feelings and is going to let the children solve the problem.

OUTCOMES OF THE "PROBLEM-SOLVING APPROACH"

The happiest solution is that Brianna: a) gives Michael the bear; b) gives Michael another toy; c) goes and gets Michael's blanket and pats him, trying to comfort him.

It doesn't always happen that way, but sometimes it does.

Maybe Brianna doesn't show any empathy toward Michael. After all, she's only two. Understanding the feelings of another is difficult at this age, though some twins have an advantage over singletons when it comes to feeling closely connected.

Let's say that Brianna starts playing with the bear and Michael continues to sob. The mother doesn't say anything, although she's still available. Michael crawls over to her and reaches up one arm. She picks him up. In the meantime Brianna has gone on to play tea party, sipping pretend liquid from a small plastic cup. The bear lies abandoned. Michael glances at it, then goes to get a teacup. There are plenty of tea cups. The squabble is over.

ADVANTAGES OF THE PROBLEM-SOLVING APPROACH

See the difference between acknowledging feelings and waiting for the children to solve the problem themselves? They always do, either by solving it directly or by abandoning it. Many problems just go away if the adult doesn't interfere too much.

Of course, you can't just leave 2 year olds to work everything out all on their own. They'll get too physical and hurt each other. The mother was ready to stop things if damage to children or property threatened to occur. She'd use protective measures, but she would still let them solve the problem. Sometimes solving the problem means holding the children apart until they calm down and quit trying to tear each other apart.

TACTIC FOUR: TIME OUT

Time out isn't necessarily a separate tactic, but can be one part of a problem-solving approach.

Used by itself or as a punishment, however, it doesn't work. Time out works fine when it is what the child—rather than the parent—needs. If a child is out of control and can't calm down, maybe he needs to be removed from the situation. When he is back to himself again, then you can get the two back together. If there is still a problem, let them work on solving it. Putting a toddler in time out away from your sight is risky. Many a wall has been scribbled on because an out-of-control child found a crayon while in time out. Twins in time out together away from your sight is even more risky. No telling what they might do to each other or to the room.

Using time out as a punishment causes resentment and perhaps even a lowering of self-esteem. Time out doesn't teach problem solving or how to get along with others. Time out should only be used when the child needs a breather to settle down. In the example above, there was no need for time out for either child.

The best thing about practicing problem solving with a nurturing adult right there is that they gain a valuable skill. Later in life, when the temptation is to do violence, they are more likely to try to solve the problem peacefully first. Even in the midst of an ugly argument, saying, "We have a disagreement, let's talk about what we can do," can make a big difference.

Imagine if everyone in this nation had good problem-solving skills and used them! It's not the only solution to violence in this nation, but it is one solution. The best thing of all is that using a problem-solving approach isn't that hard and you can start early. Toddlers are the perfect age to begin learning about the feelings and perspectives of others. ♥

"I Want Mommy!"

By Alice M. Vollmar

Twins and other multiples attach to a favored parent, it can be hard for parents to take it in stride. "Sometimes I feel suffocated," confided LeAnn Traffie, mother of 2-year-old fraternal twins. "When Nicholas came home from the hospital last night, he wanted only me and Katelin wanted me because I'd been been with Nicholas in the hospital for three days. Neither twin wanted to share me; it would be nice to have them going to their dad."

Typically, a twin or both twins attach to the primary caretaker. In the Traffie family, that's LeAnn. The Traffie twins' preference for their mom is strongest when they are ill. "No matter how gentle and loving their dad is, he's just not 'mommy,'" said LeAnn. "I think it hurts his feeling at times. Usually, he just backs off and does things I'd be doing, like making supper; but sometimes, he does get angry. That just makes it worse."

The Traffie family's dilemma is not unusual. According to Sharon Hills Bonczyk, M.PH., parent educator and manager of the Family Resource Center at Children's Health Center in Minneapolis, Minnesota, "Many young children (twins and singletons) react to stress such as illness and extended separation by becoming attached to one parent." Strong attachment to one parent is related to a child's age, gender combined with age, emotional upsets and stress, says Hills Bonczyk. Additionally, individual personality can make a difference in which parent a twin feels most comfortable with at a particular stage.

ATTACHMENT IS CYCLICAL

"With two same-age children, attachment issues can be especially hard for parents to deal with," notes Hills Bonczyk. "It can help to keep in mind that attachment to a parent is cyclical—that it comes and goes."

Wayne Hovland, father of twin boys, Wyatt and Kyle, 4, reported that right now his twins are more attached to their mother, Karla, the primary caregiver—especially Kyle—when she's walking out the door to go someplace. After the first five minutes or so, he gets past it. "I really don't mind the twins' attachment to Karla," Hovland said. "I have to work so much that there's not really time to think about it, but I do know that my turn with the boys will come."

It's common for the clinging/ dependence exhibited by some babies around 8 months to pass in a few weeks or months, then reappear during toddlerhood and periodically throughout childhood. According to many child development specialists, the cycles of attachment to one parent, and later the other parent, are part of the separation and individuation process

Countering the mommy or daddy preference

The following tactics for coping during that period in your children's lives when only one parent will do are suggested by authors Arlene Eisenberg, Heidi E. Murkoff, and Sandee E. Hathaway, B.S.N., in their book, *What To Expect The Toddler Years*: "Don't hog all the good jobs."

Share the child care fairly; trade off being the heavy when it comes to bedtime or cleanup.

"Step to the sidelines—or even off the field." Consistently, allow the temporarily less-favored parent to take over. Leave the house for a specified period—or at least be out of sight and unavailable.

"Appreciate parental differences." Remember that your multiples' lives will ultimately be enriched by the differences in your parenting styles.

"Back him up." Mom should not contradict Dad's parenting decisions in front of their multiples and vice versa. If disagreement on a parenting issue arises, discuss it and try to reach a satisfactory compromise when the children are not around.

"Flatter the father." Offer empathy and support to the rejected parent during cycles of attachment, to convey appreciation for his/her parenting efforts even though the children aren't being receptive at this stage.

which starts at birth and continues through early adulthood.

WHEN EACH TWIN ATTACHES TO A DIFFERENT PARENT

In the Nelsen family, identical twins Haley and Katie, 3, split their favoritism between the parents. Haley prefers her dad, Steve, to take care of her, while Katie prefers her mom's care. The twins' mother, Erlene, attributes this split to early bonding. "Haley was very ill when she was born and required heart surgeries. I was home with Katie, so Steve would take my breast milk to the hospital and spend time with Haley. She ended up being cared for by him a lot and bonded more with him. The twins are pretty vocal about who takes care of them, but will go to either parent if they need to."

The Nelsens make an effort to balance the care of their twins. "When the twins were younger and we went to bottle feeding, it seemed like I would automatically feed Katie and Steve would be inclined to pick up Haley. We had to, and continue to, remind ourselves not to do this," says Erlene. Steve makes a real effort to do things for Katie if she'll let him, and Erlene makes sure she spends some time with Haley alone.

WHEN A PARENT FEELS LEFT OUT OR SMOTHERED

"When my twins didn't want to share me, I'd put on a tape with different songs, and switch holding babies for each song," says LeAnn Traffie. "Also, I'd often count to 10 and then switch. Now, I have a rule: If they can't sit on my lap nicely together, then they can't sit on my lap at all." Still, LeAnn gets frustrated at times: "I have stood in the garage and cried, 'Why me?' But usually, we're able to work it out. I do think this will change when the twins are older because I know how close I became to my own father."

Wayne Hovland's attitude of accepting his twin sons' attachment to their mom, keeping in mind that it will change, echoes Hills Bonczyk's coping advice: "It's important to see this attachment as normal and to try not to personalize it. A parent may feel hurt if the attachment symbolizes a bond with the other parent. Just remember that it doesn't mean that the child needs that preferred parent more overall. Rather, the child or children simply need that parent more at that particular time." ❥

Helpful books

Sharon Hills-Broncyk recommends these books for children that deal with attachment and separation issues:

You Go Away, by Dorothy Corey, shows that when parents go away, they will return. Ages 2–5.

Annie Stories, by Doris Brett, offers an innovative way to help parents ease children's fears through storytelling. Young children.

I Want Mama, by Marprie Weinmein Sharmat, captures the sadness of a child when the mother is in the hospital and the warmth of the family circle upon her return. Ages 3–8.

Shawn Goes to School, by Petronella Beinburg, tells how Shawn wants to go to school but has a difficult time staying at first. Ages toddler–4.

1+2 = Chaos?

By Janet Gonzalez-Mena

"My oldest son was 2 years old when I found out I was pregnant with twins," said Georgi Charland of Fairfield, California. "It was hard for me to grasp the enormity of the news and what it would mean to have two babies coming at once. I didn't expect Josaiah to understand, but I started thinking anyway about ways to prepare him.

"I decided the best thing to do was to get to know some other families with young twins, so he would at least have an experience with two babies. I also looked for books about new siblings for children of his age, but found none dealing with the arrival of twins."

Charland was right; twin-specific materials are scarce. She was also wise in choosing to look for concrete ways to prepare her young child for the upcoming birth. I advise parents to start their preparations early in the pregnancy

Helping Your Singleton Adjust

Georgi Charland's story illustrates these important principles in helping a sibling cope with the birth of twins:

• Offer your child chances to be grown up—to be Mommy's and Daddy's little helper—but don't overdo it. Also allow him to be a baby. Carry him to bed, undress him and cuddle him when that's what he wants.

You might even consider letting him try a bottle again if he begs, just to see what it's like. Chances are, he won't like it, especially if you make it more worth his while to be a "grownup" than a baby. Do this by pointing out the privileges he has as an older sibling that his twin siblings don't. Expect that knowing where he fits in will be a balancing act at first, with your child acting grown up sometimes and babyish at other times. Eventually, he'll go back to "acting his age." Be careful, though, about expecting too much of him. He may seem older than he is in comparison to "the newcomers."

• Buy your child one or more dolls, if he doesn't already have one. Doing pretend play with pretend babies is a good way for him to "practice" being a grownup without taking on responsibility inappropriate to his age.

• Accept jealous feelings. Sometimes jealousy doesn't show, but underlies certain behaviors, such as bedwetting by a child who has been out of diapers for some time. At other times, jealousy is more overtly expressed by angry behavior directed at the babies themselves, or at you.

• Help your child express his feelings in words. Don't teach him it's not nice to be mad or hurt or jealous, since that may force the anger underground, where it will do more harm than good. By getting these feelings out in the open, you and he both can learn to cope with them.

Once in a while, an elder child won't appear bothered by the additions to his family until his siblings begin to move around. Walking, talking babies are bigger threats than those who just lie there! Walking babies can also create new realms of upset in a child who has already expressed a good deal of concern over the new arrivals!

• Protect your babies from any angry actions of their older sibling. Emphasize that it's okay to feel angry, but it's not okay to hurt someone. Be on your guard.

Helping You Adjust

• Don't put your "all" into preparing your child for the impending change in family structure.

• Don't try to convince your older child that this is going to be an unmixed blessing.

• Above all, don't be disappointed if you've done a lot of preparing and your child still reacts emotionally, after the birth, to what is a fact: you're spread thinner and he has to share you.

• Do accept the obvious—being a parent of three is different from being the parent of one. It's best to assume that your child is going to feel at least a little displaced, no matter how hard you try to prevent it.

• Do put your effort into helping your singleton cope with the new situation and the feelings it provokes. That's what "real life" is all about—and you'll all be the stronger for it!

by making any necessary changes in their child's life before he has to adjust to the birth of twins—and adjust to a lot of other things at the same time.

I also suggest minimizing changes once the babies arrive. For example, if they're planning to move their elder child out of his crib and stop breastfeeding, they should do so long before the twins arrive. If they are planning to put him in child care or enroll him in preschool, they should also take care of those arrangements before the due date.

Parents need to also make sure that their older child's life is "full" when his new siblings arrive. They may want to encourage his finding some playmates if he doesn't already have some. Although making these arrangements will be, in the short run, an added "chore" for his parents, the changes will make it better for him and easier for them in the long run.

Once the twins arrive, this child will especially need a life of his own, a way to show both to himself and the world that he is distinct from the twins.

Parents also need to make arrangements for their older child's routine around the time of the impending births. If the primary caregiver during that time will be Dad, for example, and he's not used to the child's eating and sleeping routines, the mother needs to help him get involved before the big day so it won't seem terribly unusual when he steps into her shoes. If this child is going to Grandma's or a neighbor's, he should first try some short visits and then some overnight stays as rehearsals for the real thing.

Preparations are one thing, but no matter what they do to prepare their singleton, moms and dads will probably face a wide range of confusing feelings on their singleton's part after his mom and the babies come home from the hospital. Charland suggested that parents consider the reunion moment carefully: "I walked in the door from the hospital with my arms empty, so I had room to hug Josaiah and put him on my lap. I feel it was important that I did what I could to make his first experience with this new situation a positive one."

An alternative other mothers of twins have tried is to come home from the hospital while the older child is elsewhere and have the babies tucked away so they are completely available when their older child walks in the door. ❤

Sibling Rivalry:
The Cost of Closely-Spaced Children

By Michael K. Meyerhoff, EdD.

Parents have debated the subject of spacing children for many years. There are two classic positions. One holds you should have children close together because they will be friends for each other and you'll get the child-rearing process over with quickly. The second is you should space children several years apart so you won't be overloaded with work.

As a result of many years of research at the Center for Parent Education in Newton, Massachusetts, on the development of young children in their own homes, we believe we've learned things about spacing children that can help parents make the decision on a sounder basis and can lead to much better results for all concerned.

Quite simply, research has proven that, in general, the single greatest source of stress for young families is closely-spaced children. The dividing line seems to be about three years. Children spaced closer than three years clearly cause considerably more stress to themselves and to their parents than those spaced more than three years apart—and the closer the spacing, the greater the stress.

WHAT ABOUT TWINS?

Of course, having twins does not involve an active "decision-making" process on the part of the parents nor does it involve any "space" between the twin children. Because very little research has been done on the spacing of multiple-gestation children, we can't provide you with much information that would be directly applicable to the relationship between the twins, and we can't be sure of the extent to which our general information is accurate when applied to the twins' relationship with other siblings.

However, the general consensus among experienced professionals is that the harsh feelings described below ordinarily found between closely-spaced siblings seems less prevalent among twins, mainly because neither one has had the "Garden of Eden" experience of being the only or primary object of parental attention. Therefore, since neither twin has "displaced" the other, intense feelings of jealousy between them are not likely.

Moreover, since the twins are somewhat used to sharing parental attention, the arrival of a closely-spaced younger sibling may not generate as much ill will as is usually the case, although a fair amount can still be expected.

However, since the arrival of twins requires at least an equal and probably greater-than-usual amount of parental attention, their relationship with a closely spaced older sibling still will be problematical, and maybe even be more so than is ordinarily the case.

A ONE-YEAR GAP

During the first seven months of life, a second child (we'll call her Sally) with a one-year-older sibling, (we'll call her Meg) experiences little or no difference in social development as a consequence of having an older sibling. A great deal of Sally's time is spent sleeping, and most other time is spent out of the way of the ongoing daily activities of Meg. During these months, Sally is immobile and caring for her is relatively easy.

Meg will be growing from 12 to 19 months of age during this time. For such a child, the presence of a new baby makes little or no difference, even though from 15 to 19 months, Meg is developing a sense of self and personal power, and probably is regularly engaged in the testing of wills with her parents.

When Sally is 7 to 9 months old, she begins to crawl. A crawling baby requires a good deal of attention if trouble is to be kept to a minimum. Meanwhile, Meg is 19 to 21 months of age and is really embroiled in negativism. She, too, must have the parents' attention and rather frequently, at that. These equally valid sets of needs simply cannot both be fulfilled all the time.

Meg finds that her parents are very often busy with Sally—in fact, too busy for her. This situation leads to the first feelings of jealousy, the first feelings that the world is not perfect, and the first acts of aggression toward the baby. This is the time when you begin to see toys ripped away from an 8 month old and other rough treatment of the baby by the older child.

As Sally moves from 9 to 12 months of age, she still requires a good deal of attention to minimize accidents and minor damage to the home. Meg, now 21 to 24 months old, also is very likely to continue to require much attention, because the decision of "who runs the home" is likely to be delayed by the events of the preceding months. The result is that Meg acquires more jealousy, more anger, and more resentment toward Sally.

Meanwhile, Sally has begun to adapt to the increased pace of aggression and hostility from Meg.

During this time, the younger child learns survival tactics. For example, she learns how useful it is to cry early rather than late. And now, the older child has begun the process of "souring," going from a situation where the world looked fantastic to one where she can't quite figure out what's going on, but knows things aren't good.

THE IMPOSSIBLE ADJUSTMENT

We have used the story above to express just how difficult a situation 2-year-olds find themselves in when they are living with a newly crawling brother or sister. It's the same situation a woman would be in if her husband one day made the announcement, "Honey, I've got wonderful news for you. Next week I'm planning to bring home someone else to live with us. It'll be a woman; she'll be a bit younger than you, perhaps a bit more attractive. In any event, she'll seem that way because I plan to spend more time with her than with you. Nevertheless, we're all going to continue to be a very happy family. You'll get used to her presence; I very much want you to love her as much as I will; and I want you to show her how much you love her."

We believe most people would have a very difficult time adjusting to such a situation. Yet that is pretty much what we're asking a 2 year old to do when there is a newly crawling baby in the same home. If an adult would find such a situation intolerable, how can we expect a 2 year old, whose whole life revolves around the home and particularly around the central people in the home, to be able to cope with the feelings that result?

The answer is that there simply is no way it can be done. The only 2 year old who wouldn't be extremely jealous and unhappy about the presence of a 9- or 10-month-old sibling would be one who had very little to lose, and the only kind of 2 year olds who have little to lose are those who have not formed a solid attachment with their parents.

In a sense, then, the nasty behavior of an older child toward the younger one is a healthy sign, in that it is proof that he has had normal, beneficial early attachment experiences and has formed a very strong tie to his parents.

As the younger child grows from 12 to 15 months of age, his condition with regard to his older brother is that of being "on guard." The older child, now moving from 24 to 27 months of age, is increasingly unhappy and frustrated. Given the survival tactics learned by the younger child during the preceding months, the result is a standoff.

That situation shifts when the younger child gets to be 15 to 21 months and, in turn, enters into his first awareness of self, testing of wills, and sense of personal power. The younger child also is moving toward the final stages of his own attachment relationship to the parents.

The older child, now 27 to 30 months, may find himself on the defensive at times. Indeed, the younger child sometimes becomes the dominant one of the pair. This is also the time when the souring of the personality of the older child often peaks, and for good reason.

When the older child lashes out at the younger child on the basis of strong feelings of jealousy, he often finds his parents, the people whose love is central to his security, showing anger toward him. This, of course, makes matters even worse because, as far as the child is concerned, they are showing him that they just don't love him anymore.

I'm sorry if all this sounds grim, but we have repeatedly seen this sort of situation in homes where the children are closely spaced. You may escape it; some people do. But if you're in a position where you're planning your family, you might consider avoiding such problems. On the other hand, if you already have closely spaced children, an understanding of what's going on may be helpful. We also have some suggestions for dealing with this situation, but first let's turn to the situation where the gap is more than three years.

SPACING CHILDREN

During the first seven months of a second child's life (we'll call him Tom), the fact that there is a 3-year-old older sibling (we'll call him Justin) at home makes little or no difference in social development. Correspondingly for Justin, the early attachment process is old business.

Since Justin's second birthday, he is spending time playing out of his home; is beginning to develop new friendships with children his age; and, in general is finding that the impact of a new baby in his daily life is very small.

Even when Tom gets to be 7 to 9 months old and is crawling and requiring more of the parents' attention, he still doesn't make much of a dent in the daily activities of Justin, who by then is at least 3 years old. Justin does not often feel the need to compete for the parents' attention with the baby. That is not to say that it never happens, but it is nowhere near as central to his life and to his daily developmental focus as it would be if he were less than 2 years old.

As a result, there is no "nose out of joint" quality in the older child's interactions with the baby. The baby is not seen as a threat, and in fact, such older children seem to genuinely enjoy the baby a great deal. Meanwhile, the baby does not often experience aggression from his older sibling.

CLOSELY-SPACED CHILDREN

Try these suggestions for helping keep a happy home with closely spaced children:

1) Be very careful that the older child does not do serious harm to the baby. He is very capable of this normal, though unacceptable, behavior, and may want to cause trouble quite frequently.

2) Try not to aggravate the difficulty by lavishing praise and attention on the younger child in the presence of the older one (visiting neighbors and relatives are often guilty of this offense).

3) An older child should be provided with more out-of-home experiences to depressurize the situation as much as possible. For example, if the older child is 2 1/2 to 3 years old, a regular play group would be an excellent idea. In any event, the use of a babysitter and excursions either to another home or to the park would help.

4) It is terribly important for the older child to have undivided attention from the mother and father on a regular basis to reassure him in the only language he can understand that he is loved just as much as ever.

Let me repeat that there simply is no way of making this situation as easy to live with as if you were dealing with a first child only or with widely spaced children. It is very important that parents understand that fact and do not try to act as if their child-rearing task was as easy as it might otherwise be. If they understand that they are in an inherently difficult situation, they will be much better off than if they ignore the fact. Good luck! ♥

EATING

Parents vs. Picky Eaters
A smorgasbord of ways to help both sides leave the table satisfied.

By Patricia M. Stein, R.D.

The groundwork for the development of healthy eating attitudes and lifelong eating habits is established during the early years of children's lives.

Unfortunately, laying this groundwork is complicated by the feisty nature of most toddlers (see "Toddler" box) who often turn mealtimes into "eating wars" as they try to assert their individuality and need for control. To discourage the outbreak of these battles, parents need to find the middle ground between being too rigid and being too permissive with their toddlers, as well as their older (and younger) children.

Child-feeding expert and author Ellyn Satter provides parents with guidelines that are designed to prevent a host of feeding problems from the start of children's lives.

The principles discussed in this article are reflected in her books, *Child of Mine: Feeding With Love and Good Sense*, and, *How to Get Your Kid to Eat, But Not Too Much.*

THE FEEDING RELATIONSHIP

It is important to divide the feeding relationship into areas of responsibility—the parents' and the children's—according to Satter. The parents' responsibility is to provide the food and the place it is to be eaten. They also set the meal and snack times. The children's responsibility is to determine how much and even whether they should eat. Period.

Parents get into trouble when their children are engaged in the "not" phase; there is a lot of power in "eating" or "not eating." And, as so many parents have found out, urging (seen as

What Eating Behavior Can Be Expected From Toddlers?

Toddlerhood—from about 15 months to 3 years of age—is a developmental stage in which most children try to prove to themselves (and to their parents) that they are independent people. They need to explore, to succeed and also to learn that they have limits. They have been described by child-rearing experts as bossy, balky, contrary, obstinate, negativistic, overly fussy and precooperative. In addition, their feelings are quite ambivalent about this new need for independence.

Physically, toddlers are growing at a slower rate than previously, so they may not be as hungry as they used to be.

Their appetites can be extremely variable, however; some days they may eat voraciously while on other days they will eat little. Instead of forcing their children to eat, parents need to relax and let their children's bodies govern their intake.

Parents can expect the unexpected from their toddlers in other areas as well. Some days they will want to do all their feeding (and almost everything else) themselves; on others, they will demand parental assistance. Children need to succeed at their endeavors and often make their own food choices based on how successfully they can eat a particular food. Spaghetti, for example, can be an embarrassing food for most adults to eat, so it may be a bit too advanced for some toddlers.

Eating Guidelines

2 to 10 Years

Milk: 2 cups (Teens: 4 cups)

One and one-half ounces of cheese or 1 1/2 cups of cottage cheese equals the calcium in one cup of milk or yogurt.

Protein: 2 to 3 portions (Teens: 4 to 5 portions)

Meat, fish, poultry, cooked dry beans and nuts. (One portion of a protein food is approximately 1 ounce or one egg, or one hot dog or 2 tablespoons cooked beans or peas.) Small children should not be given seeds or nuts because they might choke on them.

Bread and Cereal: 4 servings (Teens: 4 servings)

(Including rice, macaroni, spaghetti, etc.) One-half slice of bread, one tablespoon of cooked cereal or 1/3 cup ready-to-eat cereal per year of age is a suggested serving size for young children. Teens need the adult size serving of one slice of bread or 1/2 cup cooked cereal or 3/4 cup of ready-to-eat cereal.

Fruits and Vegetables: 4 servings (Teens: 4 servings)

One-third to 1/2 piece of whole fruit is a suggested serving size for young children or 1 to 2 tablespoons of other fruits or vegetables. Teens need the adult size serving of 1 piece of fruit or 1/2 cup of other fruits or vegetables.

Please remember these suggested amounts are only guidelines. Some days your children may want more, and some days they may want less. Let their internal food regulators dictate how much they need.

Is Picky-Eating a Bad Habit or an Eating Disorder?

In my practice as a registered dietician working with young persons who have eating disorders, I often see people whose parents have forced them to "clean their plate" or who have restricted their eating regimen for fear of the youngster getting fat. In both situations, the result has been the development of an eating disorder wherein the patient chronically either undereats or overeats.

I recently saw a young woman in her early 20s. Her parents were of the "stay at the table until you finish your supper" school of thought. She is now anorexic, consuming 300 to 400 calories per day.

Her situation may be typical of many in which the actual problem is the parents' marriage. Instead of focusing their attention on their problems, the children and their feeding problems become the major focus of attention, absolving the parents of the need to solve their own problems. The child "cooperates" by developing problems, sometimes with eating and/or other behavioral areas.

Ask yourself the following series of questions to see whether your child's picky-eating situation is more or less normal or whether it may be a symptom of larger problems.

1) Do you and your spouse argue at mealtimes? Are you or your spouse quite critical of your children or each other, especially at mealtimes or just before? Take stock of the general emotional climate of your home, apart from your children's eating habits. Are their eating habits taking the focus off the real issues?

2) Do you force-feed your children?

3) Do the children have to sit in their chairs until they have eaten all that was put on their plates?

4) Are you always going on and off diets and worrying about your weight and what you can and cannot eat?

5) Do you or your spouse exhibit some picky eating habits of your own? For example, what kind of a fuss do you make when served something you don't like or something you haven't tried before?

6) Are your children and their eating habits the entire focus of the meal?

Unfortunately, children who are forced to eat or to sit until they finish their food may develop more than eating problems. When a child's internal food regulators are overridden by external means, the child may not trust himself in other areas as well. In other words, self-esteem may be seriously damaged.

Constantly criticizing or belittling your children can result in serious problems in this area also. Perhaps you need some help in bolstering your own self-esteem. Professional counseling might help you help your children to healthier self-regard.

We have an epidemic of eating disorders in this country. Some surveys have shown that as many as 50 percent of 9-year-old girls and 80 percent of 10 year olds diet as a means of weight control.

If you are a chronic dieter, perhaps you need to break out of this cycle yourself. Consulting with a registered dietician could be of assistance to you in getting on a healthier path for yourself and the whole family.

My practice is teeming with women whose mothers were concerned about their own weight and started their daughters off at very young ages on diets of their own. Fathers are not blameless either, since several of my clients report fathers who offered them bribes to lose weight so they would be more attractive. What a message this sends to a young, vulnerable girl about her only being worthwhile and attractive if she is thin.

"forcing" from the child's perspective) a child to eat particular foods will strengthen the chances of this child becoming a finicky eater. Conversely, withholding foods from a child who is perceived as eating too much will result in just the opposite outcome—he will become obsessed with food.

To promote healthy attitudes about food, parents must be sure that their expectations are not so high in the areas of food choices and amounts that they worry needlessly about whether their child is getting adequate nutrition. Researchers have illustrated the practicality of not worrying about food choices by conducting studies with children who were rewarded for trying a new food.

The researchers found that these children were less likely to eat the new food the next time it was offered. However, children who were left on their own to try out the new food were eventually more apt to try it than the rewarded group. The message that this reward tactic sends is that certain foods are so undesirable that the child must be rewarded for eating them.

Likewise, children will quickly pick up the message that their eating is very important to their parents if, when they refuse one item on their plates, their parents rush into action trying to find something that pleases them. To avoid becoming this kind of "short-order cook," parents need to provide the food (appropriate for the children's ages); it is then the children's responsibility to eat it or not. By not "giving in" to children's manipulative eating tactics, parents give children limits, but are also promoting their independence by allowing them free choice of the foods that are available.

Older children are heavily influenced by their peers and, because of their interests and schedules, have many more opportunities to eat outside of their homes. Though parents won't be able to prevent their children's eating candy or fast foods, as opposed to a healthier diet, they need to remember that their offspring are still responsible for what and if they eat.

It is also important for parents to avoid taking personal offense if their children turn up their noses at their culinary offerings. In short, to avoid cultivating the growth of picky eaters, parents should not make an issue of the children's eating or not eating. ♥

Food Wars: Advice From the Front Lines

By Janet Gonzalez-Mena

To learn what "tricks of the trade" to use to keep order at mealtimes when toddler twins are the diners, I went to the experts—parents of toddler twins!

"Keeping them at the table—that's my biggest challenge at mealtimes," said Ginger Jordan Gregory of Napa, California. "I took Sara and Katie (who are 2 years old) out of their highchairs a few months ago," she explained, "when I discovered how well they did at a small table in low chairs at their day care home. But it didn't work as well for me as it did for their day care provider."

To solve this problem, Gregory made more of an occasion out of meals. "It seems to work better now that the whole family eats together," she admitted. "I put the girls in booster chairs up at the big table. My husband and I are somewhat of a 'draw' who keep them focused and interested in what's going on at the table. That wouldn't have worked a few months ago, but now they're old enough to conduct their own eating."

"I did just the opposite to solve my problem," said another mother, Susan Evans of Napa, California. "I gave up on the formal family sit-down dinner. It was just no fun for any of us.

"I tried having unstructured mealtimes, which worked better for my family. Now I often let the girls eat while I'm preparing the meal. If they want to get up and walk around the kitchen, that's OK with me! My goal is to make mealtime a pleasant, social experience, not a battleground."

A third mother, Theresa Snowder, also of Napa, California, explained why she changed her approach to her young eaters, Megan and Casey. "I never knew when they were finished eating because they were always wandering around. I'd take their plates; five seconds later, Megan and Casey would protest loudly that they weren't finished. So I taught them to clear their plates from the table themselves and put them in the sink. That way there was an official end to their meals, and they were the ones to decide when it was."

THE COMMUNAL PLATE

These mothers gave mixed reviews on the subject of their toddlers' eating off each others' plates. "I don't care if they do it," Snowder remarked candidly. "But they don't because they've learned not to; it's against the rules at day care.

"However, they do feed each other," she continued. "When one isn't interested in food, her co-twin will often feed her to get her to start."

Gregory remarked, "That used to be a big problem. Although Sara and Katie easily share with each other, neither likes it when something is grabbed off her plate! It's an easy problem to solve, though. I just place them far enough apart so that they can't reach each other's plate."

THE DIVIDED FRONT

The mothers were well-acquainted with their twins presenting a "divided front" at mealtimes.

Evans remarked that she didn't see herself as a short-order cook. "I give choices, but mainly in the vegetable department. I also try to find appealing ways to serve food. My latest invention is the shish kabob dinner—bite-sized things on a stick. They love anything that is a little new and different."

Snowder also said that she gives her twins

How to Begin Breaking Children's Picky Eater Chains

After answering the questions above, seek help if you think it is warranted.

Then, be certain you are offering age-appropriate foods, not something that will be physically difficult for your children to eat. As mentioned, you need to be realistic about amounts they can eat comfortably.

Establish regular meal and snack times, and provide a pleasant atmosphere at the table. Be sure to include at least one food on your menu that your children will eat. If they do not eat their meat or vegetables, don't make a fuss. They will make up for them at another time. If they refuse a food, leave it available so that they can eat it if

they happen to change their minds.

Don't let your children "panhandle" other foods from you. Have a planned snack coming up soon that will help stave off starvation or malnutrition.

Offer all your menu offerings in a neutral fashion. If your children announce they are not eating, say, "That's all right, but you need to sit with us and keep us company while we eat our meal."

Always remember the division of feeding responsibility. You are responsible for providing the food and creating the atmosphere in which it is presented. Your children are responsible for whether they eat or not and for how much they eat.

The following books are recommended for further reading on child-feeding practices:

Child of Mine: Feeding With Love and Good Sense, by Ellyn Satter (Bull Publishing Co., 1986).

How to Get Your Kid to Eat. . . But Not Too Much, by Ellyn Satter (Bull Publishing Co., 1987).

Jane Brody's Nutrition Book, by Jane Brody (Bantam Books, Inc, 1987).

Nutrition in Infancy and Childhood, by Peggy L. Pipes (Mosby Co., Inc, 1985). Note: This book is basically written for those in the health profession field.

Fat-Proofing Your Children, by Vicki Lansky (Bantam Books, Inc, 1988).

The Taming of the C.A.N.D.Y. Monster, by Vicki Lansky (The Book Peddlers, 1988).

All of these books are available from the One Stop Shop book catalog (featuring books on nutrition, exercise and eating disorders). If you wish to order one or more of these books, send a check or money order to One Stop Shop, 11111 Nall, Suite 204, Leawood, KS 66211.

choices, letting one daughter choose the vegetables for the meal and the other choose the fruit.

"I treat my children as individuals," Snowder added, "and I believe that having different tastes is part of being an individual. It's interesting, though, how they sometimes resist the individual approach. The other day, for example, when Megan asked for orange juice and Casey wanted milk, I was agreeable; however, Megan was upset that her co-twin didn't want what she wanted. I explained to Megan that she wouldn't like it if Casey insisted she drink milk, and that seemed to settle the matter."

THE UNITED FRONT

Sometimes toddler twins present a united front when refusing certain foods. Snowder said her twins often go through food fetishes together. "It's kind of a follow-the-leader thing," Snowder said. "They influence each other."

"I have a lot of confidence in my children getting what they need as long as the food offered to them is good for them," Evans remarked. "My twins' food preferences seem to go in cycles. They're interested in a certain food for a while—sometimes both at the same time—but not always. I kept track for a period of time, and they did balance themselves out nutritionally—even when they ate carrots for two days in a row or asked for chicken three times a day. I kind of cater to their tastes—whether they're divided or united." ♥

SuperTwins' Parents Suggest . . .

The Taylor, Romanoski and Swick families described below encourage table manners, proper eating habits and a short family ritual at mealtime. The large number of young children present at their table may make things more difficult, logistically, for these families, but they have devised the following routines to make mealtimes more pleasant and efficient:

• Theresa Taylor of Indianapolis, Indiana, has 6-year-old quadruplets and one older child. Assigned dinner table seating has been the rule at the Taylor house, with the quadruplets alternately seated between their parents and their older sister. "We use this method because it reduces conflict. We also use color-coded cups for the same reason," Taylor said.

Dinnertime at the Taylors is not particularly quiet. "As long as the noise is related to sharing time and not conflict, we're happy," Taylor remarked. "I wouldn't say our meals are always a 'picnic,' but the family dinner hour is very important to us, and it is pleasant the majority of the time."

• Margie and Steve Romanoski of Ferndale, Michigan, are the parents of 3-year-old triplets and an older child. Steve says that their children are used to following rules at mealtime because they consistently enforce them.

Sue Swick of Winona Lake, Indiana, has 4-year-old triplets, 9-month-old quadruplets and two older children. Sue says that a consistent routine is important to the family mealtime. "I get everything ready and put it on the countertop," said Swick. "Then it is put on the table about two seconds before it's time to eat. I dish out small portions and strategically place extra food (for refills) near the adults."

Rules at the Table: Two Experts' Views

The rules that parents devise for the family dinner hour should take their children's ages into consideration. Suggested rules that are appropriate for toddlers include staying seated, not playing with food and speaking quietly.

Marilyn Rollins, a registered dietician in Phoenix, Arizona, suggests that parents use positive reinforcement when their children use appropriate table manners and follow basic rules such as those mentioned above. Gold stars on a chart could be rewards for acting politely, using good manners, and talking in a quiet voice, for example. Enough rewards could be created so that each child is able to receive one during a meal.

Rollins also reminds parents, "Children mimic what they see and who they live with. Adults need to be good role models to encourage their offspring to use appropriate table manners."

Susan D. Parrish, a certified psychologist who practices family therapy in Phoenix, Arizona, says that the dinner hour is a good time for promoting family rituals. But she cautions parents to set reasonable goals for their children based on their ages. "Very young children can hardly be expected to tolerate long, drawn-out meals," Parrish said. "As children grow older, simple mealtime patterns learned when very young will provide the basis for more elaborate routines."

by Fran Bevington, Mesa, Arizona

Juggling Act
30 ways to feed two babies and entertain your toddler.

By Kay Lynn Isca

My firstborn son, Joey, was 15 months old when his twin brothers, James and Jonathan, arrived. To add even more confusion to an immediately chaotic situation, our family moved into a new house when the twins were 1 month old. Of the many challenges faced during those first months in the new home with two new babies and an active toddler, feeding time had to be the biggest.

Eight times a day, I sat on the floor and bottle-fed two babies cradled in my legs—a feat that sometimes made me feel like a contortionist. Twice a day on most days, I also added to this juggling act the task of keeping my not-quite-2-year-old safely entertained. (During the night and noon feedings, Joey slept; at 6 a.m. and 6 p.m., my husband helped.)

Given the confining nature of my infant feeding situation, and Joey's unbridled toddler curiosity, I had one overriding goal during these morning and afternoon feedings: keeping Joey safe until James and Jonathan finished eating. I quickly found out that "forbidding" Joey to go upstairs or downstairs was translated into, "The minute Mom's feeding the babies, I go exploring." Instead, I had to make the space next to me more interesting than the unexplored territory—at least for 20 minutes or so. Following are some of the activities that worked for me.

Soon you will work out your own survival tips for feeding time. Indeed, after six months of coping with two hungry babies and an active toddler, I saw that time-honored cliche, "Necessity is the mother of invention," in a whole new light. I hope you enjoy the special challenges and pleasures of multiple parenthood. Good luck!

1) HOME SHOPPING
Here's a use for all those sale flyers that arrive in the mail. I would quickly scan almost any ad and spot an object I knew Joey would recognize (shoe, ball, wrench). At feeding time, I would hand him the flyer and ask him to search the two-to-four-page circular until he found it. He was so proud when he "won."

2) SNAP/UNSNAP
Baby sleepers with all those crotch snaps provided great entertainment value. Joey could quickly undo the snaps, but it took lots of time for him to match the pieces and snap them again.

3) QUICK CHANGE
Challenge your toddler to get out of his clothes or PJs and dressed again. This worked best (longest) with footed sleepers.

4) "I'M THINKING OF SOMETHING . . . "
(Big, small, blue, round). Keep adding clues as needed. Again, Joey derived much satisfaction from his successes in this game.

5) MYSTERY GADGET
What could this be? Our honey dipper, garlic press and spatula each had a moment in the spotlight. Often, I was surprised at the creative uses Joey imagined for these objects.

6) PUZZLE EXCHANGE
With friends or from the library. I used to hand out puzzle pieces just a few at a time, choosing those I knew would fit together, so he would not get discouraged too quickly. With numbers and ABC puzzles, I sometimes put just three or four pieces in Joey's jar so we could talk about them.

7) SURPRISE PACKAGE
Joey loved his empty plastic peanut butter jar. Before feeding time, I'd fill it with several things—a playing card, a toy car or some blocks. At first, it took him awhile to unscrew the lid; then he'd investigate, item by item. Sometimes I'd grab familiar toys, but he stayed

interested longer when at least one item was a surprise.

8) JUNK MAIL

I saved unopened junk mail. Joey opened the envelope, "read" the letter and folded it back up (sometimes). An inverted plastic basket (mailbox) or a book bag (mail bag) extended the game.

9) CARDS

Take just three to five cards from an old deck. Ask your toddler to find the joker, find the ace, find two hearts, etc. You can switch cards and extend the game for as long as he'll play.

10) ROLL/WON'T ROLL

I'd fill Joey's jar with various round and unround things. He'd try to see if it would roll or not.

11) TELL A STORY

Add plenty of "And do you know what happened next?" Sometimes he would answer, and I could build it into the story. Other times, it gave me time to think of how to continue.

12) HATS, SCARVES, TIES

I would hide one behind a chair or under a blanket. Joey would first find it, then we'd try it on ourselves and the babies and the teddy bears. We'd make up stories about our new "characters."

13) PHOTO ALBUM

Your toddler can turn the pages while you talk about people, holidays and other special times. For us, this also helped the boys bond with out-of-town friends and family.

14) EMPTY LAUNDRY BASKET

Joey loved to "drive" the laundry basket, then crash and fall out. He "drove" to Grandma's house, to Daddy's office, and to the grocery store for milk. Then he would return home and tell me about his trip.

15) NESTED PLASTIC CONTAINERS

Hide one cookie in the smallest one. Your child has to open all of the containers to find it. Sometimes this worked well; other times, Joey had the cookie in 30 seconds!

16) PROJECT OF THE DAY

Once in awhile, Mr. Rogers or Captain Kangaroo had a simple craft activity that we duplicated. (We made this before feeding, when I could help.) Then, during feeding time, we'd look at our project, talk with pride about how we made it, and invent a story or game to go with it. Sometimes, Joey would wrap it up (paper bag or newspaper, no scissors) to give to Daddy.

17) PARTICIPATORY SINGING

"Baa Baa Black Sheep" was, and is, a favorite. Instead of three bags full each time, let your child decide how many bags and who gets them.

18) PUPPETS

Socks, lunch bags and store-bought puppets all worked well. A baby blanket over my raised knees became our stage and curtain. The babies enjoyed this activity, too.

19) WINDOW WATCHING

"Do you see . . . (school bus, leaf, snow, duck, etc.)?" Since we had moved to a new neighborhood, this activity helped us get acquainted with our surroundings a bit, also.

20) EGG HUNT

Hide small toys or anything at hand (four or five of them) around the feeding room. Joey would excitedly search, then find the surprises and bring them to me.

21) TRANSFORMERS

A sand bucket became a marching band hat. Joey marched around the room, and I was the trumpet, tuba, flute and drum. At other times, the sand bucket was the stool for the circus lions, the chair at the movie theater, a drum and a place to store treasures.

22) SHELL GAME

Take three plastic cups from your cupboard.

Hide a block or other object under one of them. Move the cups around (with your feet or elbow if necessary) and have your toddler guess which cup covers the prize.

23) SCREW AND BOLT

I'm still amazed at how long Joey would struggle to put these pieces together and take them apart. Because of the choking hazard, he could only practice this right at my side, and then with a large screw and bolt.

24) SLOW FOODS . . .

Can extend snack time. Popsicles on a heavy beach towel, for example, worked well. Have the wet washcloth ready for cleanup, though, before you sit down with the babies.

25) YARN SHAPES

We used a length of yarn or a shoestring to make shapes on the floor. At first, I made them, and Joey named the triangles, squares, circles and ovals; then he started to make the shapes himself.

26) TRAPPED

My legs formed a cage that trapped Joey until he found the secret to unlock the door. Sometimes the key was pushing my ankle, sometimes saying "please," sometimes pressing my nose or elbow. (this game began after the babies graduated from lap to infant seats.)

27) OLD PAIR OF SNEAKERS

Joey removed the laces, knotted them and tried to put them back into the holes. (He actually did this repeatedly on my favorite pair until I finally wised up and washed a pair of my husband's seldom-worn ones.)

28) PRETEND

Our small kitchen became a magic carpet, a car and a ship. Joey loved to get pretend keys from my pocket and drive pretend vehicles. (The pretend keys were invented after Joey lost his Dad's real set of keys.)

29) "I REMEMBER WHEN YOU WERE THIS SMALL"

Joey took much more intense interest in observing his brothers' tiny hands, fingers and mouths when he was trying to imagine himself at their size.

30) "MOMMY, TELL ME ABOUT. . ."

Joey would name something and we'd talk about how it's made, what people did before they had this, similar products or the origin of the name. We had more discussions about toilet paper than most people have in a lifetime! ♥

Letting Toddlers Not Eat

By Janet Gonzalez-Mena

Some parents judge their worth by how their twins eat and how much weight they gain. Once feeding gets established in infancy, most parents feel secure as they see their children double in size. The trouble starts for many families when their infants become toddlers.

Three things happen all at once. Weight gain slows dramatically, food consumption decreases accordingly, and children become much more independent about what they will eat and how much. The children who once ate half a cup of peas, even more strained carrots and a generous serving of strained liver for dinner may cut down to two peas (picked up and squashed in the fingers), no carrots, a couple of bites of bread, a taste of meat, and an apple chunk or two between them.

MAKE IT EASY ON YOURSELF

Desperate parents, those not prepared for this drastic change of habit, may resort to devices such as feeding children who can feed themselves, coaxing, begging, even bribing and threatening. Meals can become a contest of wills, even a moral issue as parents strive for balanced diets and clean plates. The hardest lesson for some parents to learn is this: good parenting is giving children nourishing food and then cheerfully letting them not eat it!

"When you have twins, making it easy on yourself is important," says Ginny Aubuchon of Suisun, California "You can't just let them walk around dribbling grape juice popsicles all over the house. A firm rule about where food is eaten keeps me sane." Ginny goes on to talk about her children's eating habits. "They're so different from each other when it comes to food," she said. "Peter just inhales food—eats everything you put before him; while Anita barely eats anything. I have to keep searching for foods she likes."

Ginny has found Anita goes through spells of hating some foods. "When she gives up something important, like milk, I find foods to replace it, like cheese or 'natural' milkshakes sweetened with fruit—bananas work especially well," she said. "It's surprising how she hates something this month, but if I try next month she may like it again. Sometimes it's hard to keep track of how much and what Anita eats because the two of them share food back and forth.

Preparing and offering food is parents' business. Eating it is children's business. It is hard to let children make their own decisions about balancing their diet, but it is important to do so. One child may eat just bread at one meal and the other eat just yogurt, refusing anything to go with it. However, as long as parents continue to offer a variety of nutritious foods, and don't dull the appetite by making junk foods available, toddlers will do a good job of getting their nutritional requirements met—at least over a span of time.

STIMULATE APPETITES

Besides offering good foods and letting children decide whether to eat them or not eat them, what else can parents do to stimulate appetites? Serving food attractively in a calm atmosphere helps. Giving the right number of choices helps, too. But if you offer your children a whole smorgasbord they will be overwhelmed and you will be resentful of all of that work.

Letting children decide what they want on their plates helps keep wasted food to a minimum. They can serve themselves some foods. Never overwhelm them with large amounts of food because facing a mountain of something may seem insurmountable. Be sensible about giving them something they love, like a big glass of milk, watching them gulp it down, and then offering the rest of the meal.

According to Magda Gerber, a Los Angeles, California expert on infants, "Being hungry is the best motivator for eating. Appetites are influenced by how you set up your children's day. Such simple factors as fresh air, exercise, and rest make a big difference in whether children are hungry or not."

In Gerber's demonstration center, small children are given a choice about whether they want to eat or not. The ones who refuse are allowed to do so. Because the center uses very low tables and chairs instead of highchairs, the children are able to get up and down to the table by themselves, so they aren't dependent on adults to decide when they are finished. However, there is a rule that children can't just keep coming back and leaving again and they can't take food away from the table. Children who are eating are required to stay seated at the table. It's surprising how well this system works when the adults are matter-of-fact but firm about it. Even the youngest toddlers come to understand what is expected very quickly.

The foods to choose from in Gerber's center are simple ones that the children can manage themselves. No one urges, "Just one more bite" or "Clean up your plate." It is expected that the children can decide for themselves when they are finished eating. If a child eats little now, it's highly probable that he will make up for it at the next meal or snack time.

PREPARATION GUIDELINES

How do parents know what foods to prepare and offer their toddlers? People choose diets based on their culture, the food available, the nutrition education they have received, and their own and family's tastes. Here are some guidelines to follow when making decisions about what to offer your toddler twins to eat.

1. Serve foods that are attractive and easy to eat. Many toddlers prefer a finger food diet to one they have to manage with a spoon or fork.

2. Serve foods in their most natural forms. The more processed a food is the less nutrition it has. Each processing step removes vitamins and minerals, and even though some may be replaced by the manufacturer, processed food never equals whole, natural food. For example, whole-grain bread is superior to white bread in fiber content as well as in nutritional value.

3. Avoid additives in packaged food. Read labels to see what the food products you buy contain. One rule of thumb is to avoid foods which contain ingredients you can't pronounce. Especially avoid artificial colors and flavors.

Better to stick to natural ones. Your twins don't need all those unnecessary chemicals.

4. Avoid additives at the table. Unless your children are already used to sugar on cereal or salt on vegetables, you do not need to sweeten or season. Unspoiled taste buds appreciate the plain, natural flavor of food. Adult taste should not be the criterion by which to judge food served to children.

5. Avoid junk food. Children full of greasy, salty, sugary snacks will automatically turn down a nutritious lunch offered an hour later.

6. Avoid food toddlers have been known to choke on such as chunks of hot dogs, peanuts (which swell when lodged in the windpipe) and popcorn. ♥

Chapter 4

IDENTITY AND INDIVIDUATION

The Biggest Challenge in Parenting Multiples: Individuation

By Elizabeth Hyde

The preschool teacher advises separate bedrooms. You're trying to schedule separate play dates. The school strongly recommends separate classrooms for each child, to avoid competition. One day your 3 year olds will ask for separate rooms; the next night they'll cry about being lonely. Suddenly, your teenage twins will polarize, one sporting green tufts of hair and a diamond in her nose and the other choosing her wardrobe straight out of Talbot's.

What do all of these situations have in common? They are all symptoms of a process called individuation, a process that begins for everyone at about 18 months and ebbs and flows throughout life, with definite peaks during toddlerhood and adolescence. As part of this process, every person—whether a multiple or not—must separate emotionally and psychologically from his or her parents; multiples have the added job of emotionally and psychologically separating from each other.

And yet at the same time, a special bond often exists between co-twins; after all, they have shared the same physical space since conception. How do co-twins find a healthy identity in the midst of this longstanding bond? And how do parents help them over the hurdles of doing so?

THE FIRST STEPS: TODDLERHOOD

Actually, I began to explore the whys and wherefores of this issue a little late, for the process had undoubtedly been going on for a few years with my twin girls before it hit me in the face. At 4 1/2, Zoe insisted one day that we go on a hike together. Alone. Just the two of us. Without Kate.

This posed problems. Touched as I was, I had a sitter scheduled for the afternoon and was very reluctant to give up that personal time and space. Nevertheless, I finally said yes, much to Kate's dismay. (Actually, Kate went into a panic, demanding that I only go on a hike with Zoe when her father was taking care of her, or when she was sleeping.) But I promised her we'd have our own hike together sometime, and went off with Zoe.

And a strange thing happened. I found myself feeling shy with my own daughter. Having spent the last few years in the presence, for the most part, of all three of my children at once, I hardly knew what to say to this girl, one-on-one. Awkwardly, I asked a lot of questions, like, "What do you like best about school?" and, "What's your favorite thing to do?" until she finally demanded, "Why are you asking me all these questions?" It was one of those moments when the proverbial light bulb went on, for my shyness with Zoe mirrored her own shyness with herself. Hey, wake up, Zoe was saying, Who am I?

All toddlers, whether multiples or not, are busy psychologically and emotionally separating from their parents. As part of this process, they will often cling to a transitional object, such as a blanket or a stuffed animal, which represents the parent to the child and creates a sense of safety. For multiples, the main focus at this point is much the same. They, too, are busy separating from their parents and, in fact, might even use their co-twins as transitional objects during this process, said Carol Tierney, Ph.D., of Boulder, Colorado. I know you, the twin thinks. I am safe with you, even if my parents aren't around.

Consider this point: Maybe your twins seem particularly close in their relationship together today. Maybe they want to be together all day long as they take those first steps away from you; however, some aspect of individuating from their co-twin may also sneak into their relationship. They may begin to squabble. They may compete for the attention of a friend. (This can result in an unpleasant tug-of-war, with the third child in the middle. Repeated fights may lead you to opt for the separate play date route, as discussed further in this story.)

But as one psychologist notes, a healthy dose of competition is not all bad. "If there is no competitiveness, the twins may feel fused together, with one identity," said Eileen Pearlman, Ph.D., a family therapist in Santa Monica, California. Competing with each other helps them to define themselves, as long as it does not get out of control.

ROOMING ARRANGEMENTS
You might observe other ways in which your twins will begin to individuate. For example, often around 4 years of age, many twins will want their own rooms. This is great if you have the space; each child can choose her own decor; she can opt for a bright nightlight or a mere crack of light under a closed door; she can exert control over her own toys. Above all, each has her own psychic space. "It's the best," Kate said solemnly to me upon waking up that first morning in her own room. And we hadn't even redecorated at that point.

Fortunately, we had a guest room to give up. If you don't, and your twins really seem to want their own space, consider a room divider, or bunk beds, both of which give a sense of separate space. If you can stand it, let them choose

their own sheets and comforters. Even though you might not opt for fire-engine-red next to pink hearts, it demonstrates to each child that you value his or her individual decisions.

Of course, many twins choose to stay in the same room together; having each other's presence provides both company and security, especially at night. Also, keep in mind that even if they do want separate rooms, they are apt to change their minds and want to share the same room again sometime. (This is where it's handy to pull out a sleeping bag and call it a sleepover.)

PLAY-TIME SCHEDULES
Scheduling separate play dates provides another opportunity for twins to individuate at this stage. They may show an interest themselves, or you may decide it's time they played with other children one-on-one. Admittedly, scheduling separate play dates is not easy, for it takes a great deal of planning and a fair amount of luck. You have to choose the date, decide upon friends (no easy task if there is one favored playmate), and then hope that those friends are available.

On the other hand, even if you find just one friend for one co-twin, you now have a built-in opportunity for your own "play date" with his twin. This need not be a major excursion to the zoo; a quiet hour or two spent reading or playing blocks will be just as meaningful, as long as your child has your undivided attention.

Sound too ideal? Maybe so. Many parents of twins will confess to being too busy and stressed out to manage much separate time with each child, let alone separate play dates with other children. Life is so chaotic that they stumble along as a de facto unit, making vague promises as they drop off to sleep that one of these days they will call Claire, and Jessica, and get the ball rolling. Which never happens.

But instead of feeling guilty, parents need to remind themselves that they are doing the best that they can. Their twins will still individuate without separate social lives at this point; and besides, this issue usually resolves itself when the twins go off to elementary school, where twins, often in different classes, naturally begin to make their own friends—which means they get their own invitations to birthday parties, sleepovers and the like.

DO "CLOTHES MAKE THE MAN" (OR WOMAN)?

What about the whole issue of dressing your twins alike? I readily admit to my own biases against it; I believe that at this very basic level, they should not see themselves as mirror images of each other. If you do dress them alike, "You may have a hard time convincing other people that you see your twins as individuals," wrote Pamela Novotny in, *The Joy of Twins*.

THE SECOND LEAP: ADOLESCENCE

Suddenly adolescence is here, and in full force. At this point, your twins will make another leap as they try to individuate not only from their parents, but from each other as well. This is usually not a smooth process. "It's a real push-pull situation," said Pearlman, for while adolescent twins are struggling to break away and define who they are vis a vis their peers, they are simultaneously drawn to the safety of twinship.

And so you may see a great deal of conflicting emotions going on between your twins at this point. There's apt to be anger one minute, a sense of clinginess the next. And don't expect this to conveniently happen in sync, either; one twin may be ready for great leaps in individuation, wanting his or her own separate friends and activities, while the other—not yet ready to individuate to the same extent—would rather continue doing things the old way—together. Then the one feels guilty for breaking away, and his co-twin feels left out and perhaps even inadequate. (And a month later you find that everything has reversed!)

The best advice for parents? Be understanding, Pearlman said. If you understand what's going on, if you know they are trying to individuate, you won't be so terrified if your twins suddenly start fighting more than usual, or dressing like polar opposites, or hanging out with different kinds of friends (as long as you approve of their behavior, of course).

Talk to your children, one-on-one, about their emotions. Ask, "How do you feel about your sister's going out all the time?" Or say, for example, "Yes, you want time alone, but you also still need time together, don't you?" Above all, don't try to push them in one direction or another. Let them decide. And if they don't agree—if they're at different points on the individuating scale—let them work things out between themselves. It's all part of growing up.

Not that you should sit back and leave everything up to them! Tierney strongly advised helping each child identify his or her interests and strengths early on—at the middle-school level, for example—so that by the time they get to high school, they have a clear idea of who they are and where they excel. For twins, this allows them to recognize the bond, but at the same time know and define themselves.

Tierney also recommended providing a clear structure so that the twins do not perceive themselves as a unit. For example, if you're disciplining Margie, and Bob, her co-twin, steps in to explain why Margie behaved the way she did, make it clear that this is between you and Margie only.

Is there any difference between identical twins and fraternal twins, as to how they individuate during this stage of development? "Everything is heightened for the identical twins," said Pearlman, "because people tend to see them as a unit." Indeed, Barbara Bengston, of Longmont, Colorado, reported that the hardest comment for her identical twin girls to take in stride was friends who would see one twin and ask, "Where's Carrie?"—as though they were on some kind of string.

And yet all twins, whether identical or fraternal, must go through this individuation process. It's just that a structure is more readily provided if you have boy-girl twins, or same-sex twins who look very different from one another.

What about competitiveness at this stage? Again, a little probably helps; and too much hurts. Of course, any parent who has two children close to one another in age must deal with this issue to some extent; but parents of twins can't fall back on the "age excuse." (For example, they can't truthfully say, "Well, Sam is a little older; maybe when you're his age. . .".)

Barbara reported that the most difficult thing for her was when one of her twins succeeded at something and the other did not. "My heart was torn between excitement for one and sadness for the other," she said.

You can partially avoid this if the twins are involved in separate activities—but inevitably, at some point, one will be likely to triumph in an activity and the other won't at the same activity, and you must celebrate and comfort simultaneously. ♥

If There Are Two of Me, Then Who Am I?
One woman's struggle to meet the most important challenge of her life.

By Joanne M. Gonsalves

Growing up as a twin was confusing for me. My sister and I heard repeatedly how lucky we were to be unique—to be twins. While being treated as clones, we were also told to think for ourselves. We were duplicates, "Pete and Repeat" as my uncle called us. We fit together but felt too odd to fit anywhere else. We were told that being twins is a privilege that is granted to relatively few, but for me it was like being invisible while simultaneously being on display.

I cannot speak for my sister. She seemed to weather events that were stressful for me with much more equanimity than I could ever muster. Over the years, I have learned to deal with my life in a much more relaxed fashion; but this was not always true.

Being a twin was not a totally negative experience, as it afforded me a measure of positive attention that I may not have had as a singleton. I do not blame my mother for my reaction to the way we were brought up. She did the best she could with what she knew, and that is really all any of us can do.

Looking back on those years, I can now at least understand her obsessive attitudes and actions, but as a child I only understood that her love seemed to me to be conditional on our being "identical" twins. We grew up hearing that we were the "pride and joy" of the family. I was not their pride and joy. My sister was not their pride and joy. The twins were. From my mother's point of view, we existed only as a twosome; and as such, we had to be identical in everything. There were no choices in dress, activities,

toys, books, etc. We did every-thing together and alike. Without being allowed the choices that foster individuality, I felt powerless and afraid well into my adult life. As a child, I believed that I existed only because I was a twin, and that if anything happened to my sister, I would cease to exist. The thought frightened me.

In retrospect, my mother must have had similar thoughts, because one of us was never allowed to be anywhere without the other, and neither was allowed out of the sight of an adult in the family. This was stifling. Not being given the opportunity to learn to function on our own, we became totally dependent on each other. I remember being frightened to be by myself. I still am on occasion, though seldom does the feeling last long. With understanding comes courage.

First grade was traumatic, because we were not accustomed to relating to children other than one neighborhood friend. Being exposed to such a large group of children after being so sheltered all our lives was the most frightening experience I can remember. I never did make many friends and related from a fear basis through grammar school. I remained a loner except for being with my co-twin and was called "stuck up" and other such names. My co-twin eventually got over her shyness and did not seem to have as many problems forming relationships with peers.

FORCED FRIENDS
Social situations sometimes became awkward. When my sister was invited to a birthday party,

my mother would insist that we both be invited. (Not that I never was; just not nearly as often.) I now realize that she was trying to keep my feelings from being hurt, but my embarrassment at being thrust unwanted on some confused child who had invited just one of us heightened my shyness and discomfort.

Very rarely would we share a friend. I think that, for another child, it was too much of a burden to keep from playing favorites. Contrary to our parents' opinions at the time, we did have different personalities, which came out when we were at school or social functions. It was natural then, for a friend to favor one personality or the other. My mother could not accept this concept, however. In her eyes, we were both the same, so friends should want to be with both of us.

As I said before, our mother was single-minded when it came to us. I felt at times that our being twins was the only thing that brought any pleasure to her life. Our accomplishments or shenanigans as a pair would bring a smile to her face, and a smile from Mum was rare indeed. Knowing this, I went out of my way to focus attention on our twinship. I would deliberately copy my twin. Because this brought positive attention from our mother, I believed it would bring it from others also.

Although this was true when we were young, as we grew older it no longer worked well. I felt bereft. If I could not interact solely on the basis of being a twin, where did that leave me? I have seen young twins playing on their twinships to get attention, and I would like to tell their mothers that maybe they don't get enough positive attention as individuals.

Our birthday was a burden for my parents. They were not wealthy. Two of everything had to be bought, so they often chose games that we could both play or something else that could be shared. I didn't mind that too much, but what I did mind was not ever having "Happy Birthday" sung to me by myself. Small point? My parents did the best they could; still, it was something "insignificant" that affected me deeply. To this day, I am obsessive about my birthday and those of my family.

FACING THE MUSIC

We were in grammar school in the Lawrence Welk era. My mother's dream was to have her twins play accordion on his show, so we took accordion lessons—for seven years. Her dream was never realized, because we were not very musical, and at least one of us would feel ill when forced to perform at school functions. Guess who?

Our father was president of the PTA for several years, and our parents were active in school affairs. At the slightest excuse, there we were, squeezing out our not-so-melodious duets. There were many more talented musicians in the school, but none of them were "lucky" enough to be twins, a fact of which we were often reminded by our classmates. Eventually, we gave up the accordion, and I sold mine to a much more talented and enthusiastic pupil.

My sister was the first-born, which somehow made her the spokesperson for us both, from deciding which clothes to wear to what sports we would join. Clothes became a source of embarrassment because we always had to dress alike, even up to twelfth grade. The one time we dared to dress differently, Mum reacted as if we were rejecting her and all that she held dear. She did not speak to us for two weeks in retaliation for that transgression. That incident reinforced my feelings of having no validity by myself. I went to school feeling embarrassed and angry at having to dress alike; but at the same time I was too fearful of losing my mother's love and approval to express my feelings or act differently. How powerful parents can be!

Even though our social education was lacking, my sister did not seem to harbor the fears that I did. She matured socially more quickly than I. She laughed and talked with friends and joined after-school activities, with me tagging along. We were not allowed to join anything by ourselves, even in junior and senior high school.

Joining everything with my sister was probably good for me in some respects, as I probably would not have done so on my own. I would have preferred to be reading or pursuing activities that did not require physical prowess. I still don't care for physically competitive games and always seem to injure myself when forced into them.

COMING INTO MY OWN

I did manage to finally make friends on my own as a teenager, but it was too stressful for me to seek out well-adjusted or popular girls for friends. (Boys were not allowed!) I was drawn to those who seemed more shy and outcast than I, and I became an enabler and a pleaser, bolstering their egos in order to feel better about myself. I went out of my way to be a good friend and never said no to any request for assistance, whether with homework or just listening to one's troubles. I still have problems saying no, especially to my own grown children. For the most part, though, I can now recognize when I am overextending myself and can choose to do something about it.

Graduating from high school proved to be the highlight of my teen years. I could finally say goodbye to an environment in which I had never felt comfortable. Little did I know that college would be more of the same. I had expected that my sister and I would be separated when we left high school to pursue our goals at different colleges, but this was not to be. We had to choose the same career and the same school, or we could not go.

My twin had chosen to be a nurse, a career which was held in as high esteem in our family as being a nun. My unspoken wishes again took a back seat. I never had the strength to go against my mother, and I was not about to start then. I convinced myself that being a nurse was akin to sainthood and imagined myself as another Florence Nightingale. I stayed in nursing for 25 years, working part time while raising my children. Ironically, my sister, who had chosen our profession, did not work outside her home for 25 years, but then went back for several years before going on to other pursuits.

After graduating from nursing school, we were both engaged to be married. Not surprisingly, we had a double wedding. This was the reasoning: My father could not afford to pay for two weddings so close together. We both wanted to be married, so why not a double ceremony? It would be fun; and it would certainly make my mother's day, I told myself. What I didn't expect was the requirement that our wedding gowns be alike. I should have known, of course; but even then I did not speak up. Our wedding was beautiful and fun. Thankfully, we did not have to spend our honeymoons together!

We have gone our separate ways ever since. Eventually, I even moved to another part of the country.

TWIN TRUTHS

I have heard all my life from singletons how wonderful it must be to grow up as a twin and how much fun it must be to always have a friend and confidante. I am sure that for the majority of twins, this may be true; but being twins is no guarantee that two people will be all things to each other.

I wish I could have been one of those twins who reveled in her twinship. It must be a special experience to have such a close relationship to another person and yet have a strong identity as an individual. My problem was that I was never allowed to see myself as a separate person, and so had a difficult time developing an identity of my own. It may be for that reason that still, when given a choice, I have a tendency to do the opposite from what I know my twin will do.

Then there are those surrealistic times that my co-twin and I turn up doing the same thing from opposite sides of the country, such as changing to the same brand of makeup, getting the same hair style or showing up in Hawaii for an anniversary with the same outfit. Years ago, that type of situation would have been stressful for me. Now it is just funny. It is a relief to finally be able to relax about our similarities. I can do that easily, now that I choose not to feel cloned. I am finally my own person, separate but still connected to my sister.

Twins are, first and foremost, individuals. They may seem identical in all respects, but each has his or her own separate inner being. By allowing choices and valuing them as individuals, their individual personalities will emerge. Then, I believe, no matter how identical they may remain outwardly, the result will be two individuals, not two halves of a whole. ♥

Encouraging Leading and Following Skills

By Janet Gonzalez-Mena

All children need to learn both leading and following skills. Some children are born with natural tendencies toward one role or the other, but parents need to help them balance out those natural inclinations by encouraging both types of experiences in a variety of situations.

Some twins create this balance by switching roles regularly. One is the leader for awhile, then his co-twin takes over. Sometimes it's a matter of place. One leads outside the home; his co-twin leads inside. Sometimes the leader and follower roles switch spontaneously during the course of a day, or even a single interaction.

But sometimes this switching doesn't develop as a matter of course. Then parents, who see the natural tendencies of their twins toward one role or the other, may inadvertently confirm their children in roles that started as just a slight inclination. One becomes the leader to his co-twin's follower.

Some parents even openly label their children. But whether the influence is overt or not, parents can limit their children's development by encouraging them to lean too far in one direction; a tendency becomes a habit. When a twin, in particular, practices only one set of skills—as his role as leader or follower is constantly complemented by his co-twin's—then both learn to feel complete only as part of the set.

KEEPING A HEALTHY SENSE OF INDIVIDUALITY

The last thing parents should do is to think of their twins as a set or encourage them to think of themselves that way. Twins must not be led to regard themselves as an incomplete whole without the other half. It's nice for twins to enjoy the feeling of belonging that comes with twinship, but it's vital for them to remain individuals at the same time.

How do toddler twins gain leading and following experiences? If they don't come by both naturally, they can learn them from their parents.

Such simple events as taking a walk can be used for a lesson in leading and following. Many times parents take their twins for a walk in a stroller. The whole complexion of the walk changes, however, when parents leave the stroller behind, find a safe place to walk, then relax and let their children take the lead. This is a good time to observe the balance between the leadership skills of their twins. If it is unbalanced, parents should initiate an exchange of leader and follower roles.

Parents who have tried the kind of walk in which their children guide them instead of the other way around, have probably found that

My Chance to Follow

I never thought much about the number of opportunities I gave my own children to lead until the day I took them to the museum of an early California mission. After driving miles to see the mission, I naturally expected my children to learn something from the experience, and I saw myself in charge of ensuring that the visit was educational.

Since one of my children was a toddler, I decided to skip the official tour, but that didn't keep me from conducting my own. Although I did take individual considerations into account, I clearly remember herding everybody around in order to see all the things I thought were important.

Suddenly I woke up to what I was doing—and to the fact that it was my expectations that were shaping this experience for my children.

I decided to try letting go. Reversing my course, I put the children in charge and followed them around for a change. It was hard when they disagreed with each other, since none was old enough to go off on his own, and it was hard, too, when they skipped things I thought were important. Still, I somehow managed to keep from taking charge that afternoon and was able to make sure everyone had a chance at the leadership role.

The afternoon was a good learning experience for all of us. In fact, I had to drag the children out—not the usual ending of an "educational experience."

they and their toddlers left a trail like snails and proceeded at about the same pace. Had they marked their path, looking back on it they'd probably find that it would go in loops and spirals, recrossing itself, backtracking, sidetracking and every-which-way tracking. There is nothing linear about a walk with two toddlers. But that's the way toddlers enjoy walking. Parents can too, if they can get out of a goal-oriented leadership role and into a receptive follower and supporter role.

Supporting the follower is also a golden opportunity for parents to encourage leadership skills in this child. If it becomes apparent that one child is doing all the leading, for example, the parent can actively encourage and promote the decisions of the follower, helping that child take the leadership role.

Parents won't find this the easiest walk they ever took, but then, it won't be the first learning experience that's easier on the kids than the parents!

Other ways to break patterns of leadership in a constructive manner include such suggestions as: "Brianna, you get to decide this time what we do first," or, "Kyle, you can choose the vegetable for dinner this time." Parents should be alert to one twin speaking for both without consulting his co-twin: "This is what we want."

Parents also need to watch out for the co-twin who is stuck in a follower role. Sometimes that child may need parental permission to follow his own desires. The parent could say, for example, "It's okay for you to stay in and play even if Travis wants to go outside." Sometimes it's a simple matter of saying to the more assertive twin, "You decided last time; this time it's Caitlin's turn to decide."

Sometimes neither toddler gets a chance to lead because parents have difficulty letting go of the decision-making role. Parents should think about how they interact with their children. Does Mom or Dad have to be completely in charge of everything? How often is a child allowed to take the lead, with parents and co-twin following along?

Of course, followers can give suggestions and advice to the leaders—parents obviously shouldn't abdicate their responsibility for their children's safety. But letting all children become decision-makers from time to time gives them a chance to experience the challenge of being a leader, too. ❀

Unique is Better Than Equal!

By Eileen M. Pearlman

What would you do if faced with the following scenario? You've offered your twins a reward, a trip to the nearest pet store to look at the new puppies, for doing a particular task. One twin finished the task and the other did not. You begin to follow through on giving your reward when your child who did not do his job asks, "Why can't I go look at puppies too?"

Would you give the hard-working twin a treat for completing the task? Would you leave his brother home to do without?

Reinforcing children for the work they have completed in a careful and timely fashion is very important. Work that the child is capable of performing, but chooses to leave undone, does not deserve a reward. Both these premises seem self-evident. But there is more to this situation than it would appear. For in this seemingly simple scenario lies a fertile opportunity for building a unique sense of self, teaching responsibility, and preparing your twins for the reality of the real world.

BUILDING A UNIQUE SENSE OF SELF

All parents want their children to have good self-concepts and high self-esteem. But what do we mean by these words? Self-concept is how each individual sees herself in the world. Optimally, this means seeing oneself as a separate, unique individual who can relate to one's self, as well as one's family, friends, employers, etc., successfully.

So how can we, as parents, help each of our twins develop a good self-concept of herself? Seeing and treating each twin as a separate, unique individual with her own wants, needs, personality, strengths and weaknesses, is one way. That means not seeing and treating her and her co-twin as a unit.

Many times, parents of twins believe that they should always treat their children equally. Whatever they give to one twin, they believe that they should give to his co-twin. But this does not build a sense of uniqueness and specialness. Adele Faber and Elaine Mazlish, in their book, *Siblings Without Rivalry* (Avon Books, 1987), state, "To be loved equally is somehow to be loved less. To be loved uniquely—for one's own special self—is to be loved as much as we need to be loved."

This unique love, then, is what enables children to build a sense of self. This is not to say that it is never appropriate for parents to give equally to both twins; but in so doing, it is important to see each twin as unique.

Rewarding each twin individually and uniquely for accomplishments also builds self-esteem. Parents must be careful, for it can have an opposite effect if done in an unkind or unfavorable way. So the manner in which a reward is given is very important.

Avoid making comparisons, favorable or unfavorable, between a twin and her co-twin. Instead, Faber and Mazlish explain, "The key is to describe. Describe what you see. Or describe what you like. Or describe what needs to be done. The important thing is to stick with the issue of this one child's behavior." There is no need to refer to the co-twin. Whatever you want to say can be said directly.

Feelings may be stirred up when one twin is acknowledged or given a reward and the other is not. Feelings such as envy, jealousy and competition are natural and sometimes unavoidable. These feelings, once acknowledged, can provide an opportunity for communication and growth for the twin, her brother or sister and her family. Parents who listen, are understand-

ing, and accept their child with all her feelings, help their child accept herself, therefore, building self-esteem.

It is important to note that some competition, once understood and appropriately directed, can lead to growth and development. This can spur a person on to stretch to great heights and achievements, breeding self-confidence and self-esteem.

TEACHING RESPONSIBILITY

Everyday experiences are grist for the teaching mill. The example given at the beginning of this article is one that provides an opportunity to learn responsibility. Making a choice, finishing a task, and learning the consequences of one's choices, teach independence and responsibility. Being rewarded for a job not finished, just because one's twin sibling gets rewarded, does not teach responsibility, it teaches dependence on one's co-twin.

Making good decisions, following through on these decisions and taking responsibility does not just happen automatically; it is a long process that is learned.

How do we teach our children responsibility? When our children discover there are choices, make decisions regarding those choices, and face the consequences of their decisions, they have the opportunity to learn responsibility. The more choices and consequences they face, the more responsible they become. This means letting our children learn from their experiences, and not bailing them out when they make poor decisions.

Foster Cline and Jim Fay, in their book, *Parenting With Love and Logic* (Navpress, 1990), discuss two kinds of parents who do not foster responsibility in their children. One type they call the "helicopter parents"; the other, they call the "drill sergeant parents." Helicopter parents feel uncomfortable seeing their children hurting or struggling, so they bail their children out.

Drill sergeant parents never allow their children to think for themselves, choosing to make all the decisions for them. According to Cline and Fay, both these styles of parenting tell children that, "You can't think for yourself, so I'll do it for you."

The more often children are bailed out by their parents, by their co-twins, by the twin situation, the less they will learn to take responsibility for themselves and grow into separate, responsible individuals. Cline and Fay believe that, by not allowing our children to fail, "sometimes grandiosely fail, we cannot allow our children to choose success." Parents who allow their children to try things on their own, make choices and see the consequences of their choices, teach responsibility. This begins in the early years with choices that are not too risky and continues throughout their lives. This is a learning process; making mistakes, or failing, is a part of learning and, therefore, growing.

The emotional climate or environment in which responsibility is experienced and taught is important. Parents who are canny, loving and understanding of their children's efforts at learning will promote future growth. These children will feel secure in their relationship with their families and eventually willing to take further risks in assuming responsibility for their actions.

Parents can help their children with decisions by teaching their children to think—asking questions and offering choices. Again, this is done in a climate in which the child is accepted unconditionally and is not judged for trying to work out her problems, or take responsibility for her actions.

PREPARING FOR REALITY

Eventually, our twins grow up and go out into the "real world," a world where they are responsible for their own decisions and actions. Each may not be looked upon as being "special" because he or she is a twin. They probably will not be rewarded because their twin sibling was rewarded and their boss wants to keep things even and equal.

Giving our twins equal rewards, according to Judy Hagedorn and Janet Kizziar in, Gemini: *The Psychology of Twins*, "does not help prepare the youngsters for reality—that throughout life what they receive and what they achieve will not be identical."

It can be a rude awakening for twins when they get older and discover for the first time that they are responsible for themselves. Therefore, allowing our twins to face the consequences at an early age prepares them for the reality of the adult world.

Let's go back to the beginning scenario. It may be easier to take both twins to the pet store. You would not see the dejected face on the child left behind, nor hear the arguments, nor, perhaps, even see her crying. But your twins would be missing an opportunity for learning and growing. Day-to-day experiences provide a rich soil in which to plant seeds for growth and development. Don't let spring planting pass you by. ❤

Keeping Parent Power Positive

By Janet Gonzalez-Mena

Have you ever noticed how a toddler will fall down and then look up to an adult for a reaction? By reading the adult's body language, the toddler discovers how she is supposed to feel.

When toddlers look to their parents for information about new situations, they are using something called "social referencing." Social referencing becomes a tool in the hands of adults—even those who never heard the term. For example, reassuring a child who takes a tumble is a positive use of social referencing.

The reassurance can come either through words or by looking unconcerned.

Through social referencing, adults influence children's feelings. Adults need to know the difference between helping toddlers cope with new and difficult situations and manipulating their feelings. When a parent spontaneously laughs at the right moment, a tense situation turns into a funny one. When toddlers face tapioca pudding, for the first time, a quick bite and a pleasant expression on the parent's face can influence babies' attitudes toward the white slime.

THE CO-TWIN'S INFLUENCE

Sometimes parents can back off completely and let a child influence her co-twin. When Amanda remains calm when a dog crosses her path, her attitude reassures Ashley. Of course, it can work in the reverse as well. If Ashley gags on her first taste of sweet potato and spits it out across the table, you can bet that action will influence Amanda's approach to her first bite.

When it's not clear that there will be a positive reaction, it's safest for the parent to provide the social referencing. If Amanda's and Ashley's mother enjoys sweet potatoes and eats them with gusto in front of the girls, there's a better chance that they will react more positively to the sweet potatoes on their own plates.

Parents constantly give children both spoken and unspoken messages on how to react to situations—whether they are aware of it or not. Unconscious silent messages come through as loudly as those voiced. We communicate through facial expressions, body language, posture and even muscle tone. If the parent who hates sweet potatoes tries to fake enthusiasm by loudly proclaiming the benefits of eating them, the children are likely to pick up unspoken hidden messages.

Once parents discover the power of social referencing to influence their children, they sometimes overuse it. They seek to control feelings, to mold and shape attitudes and influence personality development according to their own plan.

Imagine a mother who has an overwhelming desire to make her children into her idea of good, right or perfect children. Or a father who wants to make his children into smaller versions of himself—people with the same interests, talents, personality traits. These parents may overuse social referencing.

CAUTION: INDIVIDUALS AT WORK!

If parents aren't dedicated to supporting the individuality of their twins, the molding can result in one child, instead of becoming her parents' image, becoming the "duplicate" of her co-twin. Instead of discovering who she is, she might come to conform to her co-twin's image—more of a reflection than a separate person.

Then it wouldn't be the parents' "perfect child" image influencing the outcome, but the concept of a matching set.

Some children have more strength for resisting their parents' molding and become their own people no matter what their parents' desire for them. But others, anxious to please, take all the messages, spoken and unspoken, to heart and incorporate them into their personalities. They feel what the parents have indicated they should feel. They like what the parents have let them know is worth liking. They're interested in what interests the parents.

It takes strong parents and just the right child under a special set of circumstances for this to happen, but it does happen. As a result, the person grows up thinking she is someone different from whom she really is. She may discover her real self at some crisis period of her life, or she may go to her grave never knowing that she's spent her life living her parents' image of her.

It's important that parents recognize the power of social referencing and use it wisely. When a child looks to his parents for a reaction to something, the parents must decide whether it is beneficial to give it to him in that situation or not. It's sometimes best to remain neutral and let the child decide for himself how to react. After he decides, then a supportive verbal or nonverbal response from the parents is appropriate.

MIDDLE OF THE ROAD

By remaining neutral, parents can sometimes keep from making a range of mistakes. Take these two examples of adult mistakes:

A child falls down. His parent acts as if everything is all right, but it turns out that the child is really hurt. The adult response discounts the child's feelings. If it turns out that the child is seriously injured, acting as through everything is all right can even be dangerous.

Conversely, if the adult makes a big fuss over the fall, the child learns that minor "boo boos" get big attention. At the next little tumble, the child will make a fuss and expect the same attention from the parent.

The learning may go even beyond the direct

lesson. With her next mishap, the child's co-twin might carry on for the same attention she observed her sibling receiving earlier.

Social referencing starts in infancy and continues through toddlerhood, but should begin to fade in the preschool years. If it doesn't, it's continuing presence may indicate a problem.

Take the example of the slave who, when asked, "How's the weather?" looks at his master's face rather than out the window in order to answer. None of us wants our children to grow up with a slave mentality! Be aware of how social referencing works, and go easy on using it to influence your children's attitudes, feelings and preferences. ❦

Encouraging Personality Differences

By Janet Gonzalez-Mena

"Two peas in a pod" may be a good way to describe vegetables, but it is not a healthy description of twin children. The ultimate challenge in raising any child is to encourage individuality; that challenge doubles in twin-rearing. Because they were born on the same day, parents may be naturally inclined to emphasize their alikeness rather than the uniqueness of each. This emphasis invites comparisons and contrasts instead of appreciation of each as an individual.

However, research has demonstrated what sensitive parents already know—individual differences between children are apparent in the first minutes of life. But parents must look for them. If they think all newborns look and act alike, they will look for the similarities, not the differences. If they regard their twins as a unit, they may miss the indications of each one's uniqueness.

While their twins are infants, parents may be so busy meeting their offsprings' needs that they don't have much time to think about shaping their personalities. But by the time they are toddlers, each co-twin's personality becomes a big factor in his behavior—a factor parents can't ignore.

Although at the age of 1 1/2 or 2 years, it may not seem so important to differentiate one twin from his co-twin, it is in the early years that themes are set that may cause problems later in life. For example, every person needs to see himself as a person separate from his mother (a process called individuation).

Twins have a double task because they must not only differentiate themselves from their parents, but also from each other. If left until the later years, this task can be formidable.

If twins have been treated as a pair since their births, when toddlerhood arrives, they will act the way that they have always been expected to act—in similar ways or in opposing complementary roles. They may see themselves as a single unit made of two parts—each a half of a whole instead of two separate people.

Examples of playing complementary roles include one child behaving in an outgoing and social manner and his co-twin behaving in a shy and retiring manner; one may be the leader and the other the follower; one may be active and the other passive; or one may be conforming and the other rebellious. Often these roles are interchangeable and when one twin switches roles, his co-twin may adopt the opposing one automatically. It is important to help twins get beyond these roles, which begin in toddlerhood, and find out who each really is.

Fraternal twins who do not look as similar as identical twins may have an easier time developing their own personalities. However, there's an additional trap in raising opposite-sex fraternal twins. It's easy to emphasize differences by stereotyping rather than looking deeper for true differences. Parental expectations work in such subtle ways that even in the first two years, children may pick up messages such as "little girls should be cute and helpless" and "little boys should be active, strong and competent."

In my four years of interviewing families of twins, I have discovered that many parents are well aware of the importance of treating each child as an individual. Here are some of the ways those families I've interviewed do so with their toddler twins:

• Call each child by name rather than referring to both twins together as "the twins." This practice helps others relate to them separately, too. If people can't tell them apart, some will talk to them as a unit because they are fearful of calling either by the wrong name.

• Help distinguish one twin from his co-twin by using such devices as different haircuts, names on their clothes, color-coded clothes or even distinctively different clothing styles. Cut each twin's hair in a way that is different from her sibling. One mother pierced the ears of one daughter and left the other's unpierced.

• Pay attention to individual personality differences. Attention tends to be rewarding, so this kind of differential attention promotes personality development along individual lines. At the same time, parents also help others (relatives, teachers, neighbors and friends) to tune into the children's individual differences.

Many parents see a difference between fairness and equality. They know that to be fair to individuals you can't treat them exactly alike, because no two people have exactly the same needs. Equal treatment doesn't end up being fair because it doesn't take individual differences into account.

• Encourage separate friends and social lives.

This becomes more important when the children are in school, but parents' attitudes in the toddler years will influence their children's actions as they grow.

• Regard children as individuals when buying them toys. Though many toys need to be duplicates because toddlers are not yet developmentally ready to share, some parents also look for special toys that encourage personality differences. For example, one twin may like quiet kinds of manipulative activities such as puzzles or snap-together blocks. His co-twin may be more actively inclined and prefer a ball and plastic bowling pins to knock over.

• Provide for individual space for each child, thereby allowing privacy and a sense of ownership.

• Plan individual time with each child on a daily or weekly basis. This approach helps parents tune into the unique ways each of their children responds to various people and situations. Sometimes this special time for one twin occurs naturally when children have separate schedules. For example, one mother puts to bed whichever child is sleepy first, then she enjoys an hour alone with his co-twin.

While providing for individual differences, sensitive parents are careful to respect the special attachment most twins have for each other. The goal is not to break the twinship but to appreciate it while helping each personality blossom in its own unique way. ♥

Chapter 5

DISCIPLINE

My Motto: Firm, but Gentle

By Janet Gonzalez-Mena

A little girl ended up with a dislocated elbow when her father tried to keep her from running out in the street. It was not his fault. He was trying to protect her, but when he grabbed her arm and jerked her back, the tendons gave. He had no idea that would happen. He felt terrible.

I've heard two stories like that one. The second was from a friend who was a preschool teacher. She was crossing a street with her own children, toddler twins, when the light changed. Her son held back, and she jerked his arm out of desperation as she saw the wall of cars roaring down on them in the distance. His little arm came out of its socket.

This sort of thing happens because we aren't always told how fragile children are. In fact, just the opposite. I remember a pediatrician showing me how to turn over a newborn baby. He was trying to prove that kids are tough. He did the turning by taking an arm and a leg and flipping my startled son from back to front. My son was horrified; I was horrified! I still am, even at the memory.

If we were told clearly that children can be hurt when we treat them roughly, many parents would stop shaking their little ones when they want them to pay attention, for example.

I think one of the problems is we don't understand the concept of being firm and gentle at the same time. I know I didn't. I thought firm and rough went together. Soft and gentle had to do with giving—the opposite of standing firm.

WHAT IS APPROPRIATE BEHAVIOR?

Sometimes it's appropriate to be soft and giving. Other times it's important to be firm—hard and unyielding. However, it's always appropriate to be kind and gentle, whether in the hard or soft mode.

My opening examples were accidents. The parents weren't angry, only afraid for their children. But an even bigger problem is when parents injure their children because they are angry with them. Unfortunately, it happens all the time. As a general term, "child abuse" is the label given to injuries that occur as a result of parental anger. Why do caring parents need to be aware of the effects that parental anger can have on their children? Read on!

Advice like "be kind and gentle" sounds inane in the face of parental rage. Who can remember that advice or anything else when children draw parents to the very ends of their limits? The problem of parental rage usually begins about the time babies grow into toddlers and develop "minds of their own." There's no stage when gentle firmness is more called for, yet it's one of the hardest times to give it. Toddlers know how to push parental buttons and get a reaction. Parents have to be ultra-patient and gentle, yet it's almost impossible to do so with toddlers in the house. Difficult or not, gentleness is a mandate; to be any other way is to put children at risk for abuse.

I believe that every parent has the potential for being a child abuser. It's normal and natural to get angry enough to cause injury. In my opinion, parents need to recognize and accept that fact and then take steps to protect themselves and their children from the results of potential rage. My message then may seem to be somewhat paradoxical.

I'm saying to acknowledge your rage, but don't abuse your children. Is it possible to have it both ways at once? Yes. here are some hints about how to do so:

1. When anger strikes, consider putting yourself in "time out" instead of your children.

Befriending your dragon

Parental anger is a problem for everybody. I'm no exception. I know my rage well; I see it as a "mean old dragon" who lives inside me. I can value being kind and gentle all I want, but that's not my "dragon's" style at all. She's wild and refuses to be tamed. As I introduce you to that side of me, let your imagination run free while you picture what my "dragon" monster does.

One way adults help children overcome their fear of monsters that appear in their dreams is to suggest that the little ones "feed the monster." It's surprising how far nurturing can go— whether it's used to tame dream monsters, children or ourselves. The key to calming wild energy is acceptance, love and understanding your own weaknesses—what makes you vulnerable to losing self-control.

Before I understood this concept, I tried keeping my internal "dragon" in check as a protective measure. But keeping her under "lock and key" didn't work. My children are too good at picking locks, pressing my "hot" buttons, as many people call it. They learned that skill in their toddler years. As a result, the dragon's "cage door" was continually coming open and then I was faced with a raging beast who had never been socialized. She didn't know how to behave out of her cage. Naturally, I was desperate to control this wild energy.

I think it's important for us to be gentle with ourselves even as we accept that we hold wild energy. As I got to know the "dragon mom" in me, I discovered that at heart she's not bad. In fact, she has some amazingly wonderful qualities, including a fierce protectiveness where her offspring are concerned.

So I'm working on being firm but gentle with that mean old "dragon" in me. She's wild, raw energy that needs nurturing and guidance. I'm learning to give it to her, just as I've learned to give the same to my children. Firm but gentle— that's my motto. I'm learning to be my own best friend.

2. As a preventive measure, give yourself periods of silence on a regular basis. Breathe deep and long. Count your breaths. Don't do or think anything for a period of time each day.

3. Meet your needs. As the flight attendant says, put your own oxygen mask on before helping others. How can you meet your children's needs if you neglect yourself? A parent with many unmet needs is a breeding ground for parental rage.

4. Go beyond basic needs and "baby" yourself whenever you possibly can. You need nurturing too. You're a very good source for your own nurturing. After all, who knows better than you what makes you happy? Take a bath or a walk, or make yourself a delicious meal or a snack. Do what you like doing and do it regularly.

5. Get out in nature. Smell the air, hear the birds and feel the dirt and grass under your feet. Get outside every day.

As I wrote each of the previous suggestions, I could almost hear parents of multiples protesting: How can I possibly do all that? I don't have the time or the opportunity!

To avoid this parenting pitfall of feeling like you have no time to yourself, try these suggestions:

• Seek support and backup whenever you can find it.

• Don't try to tough it out until your children grow up.

• Seek out resources to help you and use them.

• Don't try to do everything yourself, no matter how much you value your independence.

• Don't be "super mom" or "super dad." Know your limits of stress and responsibility.

If you have toddlers, it's essential that you deal with your parental frustration and maintain a sense of self discipline in positive ways. ♥

The Teachable Moment!

By Janet Gonzalez-Mena

With an eye toward observing her "teaching" behavior, I watched a parent with twin boys around 2 1/2 years old pushing a cart around the grocery store. I must say that I picked the right family to observe. This mother obviously had scheduled a chunk of time for shopping, and was leisurely strolling the aisles discussing all sorts of things with her children.

As I hung out by the lettuce watching discreetly, mom let her young sons help her pick a cantaloupe. Together they spent a good deal of time touching the cantaloupes, pressing and smelling the stem end and comparing one to another.

While I puttered around a pyramid of cans farther down the aisle, she was discussing which kind of juice each boy preferred and showed how to "read" the pictures on the outside of the cans.

THE TEACHABLE MOMENT

This mother showed a wonderful understanding of how to use what's called the teachable moment. She was tuned in to her children, aware of what was interesting to them. Responsive to their questions and comments, she also made a point to give them things to consider.

The most effective education for young children occurs when parents "take advantage" of those times when the "students" are alert, calm, interested and motivated. Parents can put a good deal of effort into trying to get their children into that mode, or they can stay alert to the opportunity and take advantage of the moment when they are in that mode and open to learning.

But just knowing how to recognize a teachable moment isn't enough. Parents must be sensitive to what their children are capable of understanding. They also have to be flexible when their children's interests change, and be willing to let go of the lesson when they see that their children have had enough "school."

BEWARE OF BECOMING "SUPER TEACHER"

Sometimes parents go overboard. Here's an example from when I first started studying early childhood education. I laugh now, when I think of how much I took to heart the idea that the parent is the child's first teacher.

"Skito," my little daughter told me, while pointing out what she had swatted on her leg.

I went immediately into my teacher mode. "Let's go find some books about insects," I said enthusiastically, as I wrapped the flattened mosquito in a scrap of paper, packed my daughter and insect package in the car and took off for the library. Science lesson time. I wasn't going to let this teachable moment go by.

"We're going to learn more about insects," I announced, nudging her through the doors of the library. I found the appropriate section after some research, but by then she had wandered off to play in the picture book section. I was still searching the shelves for insect books when she left the picture books to crawl around under a table near me.

By the time I found something I thought might interest her, she had escaped outside to a little enclosed patio and was busy poking a stick into the bushes.

I called her back in, without looking to see whether she had spotted an insect. She glanced at the pictures I had for her to see, then wandered off to look at some display cases. I gave up.

My heart was in the right place, but I went overboard. Instead of being sensitive to my daughter's level of understanding, I got involved in creating a lesson that was much too advanced for my child. I didn't acknowledge that she had lost interest in mosquitoes about five seconds after she swatted her first one, though she might have been enticed into further inquiry if we had searched for more bugs instead of traipsing off to the library to search for books on bugs.

I'm not the only parent who indulges in overkill. I remember seeing a toddler once in the Laundromat who asked a simple question about the change-making machine. The mother took the ball and ran with it, giving a 15-minute lesson on math, economics and how things work. She asked a million questions and answered them all herself while the child alternated between fiddling with a shoe lace and playing in a pile of spilled soap on the floor.

My point is simple: Pay attention. What is the child really interested in? What is an appropriate response to a question? What kind of response will keep each child on his own interest track?

Sensitivity, flexibility and responsiveness are the name of the game as a parent follows her child's lead. Find it tough to follow two paths at once as toddler twins pull in two directions? Good preschool teachers manage to lead a whole class, while acknowledging and responding to individual interests of their students. It isn't easy, but it is possible. And the advantage of twins is that one child sparks the other child's interest so that sometimes they're both going down the same path.

A walk with toddler twins illustrates this concept. If parents give up the goal of covering a certain amount of territory, they'll find many teachable moments on a stroll around the neighborhood.

If they truly follow their children's lead, they'll find that children sometimes want to go in different directions, but can be gently guided to stay on the same path and be interested in the same or different things on it. Parents can use the same teachable moment with both of their twins.

DISCIPLINE AND THE TEACHABLE MOMENT

Understanding the importance of the teachable moment is an important factor in discipline. Just after children have made a mistake is when they are most open to learning a lesson. Unfortunately, parents are often so intent on making that point they wind up yelling, spanking or putting the offender in time-out. When parents arouse fear, anger or resentment in their children, the original lesson is lost.

For example, suppose a 2 year old tries to help his mother clear the table and breaks a plate? His mother punishes him to teach him a lesson about being careful. Next time, instead of remembering exactly how he handled the plate before it dropped, the child focuses on the crash and the punishment afterward. The lesson becomes: Avoid this situation! That lesson doesn't teach him how to handle plates so they don't break. It also doesn't teach how to respond when a plate does break and needs to be swept up. Finally, it doesn't teach him to forgive himself if he makes a mistake.

Parents are teachers every moment of their waking lives, whether they're sweeping up broken plates or just walking through the grocery store with their children. It's important that they give some thought to what they teach and how they teach it.

Parents are the first teachers of their children, but they don't need to make lesson plans. They need only to be aware of the concept of the teachable moment and take advantage of it when it comes along. ♥

"No Enemy" Discipline

By Janet Gonzalez-Mena

Your toddler twins are jumping on your bed, tearing each other's hair out, or throwing their mashed potatoes across the table at each other. Your goals for their behavior are not a complex issue you're going to spend time worrying about. You simply want to stop them now.

Much toddler behavior falls in the stop-them-now category—so much, in fact, that it's easy for parents to concentrate on finding ways to do just that without thinking beyond to the long-term effects of their methods of guiding and controlling their toddler twins' behaviors. Parents often can't think about that when their multiples are demanding immediate attention by doing something absolutely intolerable. They can think about goals, however, when they're not in the midst of a crisis—and they should.

THE GOALS OF CONTROL

1) Should blind obedience be a behavioral goal? It would be nice if when twin toddlers headed for the street at the same time, they could be stopped in their tracks with a single command from their parent. In this particular circumstance, that approach might work—that is, if the parent hasn't overused the command mode before this incident. However, it's just as likely that they'll run even faster, making a game of defying their parent, unless something in her voice is able to communicate to them her urgency.

Parents should never depend on a child's obedience to voice commands to save a toddler's life; physical restraints (holding hands when approaching streets or being strapped in a stroller) are far more dependable than their obedience. In this way, parents provide the control their children lack. Parents also have the chance to teach their children about the dangers of streets so that later on, when they can control themselves, they'll realize why street play is forbidden.

Controlling multiples' behavior until they are old enough to control their own makes more sense in the long run than teaching blind obedience. When young children learn to conform without question to the wishes of their parents, they also learn some lessons about conforming to authority that work against them later in life.

For example, when they hit their teen years and come to regard their peer group as their guiding authority, the last thing a parent wants is for her child to blindly obey the kids who tell him to take drugs, shoplift or steal a car for a joyride. Teens need to be able to say "no"—loud and clear.

The ability to do that starts with the first "no's" in toddlerhood, when 2 year olds find in themselves the spirit of defiance that defines them as individuals. Parents need to foster that spirit of independence, not pursue blindly obedient behavior that will work against their children learning to control their own behavior for all the right reasons.

2) What about physical punishment? A parent's goal is to control behavior; does spanking accomplish that goal? The answer is "maybe." But using pain to control behavior is a little like using strong medicine to control disease—one has to consider the side effects. Hitting children as a means of guiding behavior teaches them that violence is an acceptable means of solving problems. It also teaches them that if you're bigger and have a good reason, it's OK to hit people.

3) What about punishment that isn't physical—say depriving twins of their favorite toys? Punishment of any sort, if it's strong enough, may suppress particular behaviors, but why he should behave in a certain way may well be lost in the negative feelings the punished child experiences. Punishment may control anti-social behaviors, but it doesn't create pro-social ones. Parents can't teach a child to be kind and loving by punishing him when he's not.

Guiding and controlling behavior effectively depends a good deal on children's relationships with their parents. If that relationship becomes a fearful or angry one because of the continual use of punishment, the parent is far less effective at guiding behavior in positive directions.

4) Is there a clear distinction between punishment and consequences?

Avoiding the use of punishment doesn't mean that twins should never suffer the consequences of their acts. Consequences can be clearly differentiated from punishments by choosing consequences that reflect a direct connection between what the child did and what happened as a result. Punishment can be perceived as being administered arbitrarily from above by an authority figure. Although the parent may make a verbal connection between the inappropriate behavior and the punishment—"I'm taking away your teddy bear because you hit your sister."—there is no logical reason why one act would follow another. Through a child's eyes, it's the parent, not the inappropriate behavior, that caused the deprivation.

There are logical consequences, however, to most inappropriate behavior exhibited by children. For example, a logical consequence of hitting is the temporary separation of the child from the playmate she's hit—so she can't hit again—rather than depriving her of a favorite toy. A logical consequence of throwing mashed potatoes is this child's removal from the table. Children can also be required to clean up messes they have made to the best of their ability.

5) Do parents model the behavior they expect from their children? If a parental goal for multiples' behavior is for them to become reasonable, kind, loving, generous, sensitive, gentle and respectful, parents need to model those very behaviors—especially while they are guiding and controlling their children's behavior.

Can parents stop their children's unacceptable behaviors in kind, loving, respectful ways? Definitely, but it's a matter of attitude. If a parent conveys attentive guidance to his twins when he takes their hands gently but firmly to cross the parking lot, it's a very different message from roughly jerking them along behind him because he's mad that they can't be trusted.

If a mother puts an out-of-control child in a chair to calm her down, and sits with her quietly until the child relaxes, it's very different from her ordering a tot to serve a two-minute sentence in a time-out chair because she was bad. The parent's actions may be similar in both instances, but attitude makes all the difference in the world. In the one case, she's helping her child learn to control her own behavior; in the second, she's punishing her child because she's angry.

Convincing a child through punishment that he is bad makes it virtually impossible for parents to then teach him how to guide and control his own behavior, because once a child sees himself in a negative light, he loses a large degree of his self-esteem.

It's far better for parents to convince their toddlers that they are unqualifiedly good, but that they need their parents' help in guiding and controlling their behavior. When parents and children see themselves on the same side, working for the same goals, the chance of reaching those goals is greatly enhanced. ♥

Chapter 6

PHYSICAL DEVELOPMENT

Exploring Their Brave New Worlds

By Janet Gonzalez-Mena

Risk-taking—moving from the secure to the unknown—is an important part of toddlers' educations as they branch out in their explorations and experimentations.

Although parents may prefer that their toddler twins avoid taking risks altogether, it is from this process that their toddlers will learn and grow.

In fact, a reasonable degree of risk-taking at an early age may better enable a child to make wise decisions when he reaches his middle childhood years and teens.

However, it is imperative that parents protect their children from dangerous risks such as swimming pools, glowing fireplaces or busy streets.

While dangerous risk-taking is not acceptable for toddlers, taking small, educational risks—both physical and emotional—is. Examples of physical risks include going down a slide; stepping a foot into the cold, loud ocean; walking a low brick wall; and being confronted by a familiar dog. Even finger painting may present a perceived physical risk to a toddler who shies away from squishiness. Emotional risks include being away from one's co-twin; being left with a baby sitter; being placed in a seat next to a stranger on a bus; and sitting on the lap of an unfamiliar relative.

The perception of what physical and emotional risks constitute dangers varies depending upon age, personality, ability and time. For example, getting into a shower takes no courage at all on the part of most adults, yet many children consider that experience to be risky.

Even co-twins may disagree about what constitutes taking a risk. It may take great courage for a twin to walk across a shaky bridge at the playground, while his co-twin doesn't even consider the act a challenge. Moreover, what may be perceived as taking a risk one day ("I can't go to Sally's house today!") may seem like an easy feat the next day ("I can't wait to go to Sally's to see her new doll!").

You may find that teaching your twins how to take appropriate risks can be challenging. Here are some suggestions to help you get started:

1) Protect your toddler twins from endangering their health or safety when risk-taking. Children learn early on whether they will be protected when they explore and experiment. They feel freer to take risks when they believe that they can trust adults to protect them.

2) Don't rescue your twins unnecessarily. Allow them to take risks in which they may fail when the consequences are safe ones that provide learning experiences.

3) Encourage physical risk-taking by providing an environment that presents developmentally appropriate challenges. If your living space tends to be risk-free, take your twins to the park for challenges on playground equipment, for example.

4) Allow and encourage emotional risk-taking when the situation arises.

For example, if one twin receives an invitation to visit a friend in nursery school, and his co-twin doesn't, allow the separation. You can even plan for emotional risk-taking by asking Grandma to take one twin to the zoo while you stay home with his co-twin and bake cookies.

5) Be careful that you don't reinforce patterns that put limitations on one of your twins. A common occurrence is to encourage physical risk-taking in boys and to discourage it in girls. The consequences of this uneven encouragement often produces competent boys who are sure of their bodies and physical skills, and girls who shy away from physical challenges.

Another common pattern occurs when twins have contrasting individual tendencies.

Rather than labeling one as "brave" and his co-twin as "scared," learn to appreciate and protect the natural risk-taker while encouraging the more cautious co-twin. To encourage individual development without limiting it, view each twin as a separate person with a special set of tendencies and capabilities.

Bathing Beauties

By Janet Gonzalez-Mena

"My twins, Heidi and Jeremy, were crazy about water when they were toddlers," recalled Janet Wall, of Napa, California. "In fact, she added, "if you looked through our photo albums you'd see lots of bathtub pictures." It's obvious that baths were a highlight of her twins' early years.

Playing in the bathtub provides toddlers not only pleasure, but learning experiences as well. Early childhood educators sing the praises of waterplay as an educational activity. Toddlers get a science lesson as they discover the properties of water.

Parents need to provide nothing more than a few containers and maybe a sponge or two so that children can pour, dip, sink, float and squeeze. Letting the faucet trickle a little can also add interest to bathtime as can providing bubblemaking equipment and solution (if you have a lot of time to spend on a particular bath).

Squirt bottles may be beyond your tolerance level, but children have a lot of fun with them. Providing boats or dolls with hair to wash, or washcloths sewn in the shape of puppets can add the dimension of dramatic play. Store bathtub toys in a plastic basket or net bag, so they can drain into the tub when you are finished.

"Safety is a primary concern, of course," Wall mentioned, reminiscing. "When you have toddlers in the tub, you have to sit there like a lifeguard. You not only have to keep an eye out, but you've got to be quick—especially when you're watching two."

Because safety is of such vital importance in bathing toddlers, keep in mind the following hints for making bathtime safe for your twins:

• Never leave them by themselves in the tub—not even for a moment. Have everything at hand so you aren't tempted to run around looking for towels, for example. Unplug your phone or put on the answering machine while you're lifeguarding.

• Always test the bathwater to make sure it's the right temperature.

• Make sure the bottom of the tub is not slippery. Wall did that by putting towels on the bottom. Non-skid stickers are available, or you can put a rubber mat in the bottom.

• Keep them from burning themselves accidentally by turning down the water heater temperature.

UNHAPPY BATHERS

Not all toddlers love bathtime. Some find being naked and/or having water on their skin uncomfortable. Being born prematurely may be related to discomfort of this particular type, called "tactile defensiveness."

Some toddlers reject baths not because of discomfort but out of fear. One common fear that strikes toddlers comes when they see water running down the drain. Children may be afraid that they, too, will disappear down the drain along with the bath water! They don't take the size discrepancy between themselves and the drain into account.

Help your child who resists baths by:

1) Avoiding bathing him every day. There is no rule that says a daily bath is a necessity. Determine how often the child really needs to be bathed and then go by that rather than insisting that bathing be a daily ordeal.

2) Being pleasant, gentle, firm and persistent about getting him into the tub. Try to avoid a dramatic scene or emphasizing the difference between him and a co-twin, if the co-twin likes baths. Simply don't compare them and express the wish that one was more like the other. That approach may backfire on you as one twin decides to define himself as different from the co-twin by hating baths even more.

3) Letting the child feel he has some choice in the matter. Let him dictate how much water goes in the tub, for example, whether playtime comes before or after wash time, whether he prefers to bathe alone or with his co-twin, or who will bathe him, if there is more than one adult in the household.

SHAMPOOING TIPS

Although baths were a pleasure for both the twins in the Wall household, shampooing was not. Many children have this same problem, so the following tips may help:

• Try pouring water over different parts of the body, working up to the head, or let the child wet his head.

• Put an unbreakable mirror in the bathtub so the child can watch the lathering process.

• Let the twins help you wash each other's hair.

• Place a doll in the tub so a child can wash someone while you wash him.

• Separate hair washing from bathtime. Try doing it at a different time in the kitchen sink.

• Use a face protector (sold in children's stores) to keep water out of a child's ears and off his face.

CREATIVITY IN MULTIPLES

Whenever you interact with a child, you get a creative response.

First words become simple sentences and as the years pass, they become bold statements. Smiles, frowns, giggles, shouts, even tears and tantrums are creative reactions. The creativity that blossoms and grows and benefits child development the most combines imagination and innovative action. As parents, it is vital to foster creative thinking in an environment conducive to positive development. Encouraging your little ones to expand their horizons helps them learn, integrate language and social skills, and move to the next level of experiences with confidence. ♥

Creative Play at Home
Building creative thinking skills and self-esteem.

By Jill Case, M.A., L.PC., N.C.C.

If your multiples are babies, you are consumed by the day-to-day care of your little ones. If they are older, you probably find yourself being asked to watch or be part of their play as they explore, experiment, and test their own strengths and abilities. In both scenarios, you get to play a marvelous role in your children's emerging development, creativity, and growing self-esteem.

DIRECTING THE PLAY

How can parents facilitate their children's play? First, we must allow for spontaneous play to occur, and in our scheduled universe, this is not always easy. As a play therapist and mother of four, I get to play a lot and observe play regularly. It is important to let the kids create their own play. Sometimes big people try too hard to organize and control the activities. When this happens, the play no longer belongs to the children.

Creativity multiplied

- Let your thoughts run wild; your kids will love you for it.
- Be silly together.
- Fill trays or pans with rice, dry beans, mud, sand or water and enjoy tactile play.
- Make funny faces and laugh.
- Play "Peek A Boo."
- Use socks or paper bags as puppets and put on a show.
- Dress up.
- Have a make-believe picnic or imaginary tea party.
- Build a castle.
- Make a tent with pillows and blankets.
- Blow bubbles.
- Construct towers with empty dry food boxes.
- Act out a story.

Read all about it

The Joy of Twins and Other Multiple Births, by Pamela Patrick Novotny

Touchpoints, by Terry Brazelton

The Hurried Child, by David Elkind

Free to Be You and Me, by Marlo Thomas

Parents as Therapeutic Partners, Listening To Your Child's Play, by Arthur Kraft and Garry Landreth.

Providing creative opportunities

1. Be available to play with your children.

2. Let your children tell you if they want an active participant or an audience.

3. Make neutral statements such as "Oh, you want me over there," and "I see, you want me to wear the blue hat."

4. Directing their own play helps children build confidence.

5. Make observational remarks such as, "I was watching your face when you put the baby doll into the carriage. You looked like you were thinking hard about what you were doing, and you were so careful with the baby doll."

6. Allow for differences. There is often a lot of pressure on multiples to be the same. Encourage personal interests and styles, and remember to treat all children as individuals.

Rise Van Fleet, Ph.D., a psychologist and registered play therapist/supervisor and director of the Family Enhancement and Play Therapy Center in Boiling Springs, Pennsylvania, states that some structured activities can help children develop skills and learn discipline. It's important, however, not to overdo it. Studies have shown that children with highly structured lifestyles often become anxious. Children develop best mentally, physically and socially when they have lots of opportunities for natural play.

According to Dr. Charles Schaefer, co-founder of the Association of Play Therapy in Provo, Utah, promoting closeness and intimacy between children and their parents is one of the primary benefits of play. Research shows that social dramatic play teaches empathy, pro-socialization development, and cooperation in preschool-age children. Play also develops imagination and flexible, creative thinking.

Jennifer Doell, a registered nurse in Colorado Springs, Colorado, and mother of boy/girl twins recalls that as her twins grew older their dramatic play increased. They loved to put on puppet shows using stuffed animals, unusual hats, costumes and masks, and the back of the sofa as their puppet theater. She admits watching hundreds of zany skits, giving her twins lots of praise for their efforts and keeping a sense of humor while she picked up after the shows and put the furniture back in its proper place.

INVITE RISK-TAKING BY PLAYING IT SAFE

Whenever you can, interact with your child at eye level. By doing so, you create a respectful and safe environment in which your children can learn to trust and risk to learn. Your relationship with your children in their play activities as well as their day-to-day routine is most important. Children need safe, non-threatening, caring surroundings in which to play and learn.

From a very early age, encourage your multiples to pursue their own interests. J.P. Lilly, L.C.S.W., president of the Association of Play Therapy and father of fraternal twin boys, places strong emphasis on allowing his twins to engage in play in their own way. He feels strongly that it is reflective of their individual personalities and emerging egos.

Rhona Chalson of Norwalk, Connecticut, says that after having her son and then her boy/girl twins, she has realized how immersed she is in the day-to-day care of her 7-month-old twins. She suggests that something as simple as going to a different room can get you out of a rut and add new stimulation for your babies. Rhona also suggests putting toys in different rooms. Some toys take on a whole new look when they're placed in a new setting.

Allow your kids the opportunity to solve problems. If one twin is performing a task in his play, try not to jump in and do it for him. Some struggle helps children learn problem solving techniques. Give your child time to ponder the problem and develop solutions. A little exertion is good, but if you see your child becoming overly frustrated, you can make an observational comment such as, "Wow, you are really working hard on that. Do you need some help?" A child's sense of pride and ownership is far greater when they complete or nearly complete a task themselves. But, let them know asking for help is acceptable.

WHO WILL YOU BE TODAY?

Role playing is meaningful for young children, says Kim Foito, R.N., B.S.N., of the New Canaan Medical Group in New Canaan, Connecticut. An imaginative exchange of creative ideas encourages individuality. One child can be the teacher while the other plays the student. Children may choose to switch roles to try out different positions. By observing this creative play, parents gain helpful insights into their children's perception of school, their instructors and discipline. Role playing exposes children to events that may actually happen or that represent their hopes and dreams.

Group play can be more directive than one-on-one play. Of course when you have multiples, you always have a group! If you are participating and pretending to bake a cake, have one child "read" the directions, one get the ingredients, one pour and one do the mixing. Each child has tasks, and everyone works to achieve a common goal, thus building teamwork and cooperation, and promoting focus.

PLAY IS AN IMPORTANT LEARNING EXPERIENCE

Play facilitates gross and fine motor development, cognitive and language development, and social adjustment. Throwing a ball helps strengthen muscles and improves eye-hand coordination. Socially, play provides an opportunity to practice sharing and other social skills.

One day at the playground I observed one of my twins closely watching another boy build a creation in the sand. My son stood close by but did not utter a word. I told the little boy how much my son was enjoying watching the building take shape. The boy's father soon approached and asked the little guy how he was doing. The boy's eyes sparkled and he said, as he looked toward my son, "Great, Dad, because I have a new very best friend!" No words passed between the two children, just a shared interest and respect. Adult life should be so easy. Maybe that's one more thing adults can learn by watching our children at play. ♥

Channeling Energy Positively

By Janet Gonzalez-Mena

Toddlers are powerpacks of energy who can either be productive or destructive, as parents of toddler twins know from firsthand experience. However, co-twins do not necessarily want to do energy-expending activities together just because they are the same age. It's easy to push them both out the door together when the energy level gets too high, but try to notice what kind of activity each needs to be doing and capitalize on their different interests.

To keep toddlers' energies flowing along positive channels, try these suggestions that have worked for many parents I interviewed:

1) Provide lots of opportunities for physical outlets and challenges. Visit a playground or gymnasium if no sidewalk, driveway or yard space is available at home.

2) Allow your toddler twins to have sensory experiences such as baking, playing with sand and water, or walking on blankets.

3) Redirect activities that bother you. (Replace mud with sand or couch with a trampoline.)

4) Change the location for some activities; move water play out of the bathroom and into the yard, for example.

5) Provide emotional outlets through media such as art, music, dancing and dress-up clothes.

6) Above all, provide activities that stimulate each twin's curiosity. Allow your toddlers the freedom to explore and experiment in a safe, interesting environment.

Batteries need both positive and negative contacts to release the energy they contain. Toddler twins are different. Clever parents can, in the words of the song, "accentuate the positive and eliminate the negative" (most of it), and the energy will have much better odds of flowing freely down appropriate channels.

One mother's saga of change

Jill Draper of Napa, California, is the mother of twin boys, Justin and Jesse, who have passed the toddler stage. She believes that keeping her children's energy flowing positively was not as much a matter of directing their energy as it was of making two major changes—one in the environment in which her children played and the other in her attitude about that environment.

She discovered that playing outdoors helped relieve some of her twins' energy, but once outside, they always gravitated toward making messes with dirt and water. She constantly did battle over keeping her home and her children clean after their dirty and wet explorations until she realized how much they were soothed by them.

Deciding that she didn't have to put up with the mud, Jill cleaned up the situation by putting a sandbox in her yard. Her children spent many happy hours there playing with both sand and water—but in Jill's experience, the combination was considerably less messy than the dirt and water duo.

Jill also made changes in the boys' room so everything was touchable and explorable, which first meant making their dresser unavailable to them; they had developed a game of throwing all their clothes out of it. She also took the ladder off the top bunk of their bunk beds and put things away that she simply didn't want them handling. She childproofed their room in other ways, too—a wise step for all parents to take to help keep their young children's energy channeled safely.

Able to Scale Tall Dressers in a Single Bound!

By Alice M. Vollmar

 Able to scale tall dressers, hang from crib rails, and reach the highest shelf, twin climbers go almost anywhere. No feat seems too daring for lightning-speed duos like the Nolan twins.

"They're making a break for it," reported an amused neighbor by phone to Patty Nolan, just minutes after she left her 2-year-old twin boys playing in the sandbox in the fenced yard. Rushing outside, Nolan found one twin at the top of the five-foot chain-link fence and the other on his way up.

"After that, I stayed close to them when they were outside," said Nolan. "I had to put their crib mattresses on the floor at 18 months. At 2, Alexander and Garrett ran wildly from one thing to the next. We began going to the park a lot so they could satisfy their climbing urge on the jungle bars instead of scaling our fence."

WHY KIDS CLIMB

The strongest urge in 15 month olds is the desire to climb," said authors Frank and Theresa Caplan in, *The Second Twelve Months of Life*. "No toddler can be left unsupervised during these critical climbing periods because every task is fraught with danger. Learning to manage danger is an art that is mastered in time...if reassurance and support are freely given."

Kids climb because it's fun, said Cheryl Halverson, physical therapist at Minneapolis Children's Medical Center. "At first, kids climb to explore rather than to get somewhere. Like mountain climbing, it's there to do; and they will do it, particularly if they have the strength to. It's an adventure; they get noticed for it and get a thrill out of being up high where they haven't been. It gives them a sense of height and depth perception and the relationship of one object to another. They see things from a new perspective."

Usually, children first learn how to crawl, then pull up on furniture, walk independently, toddle, and then climb, said Halverson.

After climbing (usually) comes walking fast, running, standing on one foot, and kicking. Usually, children start to climb between 12 and 17 months. And early climbers can be a handful, due to their lack of maturity and judgment. If climbing comes later, there's usually less climbing on tables and backs of sofas.

All twin climbers require adult supervision, but early acrobats especially need it. For parents' own peace of mind and their twins' safety, Halverson recommended providing "safe places for climbers to burn off energy, express independence, and develop motor skills, such as a 'roughhouse corner' in the house with pillows or play apparatus. I'd advise parents to help their climbers learn how to safely climb down by themselves, since getting down is harder than climbing up."

PERSONALITY AND CLIMBING

Climbing is highly individual, which is why some kids climb earlier and/or more adroitly than others.

"Personality is the most important factor in climbing," said Halverson. "The active climbers are high-energy kids, constantly moving. They may have advanced motor skills, but that doesn't mean they're going to be Olympic athletes. Since they get lots of practice, they are better at it than kids who are less interested in climbing; and it's not something twins teach one another."

Like walking, climbing is something each twin does when she's ready. However, although a twin doesn't actually teach her co-twin how to climb, a daring climber sometimes prompts her co-twin to try to climb a little sooner than she otherwise might.

CO-TWINS AND CLIMBING

Parents interviewed for this story observed that co-twins who differ in climbing also differ in personality traits. For example, 2-year-old Wyatt Hovland, a less daring climber, also has a more laid back temperament than his climber co-twin, Kyle.

Fraternal twins Bridget and Monica McEvoy,

Tips for Surviving the Climbing Stage

• Childproof your house by putting away unstable furniture and breakables, putting safety latches on cupboards or doors, and using gates for stairways.

• Have as few "don't touch" items around as possible to avoid constantly saying "No." Be consistent about enforcing rules about not touching those few items.

• Keep the dining room table out of reach, put the chairs in another room. Other strategies parents have used include stacking the chairs on top of the table or turning the chairs on their sides.

• Be sure poisonous items are locked away.

• Set aside one room or area for active play with cushions on the floor and climbing equipment such as a set of wooden steps, a climbing frame, or a toddler-size slide.

• As soon as your twins begin to climb stairs, take time to teach them how to come down safely scooting down via tummy or bottom.

• Involve your twins in acceptable physical activity by taking them to a park or playing movement games with them.

• If your twins keep climbing out of the crib, lower the mattresses or put the mattresses on the floor. One mother convinced her crib-scaling daughter to stay put by remaining in the room and calmly but firmly putting the child back in her crib each time she climbed out. After several nights, the climbing out ceased.

• Help your climber when they need help, but avoid anxious hovering or constant admonitions to, "Be careful." Overprotection can undermine confidence and prevent them from learning their own strengths and limits.

---

at 2, were also at unique stages of physical activity, said their mother, Leslie McEvoy.

"Bridget is athletic and could climb wooden play steps at 11 months, while Monica just recently started doing that. Monica has been about six months later than Bridget in her climbing."

Fraternal twin Henry Beck-Erdman started climbing at 8 or 9 months. "Early on, he scaled the dresser, the diaper pail, the car bumper and the desk," recalled his mother, Nancy Beck-Erdman, "and now he nose-dives onto the couch from the end table—all without getting hurt."

His co-twin, Emma, she added, "climbs where she properly should, onto the rocking chair or the sofa. She has no interest in doing what Henry does. He's in fast motion all the time, while Emma has more endurance."

Melissa Dahl, 3, climbed out of her crib at 9 months, rides the stair railing like a horse, and generally manages to climb to get things she wants, even stepping on cabinet knobs to get onto the kitchen counter, reported her mother, Debbie Dahl. Melissa's fraternal co-twin, Michelle, climbs up and then asks for help.

Then there's fraternal twin Scott Aasgaard, an early walker (8 months) who climbed before he walked. "Nothing was out of reach," said his mother, Julie Aasgaard. "He first climbed the entertainment shelves. I kept plucking him off of things. He's very curious and persistent, while Kimberly (Scott's co-twin) is more content with whatever she's doing."

Aasgaard tells about the day that she took Kimberly upstairs to quickly wash her hair. The house was locked. Aasgaard looked out the window and there was Scott, outside riding his tricycle. He'd climbed on top of the refrigerator, retrieved the garage door opener, carried it through the mudroom into the garage, opened the door and let himself out—at age 2.

"I'd sometimes wonder how he even thought of the things he'd do," said Aasgaard with a laugh. Now, at 6, Scott's climbing is more controlled because he understands that there are consequences to his behavior.

WHAT IF YOUR CHILD CAN'T CLIMB?

"Parents need to be concerned only if a child is absolutely unable to climb," said physical therapist Halverson. "That could signal a motor, perceptual or strength problem. Perhaps the child lacks the coordination to use muscles together in the right order. To climb, some muscles cooperate and others must be relaxed. It involves using the right muscles at the right time."

In such cases, the first step is to talk with your pediatrician. If you still have unanswered questions or are worried, then talk to a physical therapist or occupational therapist on your own, recommended Halverson.

NOT A CRITICAL MILESTONE

"Climbing is a normal developmental stage," according to Halverson, "a sign that a bunch of skills have come together at the same time, but it's not a critical milestone. Even if a kid does-n't climb, he can go on to lead a complete and normal life."

And for that matter, so can parents of twins who do climb. Climbing eventually gives way to the next developmental stage, as it has for the 4-year-old Nolan twins. "Now Alexander and Garrett channel their energies to work together to build a sand castle or play catch or soccer," Patty Nolan said with relief. ♥

Climb, Boys, Climb!

By Celeste N. Schroeder

I was just a little bit proud of myself and, of course, relieved. I had just finished purchasing all the new post-modern, technological gadgets to complete the task of child-proofing our house. My husband and I had attached them to the appropriate, enticing places: the fridge, stove, cabinets, bathrooms . . . in short, basically anything in our house which performed the intriguing task of opening and closing. One more bit of relief in my day was something I truly looked forward to. Yes, life would be a bit easier! Or would it?

And then the day arrived. I should have known it would. I had already been initiated into the land of childproofing by my energetic first son, so that should have been adequate training for the dynamic duo: my 1-year-old twin boys. At first, I just saw the little feet on the kitchen chair, but in a split second, faster than a speeding bullet, Micah had accomplished his first feat of that memorable day. He was standing with the pride of a mountaineer, he had climbed the kitchen table and now glowed with pride at his accomplishment. (Of course, part of the problem was that the kitchen table was white; he must have mistaken it for Mt. Everest.)

Well, that was the beginning. And, although the climbing phenomenon began only weeks ago, since then we have been inundated with climbing expeditions in our house. As an adult, I think the furniture in the house can be pretty boring, but from the eyes of 1 year olds, it apparently represents a fascinating world ripe for exploration. Who needs colorful climbing equipment when just in our little house there is an assortment of couches and chairs, sizes and shapes of tables, bathroom and kitchen counters and, of course, two toilets—a readymade indoor jungle gym? When you think of it, practically every object can be climbed on, or used as a springboard for jumping, leaping and falling.

I should have known that I was only deluding myself when I set out to completely child-proof my house. The reality is that my twins have worked their way through all of the technology of childproofing devices, and I keep running to the store to get gadget after gadget. Someone needs to invent foolproof childproofing for twins!

But Micah's climbing expedition was only the beginning; Caleb soon discovered he could climb too, and immediately joined his brother in the joy of climbing. Their 5-year-old brother, Lucas, stood in the wings, cheering them on. I was ready to put on that old favorite song from *The Sound of Music*, "Climb Every Mountain".

Maybe I just haven't gotten with the program yet. I think Caleb and Micah are waiting for some kind of affirmation for their accomplishments. After all, for most of the last year they have been earth-bound, only recently realizing that they can experience life at a whole new level.

It really is very exciting to them; their daily agenda is being filled with ways to eventually conquer and rise above the ordinariness of floor life. But then, they haven't learned the consequences of gravity yet.

That's not to say they haven't experienced their shares of falls and tumbles, but these only seem to fuel them on to greater heights.

Of course, mastering the summit of a single household is only the beginning. The real challenge comes when one, two or even three decide to climb over from the kitchen chair, onto the kitchen table and stretch across to the kitchen counter to peer out the window—or perhaps do something interesting with the coffee pot. Of course, there are hundreds of other Olympic events for the more experienced climbers, like climbing from the bed onto the bedside table,

then jumping to the drawers of the bureau, which have been pulled out by a co-twin, then leaping off. Who needs organized athletics? All this can happen in an instant, and with greater precision, as time is invested in this sport. They don't even need a trail map; they go by sheer instinct!

So I have taken on the role of distractor, learning to look at the world from their perspective, and then trying to create equally exciting, but safer, avenues for their energy—which means I have to actually get down on the floor and see the world from their point of view. This little exercise gives me a sense of adventure in the midst of my daily routine! ♥

Toddlers in Training

By Janet Gonzalez-Mena

"I don't remember deciding how to toilet train my children," says Barbara, mother of six-year-old twin girls. "I just tried lots of things and used the ones that worked."

Do what works! Those are key words for any parent and especially for parents of twins who are toilet training multiples.

What do experts say about what works? Magda Gerber, an infant specialist in Los Angeles, California, has an extremely relaxed attitude about toilet training. She said in an interview, "You don't have to worry about it. Toilet training happens as a part of normal development because children want to be like their parents or older children they see."

READINESS

According to Gerber, readiness is what counts. "They have to be physically, intellectually and emotionally ready." Physical readiness has to do with having the muscle control to stay dry for several hours and move their bowels at will. Intellectual readiness means they know what is expected of them. Emotional readiness comes when they are willing to use their newly developed controls.

Gerber advocates no training techniques, no preparatory exercises. She sees toilet training occurring as the result of a practice started in the first weeks of life—a practice of parents asking for cooperation from their children in caregiving routines such as diapering and dressing.

She stresses involvement on the part of the child in what she calls a "diapering dialogue." Learning to use the toilet grows out from the kind of teamwork approach that emerges from the diapering dialogue. Gerber stresses the importance of the diapering dialogue for parents of twins. "Diapering in this way forces you to focus all your attention on each twin as an individual. It's the one time in the day that individual attention is built-in."

"Being relaxed is fine," says Monica, mother of 3-year-old twin boys. "But waiting for willingness is easier if you have just one baby. With my two and no washing machine, I was in a big hurry."

Monica started trying to get her boys to use the potty at about 18 months and she admits it was a long, hard struggle. "I guess they weren't really ready. With all the accidents they had I probably ended up with the same amount of washing and a lot more headaches."

PATIENCE

Maria, mother of four-year-old twin boys, started with a different perspective. She says, "My boys were late, but I just told myself to be patient. I knew that by the time they turned 21 they would walk, talk, read and be toilet trained, so I waited and didn't push them. I tried to make it easier on myself by using disposable diapers, even though I had to make some other sacrifices because they are so expensive. One of my boys was ahead of the other, even though they are identical. But I expected that, because he's always been faster. I didn't push his brother (even though it was tempting) because I knew if he wasn't ready it would be a terrible ordeal. Besides, pushing shows up later in other forms—like negative behavior."

What is "late?" T. Berry Brazelton, in his book, *Doctor and Child,* discusses the age at which normal children are toilet trained. He says that in a "study of 1,170 children, on the average, daytime training had been completed by the age of 28 months; and in 80 percent of the cases, night training was done by the age of three." ("Normal" for twins may be slightly later if you take into account that many twins are born prematurely.)

Brazelton has laid out a step-by-step approach to toilet training in his book. He suggests starting by introducing a potty (you might use two) and getting children to sit on it once a day with their clothes on. He leaves it up to parents to discover what kind of incentive will work to get them to do this. (He suggests a cookie, reading to the child, modeling yourself by sitting on the toilet.)

Step three is to continue routine sitting time and start in a week or so taking the children to the potty after they have moved their bowels to show them that the stool belongs in the potty. Step four has to do with catching them when there is some indication of a need to urinate or move their bowels.

Brazelton suggests a little praise if there is success. He also warns that step four can only be done if children are interested and cooperative. Step five has them playing naked from the waist down and reminded hourly. Again, do this, he says, only if there is no resistance. If there is a lack of cooperation, you should bring the diapers back out.

If there is success at step five, Brazelton suggests training pants instead of diapers. But he also suggests continuing to use diapers for naps, night time, visiting and shopping until "well after the child has been dry for a long period." He assures parents that his method works. He points out that of the 1,170 children whose parents used his method, 940 of the children trained themselves for bowel and bladder simultaneously and accomplished it almost overnight."

Brazelton does not state in his book how his steps work with twins. Sarah, mother of a set of grown twins, reacts to Brazelton's advice:

"The problem with those steps is that my kids were so different in their development. My son wasn't ready nearly as early as my daughter and whenever I concentrated all my attention on just one for very long the other was off climbing the kitchen counter. So, you see, I couldn't very well have gone through each step unless they happened to be both willing and ready at the same time. It might work for children who were more similar in their development."

Both Gerber and Brazelton see toilet training as a process that occurs over a fairly long period of time. In contrast, Nathan Azrin and Richard Foxx, in their book, *Training in Less than a Day,* claim that half a day of concentrated effort will accomplish the feat. Using demonstration (a doll that wets), rewards (lavish praise and snack items), drinks to fill the bladder (drinks are also rewards) and practice, practice, practice, they claim children who are ready can be trained in one three- or four-hour period. The key again, as with Gerber and Brazelton, is readiness, plus individualized attention. The difficulty with using Azrin and Foxx's method with twins is finding a way to devote all that time to just one of them.

It's up to you. Do you want to follow a method or "play it by ear?" Whatever you decide, the following tips may be useful:

1. Help children feel physically secure as well as independent by using sturdy potties that sit on the floor and don't tip.

2. Dress children in loose, simple clothing they can remove themselves (elastic waist bands rather than overalls for example).

3. Try to be patient and relaxed. Avoid power struggles. You can't win them. If you have an emotional stake in toilet training, it will work against you.

4. Be gentle. Harshness connected with toilet training has harmful long-term effects.

5. Don't use competition or comparison as a motivator. You have enough natural competition without promoting it.

GOOD LUCK! ♥

"It Worked for Me!"
Potty-Training Tips

By Colline Schibig

Editor's Note. Colline Schibig sent 25 surveys to mothers of multiples around the United States asking them for their experiences when potty training. A Mothers of Twins Club in Houston, Texas, sent her the results of their own independently-run survey of potty training. She used their statistics along with her own surveys in writing this article. Though hers was not a scientifically run survey, Schibig believes that the respondents had as much to say as many of the so called "experts" on the subject. We join her in hoping that these firsthand experiences are helpful to those beginning, or "in the middle" of, this child-rearing stage.

Few child-rearing tasks seem to worry parents of singletons or multiples more than potty training. At Mothers of Twins Club meetings across the nation, conversations invariably lead to the "problems" of potty training. When a few mothers proudly announce that their twins have "finally" become trained, a chorus of cheers goes up. Parents who are still struggling with the task can hear discussions of various potty training methods, including the pros and cons of child-sized toilets on the floor vs. small toilet seat inserts for the regular toilet and whether or not to use candy as a "bribe" and/or reward.

We've all heard stories about babies who were potty trained at 6 months of age. This is physically, as well as intellectually, unlikely since most children under 2 years of age are not developmentally able to be trained in this endeavor. Therefore, it is the parents of these children who are truly "trained."

One mother I spoke with from California admitted that her mother, known as Granny, tried to potty train her 6-month-old son. Granny held him over the potty on her lap at exactly 10:30 am. because she knew that was when he did "big potty" after breakfast. She would make grunting noises and pretty soon the baby would, too; then he did his "big potty."

The mother of the baby saw that it was only Granny who was trained and asked her to stop doing so. When the child was 18 months old, he quickly learned how to use the toilet from watching his daddy. He did it then because he wanted to.

The information for parents to remember is that there is no need to rush into potty training (no matter what your mother-in-law says.). Trying to train your twins at too young an age will simply set them up for failure.

Children usually let their parents know when they are ready by showing an interest in the toilet and by asking questions about its purpose. Most children want to copy their parents and do exactly what they do.

When one (or both) of your twins comes to you with questions and an interest in going to the bathroom, then it is time to tell him how adults use the toilet and how he can do so, too. Another indication of readiness is a child's keeping her diapers dry for longer periods of time or waking up from a nap or in the morning with dry diapers.

When asked at what age they attempted to potty train their twins, most of the mothers I interviewed said at 18 months to 2 years. Several waited until 2 1/2 years of age. Those who waited the longest to start training their children had the quickest success. Staying dry at night usually took several months longer for the children to learn than keeping dry during the day, although several mothers said that their children were totally potty trained—day and night—at the same time.

It's easy to become frustrated when you are potty training twins. It always seems that everybody else's child is trained and it doesn't take long to get tired of hearing, "You mean Emily and Jay aren't potty trained yet?" Try to ignore these comments; letting your children know that you are upset with them when they won't use the potty only makes matters worse.

Ruth Lebovitz, of Franklin, Tennessee, made an important discovery while potty training her boy/girl twins. She said that a big mistake she made when initially potty training was not knowing that it is something a child does for himself so that he is more comfortable. She believes that it is important for the child to realize that it is his "problem."

Lebovitz said that she made a mistake by making the whole issue of potty training a personal battle; failure meant a disappointed parent, not an unhappy child. She was outraged that Robin (her daughter) was urinating inappropriately in the hall (or wherever) before making it to the bathroom! Once she turned her thinking around and had Robin clean up after herself and change her own clothes, Robin began reaching the bathroom before "an accident" occurred.

Lebovitz is not the only parent who put the potty training responsibility on her children. Diana Roye of Houston, Texas, began training her fraternal twin boys at age 2 1/2. As they got older and stayed dry longer, especially at night, she put more and more responsibility on them. They were changing their own clothes and sheets and taking them to the washer. At night, Roye dressed her twins in training pants with

plastic pants over them, used a mattress pad and plastic sheets on their beds and made sure they had plenty of spare pajamas and sheets handy before everyone went to sleep.

POTTY CHAIRS

A good time to purchase potty chairs is before your twins show an interest in using one. Some children need time to get used to just seeing the chairs in the bathroom and to become familiar with them.

There are several different styles of potty chairs available to parents. Some have detachable trays, so small that toys can be played with while the child is sitting there; others even include seat belts.

I believe that these "extras" are unnecessary because children need to learn that the bathrooms are for "business"—not for play. I believe that parents should never force a child to sit on a potty chair or let him sit on one "all day" playing or dawdling.

Since potty chairs are not usually used for too long, a good place to buy them are at twins clubs' clothing and equipment sales. As long as the chairs are still in good condition with no edges broken that can hurt a child, there is no reason not to save money and buy used ones since you will probably buy two.

Most mothers of twins I interviewed recommended buying two chairs so that each child has a chair of his or her own.

Though they usually come with a detachable front shield, or guard, to be used when training boys, most mothers told me that they didn't serve much purpose. Because the shields come on and off, parents should be forewarned that they can hurt little boys and, at the very least, can pinch.

Lois Elliott of Charlotte, North Carolina, potty trained her twins without the use of a separate potty chair or little seat that fit onto the regular toilet. Instead, she sat them on the commode backward so they had something to hold on to. She says that they were easily potty trained at 2 years of age by watching themselves go to the bathroom!

Though most books on potty training say that bowel training will most likely be learned first because bowel movements usually occur at regular intervals, more than two-thirds of the mothers of multiples I interviewed said urination control was accomplished first. A few said that urination and bowel control happened at the same time.

BRIBERY

What about trying bribery? All the mothers I interviewed admitted they used some sort of incentive. Hugs and kisses were given freely, but big rounds of applause seemed to be the most popular gift.

The people I interviewed did not use candy or food bribes as rewards as much as they used new big-girl and big-boy underwear! One mother said that her identical twin girls did not like the terry cloth training pants and would not wear them. When she bought plain, cotton big-girl panties, her girls loved them and only had two or three accidents in a week.

An original method of potty training came from Nita Landes of Rochester, New York. She has boy/ girl twins and two singleton boys that are all grown up now. She trained the boys by painting a bulls-eye in the bottom of the toilet with nail polish and told them to aim for that. They were trained without much difficulty! When they went out, Landes took a Prince Albert tobacco can with her and told the boys to "go" on Prince Albert. It worked!

If you think your child is ready to be potty trained, but no method seems to be working, maybe you should let someone else try it. My own daughter, Emily, was almost 3 years old when she was potty trained with the help of some M&Ms for reinforcement. However, her twin brother, Jay, was not so interested, even in the M&Ms. Jay told me that boys wear diapers and girls use the potty. I tried and bribed and begged to no avail. Finally the summer that he was 3 1/2, I went out of town to a convention.

My dear friend, Frances, kept both the children the entire week I was gone, and by the time I got home, Jay was potty trained!

Since many mothers of multiples and single-tons work outside their homes, many children are potty trained at their day care center, sometimes even without the day care worker's knowledge, as the following story shows: One mother reported that the only day care she could afford and wanted her girls to attend required that all "students" be potty trained. Terry assured the day care owners that the girls were potty trained, even though they were not.

The night before their first day at the day care center, Terry spent four hours in the bathroom showing both girls how much fun a potty was. They seemed to agree as they both climbed, crawled, stood and moved each potty chair all around the room—then proceeded to need their diapers changed!

The next morning, the girls excitedly went off to day care wearing training pants, armed with plenty of spares. Upon arriving, Terry explained that the girls were new to training pants and might have an accident. The day care worker assured Terry that everything would be fine.

At the end of the day, Terry sheepishly walked in to pick up her girls, expecting a frustrated teacher. However, to her surprise, she was handed back all the spare pants completely dry! All the girls talked about that night was how everybody got to march to the potty! From that day on, diapers were a thing of the past.

This story reinforces the basic principles of potty training: Don't worry about it. Never force a child to sit on the potty when he doesn't want to. Applaud his successes; ignore the failures. Children naturally want to grow up and mimic their parents. If parents are helpful, supportive and patient, their twins will "train" themselves when they are physically and developmentally ready. ❦

Potty Training in Pairs
Let your twins lead the way.

By R.C. Barajas

As parents of multiples, we breathe a collective sigh of relief when our babies "settle." They sleep through the night for the most part and begin to express their wants and needs somewhat verbally. In general, as some of the dust settles, they become a little more predictable.

They also start to show their true, individual colors in the battle of wills department. Which brings us to the subject at hand. Potty training multiples. An important thing to keep in mind as you approach the daunting task of separating your children from their diapers, is that in entering that battle of wills, you all lose. The bathroom is not a war zone, the diapers are not the enemy, and we cannot impose our timetable on our children. As parents, we undertake potty training to impart an essential social skill, not in order to exert our authority. When the children are physically and developmentally ready to learn that skill, they will do so. Reluctant children may have to be encouraged, frightened children may have to be reassured, but eventually, learn they will.

RESPECT INDIVIDUAL READINESS

Unfortunately, there is no package deal in potty training multiples, and it's not cheaper or easier by the dozen. Each child has his or her own agenda, and what works for one eager child has no promise of having the least effect on more reticent siblings. Parents sometimes end up straddling the fence as one sibling finally dons the underwear and the other grips even tighter on to the diapers. Vicki Lansky, in the book, *Toilet Training*, cautions: "Concentrate on treating the twins as individuals, not as a matched pair. Never compare the progress of one against the other. Don't impose one child's readiness on the other by comparing or blaming."

Meg Hogan, of McLean, Virginia, found that while Rachel, one of her fraternal girls, trained readily, Rebecca, generally the feistier of the two, resisted the whole process. Among the things

Signs for Potty-Training Readiness

According to, *Toilet Training in Less Than a Day*, by Nathan H. Azrin, Ph.D., and Richard M. Foxx, Ph.D., most children are capable of being potty trained at about 20 months of age if they are developmentally ready in the following areas:

Bladder control—If a child can stay dry for several hours, urinates a good deal at one time rather than dribbling throughout the day and seems to be aware of when he needs to urinate (by special postures he assumes or expressions on his face), then he probably has enough bladder control to begin toilet training.

Physical readiness—Being able to walk without assistance and demonstrating good finger and hand coordination makes a child a good potty training candidate.

Instructional readiness—A child's being able to understand and complete simple directions is a signal that he is intellectually capable to begin training.

that helped overcome the stumbling blocks were incentives such as candy (the old parent's helper), videos, and the social pressure of school. But in the end, Meg reiterates an unwavering truth of potty training: When they were ready, they were ready.

Readiness is really the key factor, and that readiness may strike your children at different times, reflecting their unique personalities. Says Betty Rothbart in *Multiple Blessings*: "Toilet training is a great time to reaffirm children's individuality."

WHEN IS A CHILD READY?

Some families sail through the trials of potty training relatively unscathed, as did Janie Krag and her identical girls, Kelly and Alyssa, of Los Gatos, California. Reading books together helped to spark interest and curiosity, says Janie, but the truth is, the girls were ready and willing and Mom hit the ground running.

Katie Schwieder's identical twin boys, Andrew and William, of Atlanta, Georgia, were the third and fourth children in their family. "By that time," says Katie, "we were pretty low-key about the whole thing." Katie made sure not to introduce the potty until the boys were mature enough to move ahead. "Potty training is one of the first steps towards building self-esteem," she believes. The boys did not compete, but rather cheered each other on with each success, and though one was dry at night well before the other, there was never any teasing or gloating.

Rosemary Kendall, Ph.D., a parenting instructor in Fairfax County, Virginia, lists some signs to watch for before beginning to potty train your children.

• The child can stay dry for several hours at a time.

• The child gives evidence when having a bowel movement.

• The child indicates interest in using the toilet or complains about being wet or soiled.

• The child uses and understands language.

• The child likes to be neat and tidy.

• The child likes to imitate adults.

Dr. Kendall also points out that there is certainly a cultural component to potty training that can affect the age at which parents consider their children ready. The average age for potty training in the U.S. is 28 months. In much of the world it is not uncommon for a child of 2 or younger to be already proficient on the potty. In the U.S., parents, educators and doctors emphasize the independence of the child, and so training does not begin until the child can take upon him or herself much of the responsibility for his or her own toilet learning. They learn to listen to their body's signals and to act upon them, rather than have an adult sit them on a toilet at regular, frequent intervals during the day.

The challenge in potty training multiples is not that we have more than one to train at a time, but in allowing each child to show us his or her own signs of readiness as the individuals they ultimately are. Although they share a birthday, it has little bearing on when their internal clocks are set to don that Lion King underwear. There may be an uneven few months with one child prancing around in the glow of newfound freedom, while the other wad-

dles obliviously along with serious "diaper bottom," but it is a small consequence for allowing our children to set the pace for this momentous development in their young lives.

Betty Rothbart reminds us, "Praise their efforts to try. Above all, express calm, unpressured confidence that each will learn this skill." It will, in time, happen. The diapers will be left by the wayside, and those days of bags, wipes and paraphernalia will be just an ever-fading memory. Calling on our diplomacy, patience and parenting skills and our faith in our children, will set the tone for success. ♥

You can lead a horse to water, but . . .

Fraternal twins Julian and Gabriel share clothing, a room and toys, but little else. Gabriel painstakingly constructs a tower. Julian demolishes it. Gabriel sits quietly and "reads"; Julian does gravity experiments with books over the banister. Gabriel zigs, Julian zags. Both boys had been routinely peeing in the potty. They each had a chart covered with colorful stickers as evidence of their successes. A drawer-full of character briefs proved they were ready to use big-boy underwear. I freely dispensed jelly beans when they asked to use the potty while still dry. And there was praise, praise, praise.

But all this was not enough to get either boy over the poop barrier. A screeched, "No poop in the potty!" ended most discussions on the matter.

Finally, the promise of microchip-enhanced Star Wars toys piqued their interest, but soon I saw that the mere offer was too abstract. Perhaps they needed proof of my sincerity. I purchased the toys and held them out in all their splendor like carrots on sticks. Incentive. Bribery. Whatever. Gabriel took the bait. He marched to the bathroom and pooped in the potty three times in thirty minutes. One down, one to go, I thought smugly.

I then let Julian hold the other Star Wars toy in its enticing box. I reminded him that he, too, could have the prize if he pooped in the potty. He beamed up at me.

"No thanks," he said.

He handed the box back to me and galloped out of the room with a big grin and a full diaper. It's the "one to go" that will get you every time.

Toilet-Training Times

By Harriet F. Simons, LICSW, Ph.D.

In our society, toilet training is a critical rite of passage—more for parents, it seems, than for children. Unlike walking and talking, toileting does not hold any obvious advantages to children. However, this goal may appear to be doubly advantageous to parents of multiples, who are understandably tired of the burden and expense of having two or more toddlers in diapers.

One mother of twin infants of differing sizes, plus a toddler, remembers sympathetic stares when she bought three cases of diapers—one in each size. The urgency attached to toilet training may be even greater if the mother of young twins becomes pregnant. One baby's due date might also become a toilet training target date for the older siblings, should the prospect of three in diapers be overwhelming. (On the other hand, some parents feel that having a child in diapers is actually easier than supervising that stressful transition period during which "accidents" may occur frequently.)

While having twins in their family may increase parents' desire to toilet train their children, just as they'd like them to walk instead of having to be carried, for example, some twins may not be ready, willing or able to be that "grown up," and might actively resist pressure in that direction. Parents must, therefore, weigh their understandable desire for certain phases to progress with realistic developmental expectations.

Toilet training illustrates to a great degree how twins are individuals, and how dissimilar their individual developmental paths may be. In fact, the very desire for individuality, coupled with the autonomy issues that toilet training evokes in all children, may interact to cause twins to respond very differently to the same approach at toilet training.

WHEN TO BEGIN

Parents who begin toilet training a child at too young an age usually end up spending more time in "training" than those parents who wait.

Pediatrician Benjamin Spock, M.D., does not recommend performing any training activities in the first year. While he grants that parents can "catch" their children at the correct time and eventually elicit a conditioned response to eliminate when placed on the toilet, he points out that such children are not really cooperating willingly. In fact, he fears that children trained in such a way will be more likely to rebel later with prolonged periods of soiling or bed wetting.

According to psychologist Burton White, Ph.D., "If you attempt training when he [your child] is between 14 and 24 months of age, you will run headlong into the rise of negativism. That is the worst possible time to try."

Dr. Spock, however, feels that by the second half of the second year (18 to 24 months), many children begin to display signs of readiness. Elizabeth Noble states in her book, *Having Twins*, that while no child under 18 months will have adequate neurological development to be successfully toilet trained, most authorities do not recommend trying to toilet train twins before 2 years of age. In short, there is obviously no single answer as to identifying the optimum time to begin.

Some signs to watch for which may indicate readiness are:

• Diapers which are dry for a couple of hours.

• The ability to understand and follow simple commands.

• A dislike of being wet or soiled.

• Indicating verbally or with a physical signal when a bowel movement is coming.

• an inclination toward tidiness and orderliness (such as putting things into containers)

• A desire to imitate older child or adult behaviors.

• Pride in learning new skills.

However, bear in mind that a child may not demonstrate many of these behaviors and may still be ready; these are suggested as guidelines only. One mother remarked that her child would never have been toilet trained if she had waited

Toning Down Reactions

Since toilet training is such an inevitable part of parenting, there is no scarcity of opinions on the subject. To the contrary, relatives and friends may all have their own "surefire" approaches which they will zealously recommend.

Unfortunately, unlike other developmental achievements, toilet training becomes a matter of public knowledge and comment, particularly if a somewhat older child is obviously still in diapers. Day care centers and nursery schools which require toilet training for admission exacerbate the public pressure. Fortunately, parents of twins may, to some extent, be exempt from external pressure by the very virtue of having twins; however, this does not allay the internal pressure.

New mothers often compare the progress of their children, which can lead to feelings of competitiveness and/or failure. While other developmental gains are more elusive (how do you compare the beginnings of insight or compassion?), toilet training is a tangible, observable behavior which may affect new parents' sense of competence. First-time parents may have a greater need for reassurance that they and their child are "normal."

One mother reported that her firstborn was late in achieving toilet control; but she was able to commiserate via long-distance phone calls with a college friend whose daughter was the same age and was also still untrained. When the call finally came to announce that the friend's daughter was out of diapers, the young mother felt abandoned and was amazed to feel the urge to abruptly cut short the conversation. Perhaps more surprisingly, toilet training her twins later was a matter of much less urgency and certainly less ego.

Your approach to this issue taps into individual feelings about yourself, parenting and roles within your family, as well as your understanding of your own children and their individual needs. Hopefully, it will not become a forum for "proving" your parenting skills or comparing your children's progress. However, these dynamics are very real, as illustrated herein, and, coupled with the often seemingly overwhelming work of caring for two babies in diapers, can lead parents to try toilet training when they feel it is necessary, rather than when the children appear to be ready.

Although parents may reason that there is little to lose by just trying, the process once begun seems to take on its own momentum and can result in feelings of failure on the part of both parent and child if not completed successfully.

The authors of, *The Early Childhood Years*, Theresa and Frank Caplan, caution that in the matter of toilet training, children fare better without too much parental interference. Letting children learn themselves without coercion, they say, is usually more successful than efforts to "train" them. Author Vicki Lansky's, Best Practical Parenting Tips , states it succinctly: "Remember that if you try to push things, you'll only be training yourself." Pediatrician T. Berry Brazelton, M.D., concurs, citing data which indicate that children, on the average, achieve daytime control at 28.5 months of age. Since it is impossible to speed up physical maturation, parents who try to "force-train" their child become engaged in a battle of wills which leads to "mutual misery" and a "warlike atmosphere." Penelope Leach, in her book, *Your Baby & Child*, agrees that parents cannot win by imposing their will, and advises parents to "tone down" their reactions in order to diffuse a potentially loaded situation.

Easy Training Tips

• Purchase two potty chairs and let the children get comfortable sitting on them (most children prefer these to using the big toilet).

• If you are comfortable with the notion, let the children watch you or older children using the toilet.

• Put the child on the potty prior to a diaper change. Ask the child to tell you when he feels the need to eliminate; when he does, take him directly to the potty whenever possible.

• If you decide to try one of the purported rapid training techniques which require constant one-on-one attention, arrange for someone else to care for the co-twin during the day of intensive training.

• Take a portable potty with you during those days of intensive training. It is hard enough to locate a bathroom for one child without having another toddler along on the mission.

• Explain to each twin when he is ready to use the toilet that he will no longer wear diapers but underpants (exhibiting attractive "big boy or girl" underpants for later use can be motivating).

• While it might make excellent logistical sense to you, don't expect a co-twin to use the toilet just because his twin needed a trip to the toilet and you'd like to avoid another. Using the toilet prior to feeling a sense of urgency is cognitively and physically difficult during toddlerhood.

• Praise the child's success, but don't overdo it; never punish or shame for "accidents" or a reluctance to try.

for him to have dry diapers, although the training proceeded smoothly once initiated. Parents are ultimately the best judges for each child and must make the decision they believe is best for their family.

TWIN DYNAMICS

While experts note several common criteria for determining when a child is ready to be toilet trained, there are no guidelines for when (or if) to begin "team" toilet training. The issue is complicated when two children are involved: Do parents start training both when the first is ready, wait to train both until both are ready, or train each as it seems appropriate to their individual levels of readiness?

Although there might appear to be less duplication of effort in training twins together, this may not, in fact, be the case, especially if there is a sex difference. One mother of boy/girl fraternals reported that her daughter trained herself at 2 1/2, while her brother was content to wear diapers until 3 1/2. The mother felt so lucky to have one out of diapers that she was quite content to have her other twin take his time.

Authors Theresa and Frank Caplan point out in their book, *The Early Childhood Years*, that in no area of functioning are individual variations more striking than in toilet learning. This is especially true of twins. One twin is not being more "cooperative" than the other when he learns toilet habits quickly; he may simply be at a stage of greater readiness.

Some parents fear that the later-trained twin will get discouraged or abandon attempts at using the toilet altogether if his co-twin has already mastered this task. One mother of girl twins feared her twins' tendency to pick complementary activities would mean that, while one opted for toilet training, the other would automatically rule out that possibility!

The Parents Book of Toilet Training, by Joanna Cole, tells about a set of boy fraternals who demonstrate the effect of individual differences. Both shared the thrill of accomplishment when the first child successfully used the potty at 2 years of age. Although thrilled at his brother's accomplishment, the co-twin had no interest in using the potty himself. At 2 1/2, the first twin was wearing underpants all the time while his brother had yet to try. Several months later, after demonstrating no interest in this achievement in the meantime, the co-twin trained himself in two days and never had any problems with toileting after that.

This example illustrates the point that toilet training is more than a physical or developmental issue; it also reflects learning styles and risk-taking behavior. As is so often seen in walking, some children like to explore and learn by trial and error; others prefer to take it all in and wait until they are good and ready, confident of success.

While parents may be tempted to use the "trained" twin as a model, such an approach may exacerbate normal competitiveness. In fact, it is important that the twin who is using the toilet or potty be restrained as much as possible from teasing his co-twin about his not doing so. This is a good time to point out individual strengths and diversity in areas far afield from toileting.

Some techniques of reinforcement which are suggested in training single children might not be advisable for twins. For instance, a chart with stars, or awarding a special treat, might serve to overemphasize differences. Although parents may "soft peddle" the difference in achieving control, co-twins themselves are quite cognizant of what each is doing.

Some parents of singletons look forward to their child attending nursery school or play groups so he will have some exposure to children who have been toilet trained, hoping that "peer pressure" will accomplish what parental urging could not. Twins have a perfect opportunity to learn from one another and usually do so, sometimes without their parents' knowledge. Elizabeth Noble illustrates the case with the example of the twins who took longer to be potty trained than their older sibling. On the other hand, she reported, once initiated, "the job was much easier with the twins as they learn a lot from each other through imitation."

The amazing thing about toilet training is that, once accomplished, it rapidly ceases to be of importance. A mother of twins at her first grade parent/teacher conference was asked about differences between her twins. Who was trained first did not even enter her mind! In this, as in so many parenting challenges, a sense of humor and perspective are crucial. Remember that parents even parents of multiples, all seem to survive this stage of their children's growth. ♥

The End of an Era

By Janet Gonzalez-Mena

Thump! I remember that sound as plain as day—the sound my son made when he climbed out of his crib for the first time. He managed the feat easily, swinging both of his feet over the bars of his crib, dropping or slithering down the side, and landing without hurting himself.

But the thump I heard was definitely him hitting the floor. I leapt at the sound and met him at the door of his room, as he came waddling toward my bedroom with a big grin on his face. "Free at last!" his smile said to me.

Climbing out of the crib is a big moment for tots, and the end of an era for their parents. With their newfound freedom, children can't just be put to bed and be expected to stay.

So what do parents do when cribs can no longer contain their toddler twins?

BEYOND THE CRIB

For some parents, this event prompts a move to "regular" beds. Other parents continue to use the cribs, but leave the sides down, so it's not so dangerous for them to climb out. Others take out the crib mattresses and put them on the floor so the danger of climbing is eliminated. Cribs can be used for years—the standard crib is called a six-year crib—but most parents get rid of baby furniture long before their children reach kindergarten age.

Replacing the furniture is the easy part. The hard part is getting children to sleep when they are no longer physically confined.

If the going-to-sleep routine has been fairly easy all along, the lack of confinement probably won't create problems once the children get used to the change. But children who fight bedtime or have trouble settling down can make things hard for parents once they find themselves with freedom from crib bars. What do parents do then?

It may take a period of constantly and patiently hauling the wandering child (or children) back to bed every time she gets out. It may seem to take forever, but most parents find that, if they are consistent, their children do eventually learn to stay in their beds.

Some parents find that it helps to put their children to sleep in a very routine way at the same time every night so the children are used to the regularity. Others look for signs of sleepiness and put them down then. Both the by-the-clock parent and the on-demand parent may use a bedtime ritual designed to settle the children down and give them the message that it's sleeping time. Usually, rituals are created jointly by parents and children and may include music and a story. But they may vary, even within the same family.

"Tickie!" demands Shelby, thrusting a foot in her mother's face. Since she learned to climb out of her crib at about age 18 months, she's found she can enjoy her mother for a longer period of time in the evening. Now she's allowed to stay up a bit after bath, jammies and toothbrushing so she can snuggle on the couch. When she asks for her foot massage, it means she's starting to get sleepy.

Her mother knows the pattern well and scratches the sole of her daughter's foot until she notices Shelby start to play with her fingers, stroking them very gently, always an indication that it's time for sleep. Her mother gets up and puts her into her bed, and then sits with her a short time, scratching her feet until Shelby, predictably, drops off.

Amanda, who hasn't yet learned to climb out of the crib, snuggles nightly with her daddy and a special blanket while Shelby is getting her "tickie." It's easy to put her into bed after the snuggle, because she goes right to sleep with her thumb and her "blankie" to help her along. She has her own comfort devices and doesn't need adult help usually, though she does enjoy a foot massage, too, now and then.

Children have their own ways of going to sleep. For a few children, it's easy. All they have to do is get into a horizontal position when tired, and their eyes close just like those dolls with weighted mechanisms inside their heads. But most need more than a horizontal position. Many have developed self-soothing skills. Shelby strokes her fingers; Amanda sucks her thumb. In addition, Amanda has a comfort device—her "blankie." Other common comfort devices are special pillows or stuffed animals.

Toddler twins who have slept in separate cribs may choose to sleep together once they can get to each other. If this arrangement is disruptive to the children's sleep or is otherwise

Keeping Them Cozy in Their Cots

• Be kind but firm. When they get up, insist that they go back. Escort them if they don't go on their own.

• Be clear in your own mind that bed is where you want them. If you're ambivalent, they'll know it.

• Make bed a place where they're used to sleeping. It helps if they know when they climb in what they're supposed to do there. Don't use beds for punishment.

• If the environment doesn't already say "sleep," consider ways you can transform it. Create a peaceful atmosphere by lowering the light and eliminating noise. Soft music can help. Put toys out of sight, as much as possible.

• If you don't already have one, create a bedtime ritual that includes an unwinding period and takes individual needs into consideration.

• Encourage self-soothing skills. The more that each child can calm himself, the easier your job will be when it comes to bedtime.

• Some children settle down better with a heavy blanket on top of them. Try this and any other safe "tucking in" measure, like putting covers tightly around them, to reassure them that they're safe and cozy in their cots.

not in the children's best interest, parents may choose to teach their children to sleep apart through gentle training and constant insistence that they get back in their own beds.

TO SHARE OR NOT TO SHARE

Once toddlers have the ability to climb into their parents' bed on their own, many will often do so. If parents want to keep their bed a "no-kid zone," it's important for them not to be wishy-washy about this rule.

Bedtime conflicts can trigger enormous power struggles if parents become too "heavyhanded" when dealing with their toddlers.

It's important that when parents put their children back in their own beds, they reassure them that they're not being abandoned. The children need to know that the parent is still close by. It may take continual reassurance and reminders on the part of the parent, however, before children finally soothe themselves and fall asleep.

Problems getting toddlers into bed and keeping them there often have more to do with parental attitude than the techniques they use. A parent who has been gone all day may have some internal conflict about making his children go to bed instead of spending time with them. Even though this parent may be firm about bedtime, the children pick up on his ambivalence and react to it by resisting sleep.

The parents who have the easiest time getting children to sleep are those who are sensitive to their children as individuals and are clear about their need for sleep.

It becomes especially difficult to deal with bedtime when toddlers are overly tired. An evening out can disrupt sleeping schedules and make bedtime extra difficult. Or if parents miss the signals that it's time to put a child to bed, they may find that he has gotten wound up and may be hard to settle back down. Some children stay up until they drop from exhaustion because no one reads the earlier cues. Timing is critical when it comes to putting children into bed.

Persistence is also important. A firm but gentle insistence on "back in bed" is the way to deal with the question, "What do I do when they learn to crawl out of their cribs?" ♥

Chapter 7

LANGUAGE DEVELOPMENT

One Family's Language-Learning Adventures

By Bethany Reid

"Silence was the soundtrack that accompanied my picture of motherhood. Sure, I had a realistic side, but during the seven years my husband and I worked our way through infertility treatments and then adoption preparations, I was motivated by a mental picture of myself rocking a cherubic infant, the two of us alone in a wordless reverie. Then, with a single word, the silence was shattered: Twins!"

In the three months I had to prepare for the arrival of our fraternal twin daughters, I was never able to imagine myself with two babies. I had a feeling, though, that things weren't going to be too quiet around my house.

I went to the bookstore and bought every book available on raising twins. There I discovered all the stories about two-hour, round-the-clock feedings for low-birthweight infants, and about toddlers who worked together to pull the furniture down. Nothing fazed me.

In fact, I read the passages out loud to my husband, Bruce, and we were both utterly charmed. He went out to buy special bolts to secure our bookshelves. I went to the library to look up books on prematurity.

Nothing I learned about twins worried me until I read that twins often experience language delays. It may seem an exaggeration to say that I felt a genuine dismay, but as a teacher I have a heightened awareness of the benefits of good language skills.

Yes, I had harbored a blissful, silent ideal of motherhood, but all along I had competing expectations of books, babble and even some precocious conversation. Learning that I could not take these for granted helped me to to begin to entertain a more complex view of what mothering twins might entail.

It also made me question my abilities. Could I provide enough stimulation for two babies at the same developmental stage, day in and day out? If twins—as one author and mother put it—get "half as much" of everything, including parents and parent-talk, was I ready to start talking twice as much?

It wasn't a difficult decision. I wanted these babies, and I wanted whatever was best for them. If talking twice as much would help them to develop good language skills, I was willing to go for it. I envisioned myself prattling away to two interested, engaging little faces.

Still, I was unprepared for the reality of Annie Rose and Pearl Alix. Are any of us ever fully prepared for the impact our children make on us? Fortunately, they were full-term, healthy and gorgeous. Because their terrific birth mother shared the hospital experience with my husband and me as much as rules would allow, we were able to introduce ourselves with an onslaught of chatter from day one.

And perhaps because I was spared the physical ordeal of birth, my idealizations survived the twins' birth intact. I was certain that once we got Pearl and Annie home, the alphabets and English lessons would commence in earnest.

REALITY SETS IN

At first, Annie—the 5-pound, napless wonder—had the edge. She was on the receiving end, so to speak, of spirited exchanges during changes, bottles and baths. I thought it predictable that she should be our babbler. At age 2 months, when she scolded her father for trying to put her to bed, we were ecstatic. We called the grandmas long-distance: "Annie is speaking in complete sentences!" Since then, I've read that even hearing-impaired infants babble. So much for our superior parenting.

Pearl, who preferred to snooze through her bottles and changes, would wake at 11 p.m. and stay awake until 2 in the morning. I, of course, was awake with her—determined to follow the "low lights and murmurs" guidelines for getting her switched to a more acceptable schedule.

As a result, from the vantage of her Snugli, little Miss Pearl didn't hear much adult conversation. Although for a while I was stumbling through the daylight hours as well, once we'd established a routine, I began feeling like myself again. But my goal to "talk twice as much" took a back seat to the joyful business and busyness—of caring for our delightful little daughters. I didn't have time to worry about language development.

My interest in the subject was piqued again earlier than I would have guessed, when at 6 months of age, Annie and Pearl were asked to participate in a language study at the University of Washington in Seattle. Bruce and I were flattered (as if our darlings had merited the honor by doing anything besides being in the card file, and being the right age at the right time), and readily accepted the invitation, in spite of the difficulties of transporting two babies across town in January and at nap time—three days in a row.

The study was one of several conducted by Professor Patricia K. Kuhl, a noted researcher in language development. As subjects in the experiment, each baby had to sit on my lap observing an amusing but not too engaging parade of toys, while listening to a randomly timed series of repeated syllables, such as "ga" and "la". When the syllable changed, a box lit up and, inside, a toy bear beat on a drum. The baby learned after only a few repetitions to turn her head to look for the drumming bear before the light switched on, signaling that she recognized the difference between the two sounds.

Pearl and Annie excelled. I was pleased to learn that they had completed their testing early, when only 30 percent of the studied 6 month olds are projected to finish. I was more than pleased: I boasted about my little geniuses to everyone. Much later, it occurred to me that their patience and good attention spans may have had as much or more to do with the girls' success as did any special ability with language.

Dr. Kuhl's work, ongoing for about 10 years, is not specific to twins. Rather, she has discovered that all babies in the first half-year of life learn to identify sounds significant to their language, and to screen out sounds not significant to their language.

That won't surprise many parents, but it has far-reaching implications. Among other things, it has enabled a new evaluation of "motherese"—the baby talk that child development experts denigrated a generation ago. Now it seems that the drawn-out vowel sounds and accented consonant sounds of baby talk are crucial to language development.

In short, when parents say "baby want the rattle," we emphasize sounds that are usually "rattled off" more sloppily. The emphasis on "prototypes" of our language, Kuhl believes, helps lay the groundwork for infants to begin processing real language. If twins hear less language even in their first six months of life, then it may make sense that their first words usually spoken around age 1 will be delayed.

But do twins hear less language? Participation in the study prompted me to learn more about language development specific to twins. Idioglossia, or autonomous speech, has been the topic of many researchers' language studies for the past several decades.

In addition to noting that many twins develop a private language, a belief in delay of language acquisition for twins also persists in the scientific community. In fact, some researchers have found an experiential basis for delay, but the phenomenon is much more complex than its myth.

IT'S NOT INEVITABLE!

To begin with, language development delays in twins versus singletons is a tendency, not a rule. Some boys talk earlier than some girls, in spite of their "tendency" to speak later. Certain younger siblings begin talking at an earlier age than their big brothers or sisters. And some twins are terrific with language from the get-go.

Where delay exists, some observers point to the home as the predicating factor, not a biological or psychological disability inherent to twins! Instead, the "triadic" relationship, versus the usual "dyadic" one between a parent and a single baby, is a practical difference in homes where two or more infants must share one primary caregiver. And research shows that "zero spacing" of twins exaggerates the effects evident between conventionally spaced siblings.

Though one study demonstrated that twins hear just as much speech as do singletons, much of the research indicates that mothers of twins speak less often and more briefly to their children one-to-one. Mothers of twins may also tend to be directive ("Billy, come here!"), rather than conversational ("Billy, what are you drawing?"), simply due to the amount of caregiving details they have on their "to-do" lists.

Not all of these findings are convincing. Many researchers appear to be looking for deficiency, perhaps to prove their theories about nature versus nurture. Others fail to isolate "the twin situation" as the only compelling factor affecting language. Large families, older siblings, financial stress, and illness, including prematurity, can all play a role in language development. In studies where these factors were eliminated, twins fared much better.

One such study is that of Svenka Savic, widely cited in books on raising twins. Savic asserted that the way twins learn to speak is not inferior to the way singletons learn to speak, only different. Using the scale developed by psychologist and child development theorist Jean Piaget, Savic suggested that twins engage in a more advanced form of speech—social speech—before the less advanced "egocentric" speech.

A more recent article gave an example of this, maintaining that twins often "name" their rela-

A Language-Building Strategy

Has my strategy to "talk twice as much" been the right strategy to help Annie and Pearl with their language development? Actually, it wasn't a bad idea. But in the meantime, I've picked up a few more practical guidelines for helping young twins (or supertwins) develop good language skills:

1. Much of the time, parents of multiples interact with their babies en masse, so take opportunities for individual interaction when and where you find them. While changing a diaper or adjusting a carseat, narrate your actions and name or "label" whatever is appropriate to the situation.

2. If you're lucky enough to have twins who entertain one another, try not to leave them on their own for too long. The existing research demonstrates that adult interaction and especially interactive parent-child chat, of any nature, is extremely valuable for language development.

3. Call your twins by name when you speak to them, and wait and listen for each to respond. When you address them together, get into the habit of expecting a response from each.

4. Read to your twins individually when time allows. Expressive reading aloud geared to an individual child is crucial to the development of good, and maybe superior, language skills.

5. Even while your young twins are still prattling nonsense syllables, try to be an attentive and responsive listener. Perhaps the "cocktail party" model will work for you—you know, where you try to follow two or three fascinating conversations at a time!

6. Don't talk until you're hoarse. Remember that even the "experts" can't control all the variables that go into when and where your twins will begin to talk. So relax and enjoy your precious little ones!

tionship before they name themselves, giving the appearance of a delay in their language development.

Another more recent study found twins "performing in the normal range" for language skills. Researchers assessed 40 multiple-birth children who, though they tended to use a shorter "mean length of utterance," showed more dexterity in adapting their language to different conversational partners than did singletons.

Research indicating a difference between the way twins acquire language and the way singletons acquire language is often contradictory. One claim is that the more similar the twins, the more pronounced the delay. Thus, identicals tend to be more delayed than fraternals, and fraternals of the same sex tend to be more delayed than fraternals of the opposite sex.

One researcher concluded from this generalization that early separation of twins was the best way to avoid language delay! A 1989 study, however, found no difference in language acquisition between 13 sets of identical twins and 13 sets of fraternal twins.

LONG-TERM EFFECTS

What are the long-term effects on twins who originally experience delays? On this point, researchers agree: Most twins do catch up with their singleton peers, usually around school age. This point can't be overemphasized. The fact that many delayed talkers catch up in expressive language—words said—indicates that their receptive language—words understood—is not delayed.

Even as I felt bogged down in the mounds of material available on this subject, my 9-month-old daughters were beginning to try out their first real words: "gog" for Pearl; "ruff" for Annie. They were also developing a repertoire of sounds for each other and beginning to play and giggle at one another.

Even at this tender age, I suspected that having a built-in age mate wasn't detrimental to my daughters' development. When I later asked other parents of twins about their experiences, I heard as often about early and on-schedule talkers as about late ones. And a dear friend of mine, an identical twin, informed me that not only is she a writer considerably gifted at language skills—but so is her twin!

In fact, I'm beginning to wonder if the necessity for twins to accommodate their relationship as they learn to speak couldn't ultimately make them better communicators. In any case, I now know that twins occupy a wide spectrum in regard to language skills, as do singletons. My fears about developmental delays for my twins have vanished.

Annie and Pearl have almost reached their first birthday, and their "Da" and I have watched them learn, by the simple virtue of their being human, an amazing amount. Along the way, we've discovered that we value their twin relationship as much as we value their amazing uniqueness as individuals. Gone is my old fantasy of the quiet singleton!

Are they prodigies in the language department? Probably not. But Pearl has a small recognizable vocabulary, and Annie has an extremely useful expression, "ditdah," that seems to mean something or other. And they babble like gangbusters. They rattle off incomprehensible strings of words, then crack up laughing—strong indicators that they're already telling each other knock-knock jokes.

Obviously, their daffy parents are still bragging them up (at least twice as much) to anyone who will listen! ♥

The Art of Doing Nothing

By Janet Gonzalez-Mena

"I've got lousy leisure skills," my friend complained to me. "If I'm not being productive, I go crazy! My son also has lousy leisure skills, but he's the opposite of me. All he ever does with his free time is watch TV. You should see the two of us together on vacation. It's pitiful."

Sad! Two people who don't enjoy their free time. How do people end up in adulthood with poorly developed leisure skills, anyway?

As with most things, it starts in childhood. Children are born with the potential for developing excellent leisure skills, since they start out life with nothing but free time. And, in fact, they are capable of filling it very well. One of the qualities of young children is their ability to find something to do, especially in an environment that encourages exploration. When adults see children with free time, however, they have the tendency to fill it for them.

I know all this because I was, at the beginning, just such a parent. I remember thinking how bored my first baby must be when he was just lying there with "nothing to do." I thought that because when I lie around not doing anything, I'm bored; and I projected that feeling onto my child. It took me a long time to discover that my baby was not me!

Those parents who see their job as distracting their babies from "boredom" need to consider the fact that a tremendous amount is going on inside a baby's head, even a very young one. Fully experiencing the world around them is plenty of activity for most babies.

Many parents worry so about their babies being bored that they constantly haul them around. I remember carrying my baby from room to room as I moved through the house. I hardly ever left him in one spot long enough for him to really absorb all that was coming in, let alone contemplate his navel or the universe! I believed that constant change was good for him.

By the time he was a toddler, therefore, he was used to the idea that it was my responsibility to entertain him. He didn't consider himself capable of entertaining himself for very long.

I wasn't the only parent doing all this entertaining. With some of the experts pushing early stimulation, many parents still think that it's their job to keep their children busy. Parents even convince themselves the children are learning something.

But many of those toddlers grow into preschoolers who are hooked on the tube. When given the chance, many dedicate more and more of their lives to TV. Leisure skills in such children are lost as TV-watching replaces valuable play time. Although parents don't mean for this to happen, children learn that they must be entertained or they will be bored.

Some parents, eager to take advantage of their children's precious early years, or perhaps to keep their children from spending too much time in front of the TV, over-schedule them or over-structure their activities. These same parents may also be making up for all that they missed as a child. Again, leisure skills are lost as children don't learn to make decisions about how to spend their time in ways that allow them to tune into their own needs, feelings, aptitudes and interests.

What's needed, really, is a good balance. One extreme is to sign children up for every lesson available and then frantically drag them around town, keeping them busily occupied in between. At the other extreme is keeping toddlers in a bare room all day. Obviously, neither works well for either parent or toddlers.

A balance includes toddler co-twins having time with nothing planned except to enjoy each other in an environment that is appropriate to their age level—one that allows the youngsters to pick and choose as they explore it. In addition, it's wonderful to plan simple, uncomplicated activities that toddlers enjoy. Invent things that they can do in their own individual ways and in their own time.

Child choice is a key here. Water play or

blowing bubbles are standard toddler activities. A short walk to the park followed by exploring the sandbox and swings is another time-honored toddler activity.

Watch out for a need to keep them constantly occupied. The keep-them-busy attitude of the parent can produce misguided notions of productivity in the child.

Leisure skills are vital. Children master them by being given free time that they can choose to use in recreational ways—active ways that don't involve being entertained from the "outside." Recreation means renewal, which is lost in the face of constant distraction.

Most of us busy parents could use a few more leisure skills ourselves. If we model them for our children, they'll get the best lesson of all. Besides, most of us will live long enough to come to a time in our lives when the work stops. If we "recreate" as we go along, we won't be so stuck when our children grow up and we suddenly find ourselves with nothing to do! ❦

The Importance of Early Interaction

By Janet Gonzalez-Mena

Early education is a hot topic lately. This year brain development was the focus of everything from media to government. *Time* magazine featured it in a cover story, a prime-time television special called, *I Am Your Child*, explored brain development, and it was a topic of discussion at the Presidential Summit for America's Future, held in Philadelphia.

The conclusion of all this coverage: Early education is important. The experts agree that if you ignore the beginning years, the effect on a child's brain can be disastrous. They also agree that it isn't schooling that young children need. Instead, what they need is play. Children learn more by playing with toys, boxes and people than any formal lessons we could ever think up for them. Flash cards and worksheets are out.

Building blocks, modeling clay, dress-up clothes, dolls and empty cardboard boxes are popular.

MAKING CONNECTIONS

"Making connections" are two key words that appear in all the various reports on brain development. Interactions lead to brain connections. When toddlers play peek-a-boo, for example, they are creating actual physical and chemical connections in their brains that advance the ability to think and reason. When children interact with objects they also make those connections. As toddlers pound modeling clay, stagger after a push toy, stack measuring cups to create a tower or explore a cardboard box, they are increasing their brain development.

A GOOD USE OF TIME

We now have some convincing scientific evidence that play is a valuable use of toddlers' time. When parents understand play, they tend to encourage it instead of just tolerate it. Toddler multiples play by exploring their environment, taking things apart, experimenting with everything in sight and inventing ways of doing things you never thought of—all in the name of brain development.

Of course, squeezing the contents of a toothpaste tube onto the carpet may be playful as well as inventive; parents have to put limits on some activities. The challenge is to set boundaries without squelching creativity. They must distinguish between activities that are truly unacceptable from those that are merely unusual. If toddlers want to line up the puzzle pieces and make them into a choo-choo train instead of putting them into the puzzle the way they belong, they are being creative. Why not let them?

Toddlers are bundles of curiosity and that can get them into trouble. Not only do they squeeze toothpaste tubes, they unroll toilet paper and even try to rip things apart to see how they are made. Parents can cope with this kind of behavior better if they consider that this driving need to explore and understand is an essential trait of toddlers.

PARENTS' ROLE IN PLAY

Toddlerhood is the time to nurture inquisitive spirits. Much of toddlers' play is pure experimentation. Play is play whether children are singletons or multiples. One of the benefits of being a multiple is a built-in playmate. The disadvantage is that they have to share their parents so their interactions with adults are more limited than those of singletons.

When parents are available to children while they are playing, they can take numerous roles. Sometimes directing the action is important, but this, too, should be a limited role as children need the freedom to play the way they want.

The most effective roles of parents are supporter, mentor, collaborator and safety monitor. For example, when problems arise, parents can support the children in seeking their own solutions. If that doesn't work, the parent becomes a mentor by talking them through the situation so they can learn the skills for solving their own problems in the future. Even toddlers who have limited language can benefit from this approach, as parents model the skills the children will eventually learn. Problem solving, which arises regularly as children play, creates many brain connections.

The role of safety monitor is a vital one. Only when children feel secure can they freely engage in play. It's up to parents of multiples to arrange the environment so that no one gets hurt and to monitor the interactions taking place in that environment.

All these roles are very different from the teacher role. Though the adult may want to sit toddlers down and give them lessons, toddlers resist that approach to education. They're not programmed to sit still and listen. Their urge is to be playful. We now know that they are doing what is best for them—and their brain development. ❦

Flush Out That Talk!

By Janet Gonzalez-Mena

"Poo-poo-poo-poop," chants 2 1/2-year-old Caitlin, playfully relishing the sounds coming out of her mouth.

"Potty-potty-potty," her co-twin, Briana, chants back.

Why would two sweet little girls need to say such things?

Caitlin and Briana are learning about body functions and about language at the same time. Both are fascinating subjects to some children of their age, though the ability to manipulate either may not come quite so early to all. Many children do not show interest in bathroom matters until the preschool years.

Caitlin and Briana, at 2 1/2, are very involved in toilet training. They've recently learned to use the potty and are proud of their accomplishment. They may even be "crowing" about them in their chants.

WORD POWER

At the same time these two are learning to control their body functions, however, they are discovering that words and sounds are interesting. Just as they explore the objects in their physical environment, so too do they explore the words that come their way.

During their explorations, they are bound to discover that some interesting words are also powerful. They learn this from the response they get from others.

Most parents respond mildly to the kind of bathroom talk illustrated by Caitlin and Briana's chants, and it is most likely that the girls will soon outgrow their new game.

But innocent little chants that play with bathroom words are just the beginning. Before long, Briana brings the term "poo-poo head" home from a visit to her cousin's home. The first time she uses it at home, she is just trying it out, like any new word.

"You poo-poo head," she shouts at Caitlin, just the way she heard her older cousin say it.

Her mother's mouth drops open and then clamps shut as a frown creases her forehead. She leaps up from the couch and rushes over to her daughter. Grabbing both her arms, she looks her straight in the eye and says with great emotion, "That's not nice. I don't ever want to hear you call your sister that again!"

Well, that's all it takes.

Both children, stunned by their mother's reaction, make a big discovery. Words have power.

Caitlin now knows that she has been insulted and she knows also, from her mother's reaction, that she too should react when called these words.

Both girls also learn that if they want to get a rise out of their mother, all they have to say is "You poo-poo head" in the right tone and context.

Once children learn about the power of words, however, they want to use them. It's exciting to get such a strong response. And although Briana is quiet after that first incident—no more bathroom talk for her today—you can bet that the memory of their mother's reaction is ingrained in both girls. Next time either of them wants attention, or needs to feel powerful, she will probably pull those words out and use them again. She may even pull them out just to test them. Will the effect be the same every time? she'll ask herself.

Briana and Caitlin are on their way to learning what adults know so well—that words can hurt, heal, soothe, calm, excite.

Children start using forbidden words because they don't know any better. They hear them and imitate what they hear. If the adults in a child's life use adult versions of bathroom language, their children are bound to use those words too. They become a part of their vocabulary. If they keep hearing them, they'll continue to use those words even if they are told they are wrong, bad or distasteful.

They may also take on the label they've been given for people who use that kind of language

and think of themselves as "bad" because they use "bad language." It can be very confusing to children who hear those they love use language they have been told is wrong.

It seems reasonable that a parent could stop the use of inappropriate language by expressing continual disapproval. That only works if the habit isn't too ingrained and if the child

Clean-up crew to the rescue!

So what can you do about "cleaning up" a child's mouth? Forget the soap and water. Here are some far better ways to deal with bathroom talk:

1. Ignore it. Without a strong reaction, most bathroom words fade away over time. If a word is being used as a way to get your attention, ignoring it is by far the best response. There's no reward in yelling "You poo-poo head" at someone who turns and walks away.

2. Tell your child your feelings regarding those words. If you feel uncomfortable about ignoring certain expressions, say "I don't like to hear you say that—it really bothers me." (This direct feedback only works if the child cares that it bothers you and is willing to stop.)

3. Teach your children the same techniques. Ignoring annoying behavior to make it go away is a lesson that most of us take a lifetime to learn, but it doesn't hurt to start teaching it early. Also, teach your child that he can express his feelings about being called names—even though that may not be effective in stopping the name calling.

4. Teach alternative ways of expressing feelings. Give your children words that you approve of besides name calling and bathroom talk. One mother whose children were determined to use "dirty words" made up some "pretend dirty words" as substitutes for the real thing.

5. Set some limits. If they can't make bathroom talk go away by ignoring it, some parents assign a special place where inappropriate language is allowed. "Go to the bathroom for bathroom talk," is a rule in some homes. This can be done without a punishing attitude, but just as a way of sparing the rest of the family words they don't care to hear.

6. Model language you want your children to use. It's important to set a good example. Screening movies and television programs helps too. Children have a knack for picking up those very words we never want them to learn.

feels like pleasing. Toddlers are known for contrary behavior, so assuming that they are inclined to please adults is not always an accurate assumption.

If parents keep in mind that their children tend to repeat that which makes them feel powerful, they'll see how important it is to defuse bathroom talk by ignoring it or downplaying it. Above all, they should keep out of power struggles. Parents can't win them. As in toilet training, there's no way a parent can control what comes out of a child, so they can save themselves the energy and frustration. It just adds more power to already powerful words when parents make a big fuss.

There's nothing bad or abnormal about toddlers using bathroom talk. They're doing what children have done since the beginning of time—learning to use language in all sorts of ways. ♥

The Ecstasy of Excess!

By Janet Gonzalez-Mena

Power struggles between parents and children are often the result of parents not letting their children get something out of their systems—not letting them thoroughly do something they really need to do. Of course, limits and balance are also important, but both can catch parents in the trap of a power struggle. That's where occasional excess comes in.

Here is an example from my own life: As a child, I loved to read, but felt I never got enough time for it, so I used to sneak a flashlight into bed and read under the covers. Once my mother discovered my nocturnal activity, she put a stop to it.

Not long after her ban on my late-night reading, I devised a plan to end my frustration: One rainy vacation, I gathered up a lovely stack of books, settled myself in an easy chair by the fireplace and started reading. I did nothing for days on end but read. I've never gone through such a reading orgy since; but I look back on that vacation with warm memories. It was good for me to be so excessive.

Another personal example of the benefits of excess is more recent. My daughter and I had been locked in a furious power struggle over bedtime for years. I wanted her in bed early; she wanted to stay up late. This issue started in infancy, when she refused to lie down in her crib and would go to sleep standing up. By sixth grade, we were both sick of bedtime arguments.

The first night of that summer's vacation I announced to her unexpectedly, "Go to bed whenever you please. I'm not going to tell you anymore." So she stayed up all night. Not just one night—for many nights. She became a nocturnal creature.

Her day began sometime between lunch and dinner. She was just getting warmed up to work on some project when I went to bed. I'd get up in the morning to find a sleepy girl getting into her pajamas; on the counter would be the brownies she had baked at 2 a.m. Sometimes she even did housecleaning by moonlight!

I thought this was strange, but I told myself, "She's just getting it out of her system." I was right. Once she had thoroughly experienced being the boss of her own bedtime, she switched back to a normal schedule—and, wonder of wonders, it was a sensible one! She began putting herself to bed at an appropriate hour and has continued to do so to this day. I never again had to say a word about staying up too late. She became the one worried about getting enough rest for the next day, so I didn't have to.

Another example of excess can be found in the wild or mischievous play of young children. Of course, no parent likes his or her children to act rough and rebellious under the guise of play, and I'm no exception. Children running around screaming—out of control with hilarity—can grate on parents' nerves, to say the least. But oddly enough, playing to excess is an ancient tradition in many societies and is a form of celebration found in cultural rituals around the world. The play experts call it "illicit" or "festive" play.

Festive play is an example of going overboard, but sometimes children just need to take that plunge. A reputable childcare program has learned to work just such a liberating ritual into its normally sedate routine; although the program keeps its children fairly neat and well-managed most of the time, one day of the year is dedicated to wild abandon. That day is mud day. When the weather is declared just right and the parents have been advised, the staff puts bathing suits on the children, runs a hose on the dirt in the play yard, then turns the children loose. The kids go overboard wallowing in the mud. Of course there is a big mess at the end of the day, but hosing down the children is part of the fun. Mud day is an event that is remembered into adulthood by the children who participate in it.

Imagine for yourself, if you can, that you have a mud hole in the back yard, and it's a constant problem to keep your toddler twins out of it. Of course you're not going to have mud play every day—it's too much trouble. Besides, it may not always be warm enough, and it's hard on clothes. There are many reasons not to let your children play in the mud; but if, for once, you ignored all those reasons and tried it out, you might be surprised at the benefits.

If you've never experienced excess yourself, it may frighten you. After all, if you go overboard, how do you know you won't drown? Can you picture yourself climbing back aboard the ship of decent behavior again? And, if you can't, do you say to yourself that it's best not to take any chances?

Not to fear. You can climb back aboard, and you will. So give yourself a little rein now and then and your kids too. You will all be better for it. ♥

How Do Emotions Affect Learning

By Janet Gonzalez-Mena

I sat in a filled auditorium waiting for a lecture on "The Link Between Thinking and Feeling." The lecturer did not begin on time due to problems with the slide projector. The minutes crept by, and the audience grew restless.

Finally, the speaker walked to the lectern and commanded "Slides!" to his assistant.

The lights went out, but nothing happened. Tension grew. A light flashed on the screen and quickly flickered out. Darkness again. Suddenly there was a loud crash as though 100 slides had spilled out onto the floor. The house lights went on, revealing a distressed assistant in the back of the room.

But our attention turned back to the front when the lecturer threw his notes down and stomped into the wings. The audience gasped and held its collective breath. Before we could let it out, the lecturer returned to the podium and asked, "Well, how are you feeling, and have you learned anything yet?"

I got the point immediately. The emotional overtones of the session had completely obliterated anything I might have gained from his lecture. He gave us a firsthand demonstration on how emotional climate affects the ability to take in and understand information.

Think of toddlers in the bathtub faced with a furious parent trying to teach a lesson about keeping the water inside the tub. What lesson do the children remember? It's hard to tell. Think of toddlers who live in a household where angry feelings between parents are the rule. How does it affect them? Even a little lesson like staying off the coffee table changes when emotional overtones in the house are present.

Of course, parents get upset about their children's behavior, and about each other's behavior sometimes. However, it's good to be aware that these feelings affect learning. If you're furious about what your child did to her co-twin,

Don't Cry Over Spilled Milk

So what can you do to help keep the emotional climate at least neutral, if not positive?

Here are some suggestions:

Keep your perspective. It helps to remember that toddlerhood is a stage and it will pass. The negativity and defiance come because toddlers are working on issues of autonomy. They are trying out their power. Keep your perspective on the matter, and it may help you keep your temper.

Save the lessons if you get too angry. Just get through the situation. Sit down afterwards with your child or children and reflect back on what happened. Talking about things when you have all calmed down helps.

Keep out of power struggles. Sidestep a power struggle when you perceive that you're headed into one. Don't be as stubborn as your toddler; use your adult intelligence to figure out how to keep from bumping heads.

Be aware of the possibility that your child (or children) may be seeking negative attention. Some children find that they can get parents to spend plenty of time and energy on them only when they misbehave. In a sense, they learn to misbehave. When that happens, parents must demonstrate that attention comes from positive behavior more readily than negative behavior.

Talk in the trenches . . .

From bulletin boards on the **TWINS** Magazine Home Page

Older siblings are important, too. I have a 5-year-old son and 3-year-old boy/girl twins. Since they were born, my older son has been consistently left aside by the curiosity of strangers who ask the most incredible questions about the twins. I learned very soon to introduce him into the conversation as soon as it started as the wonderful older brother of the twins. It helped get him some attention. Also, whenever we went out with someone else, I sat one of the twins with his/her brother in the double stroller and the other twin in the single one. This way the twins weren't so notorious, and we were able to peacefully do whatever errand or just walk as we had planned to do.

Maybe you could just praise your older child in front of strangers to try to wake them up . . . Something like "Yes, they are twins, and (the boy) is their great older brother"

Jealous older singletons

I am the mother of three girls. One is 3 and the twins are 3 months. I try to give my 3-year old attention, but it never seems to be enough. Today, while we were watching TV, I was holding her on my lap and the twins woke up. She started to cry and scream, "No, you can't feed them. You need to watch TV and hold me." I told her she could sit next to me while I fed the demand that she could sit on my lap when I was done, but she still cried, yelled and stomped her feet. I don't know how to deal with her jealousy.

It has been a long and rocky road dividing my attention up equally (between my twin girls and my older son) and dealing with the jealousy. I tried to spend every one of the twins' nonwaking hours making up time with my son. We started home preschooling him and that seemed to take the edge off of the jealousy, since preschool was something just for him. It is 10 months later, and we still have bouts of jealousy going on, but now it's with all three of them!

Problems? Solutions? Issues To Discuss? You can post your messages or send e-mail to **TWINS** Magazine at www.Twinsmagazine.com.

for example, let her know that you won't allow that behavior—but wait until you calm down to help her understand the situation. If you're upset about rough treatment of the cat, stop it—but save the lesson on how to pet the cat for when the emotional climate is right.

It's not easy for parents of toddlers to continually create an emotional climate that is conducive to learning. Toddlers can challenge their parents in ways that trigger emotional responses in even the most mild-mannered person.

A big shock for me as a parent came when I

discovered how different toddlerhood is from fantasy. Those sweet, innocent babes that just lie there become walking balls of fire once they get up on their feet. And by 2 years of age, there's no stopping them! Toddlers demand a different kind of parenting from what they needed as infants. They need parents who set limits and enforce them in a firm, but calm, way.

THE POWER OF FIRMNESS

Being firm is a real switch for many parents. Infants don't call for firmness—but rather, responsiveness. Reading their signals and meeting their needs are the primary concerns. The question is, what are my babies trying to tell me, and how should I respond? Toddlers still have needs, of course, but those needs often lead them into behaviors their parents never even thought of. And besides having needs, they also make impossible demands. The best parental response in the face of a good deal of toddler behavior is firmness.

A firm but calm response is easier said than done. It's very difficult to keep from losing one's temper in the face of some 2-year-old behavior. How many parents are able to face toddler defiance and negativity calmly?

It's hard, but important, to create an emotional climate that is conducive to learning. If you understand that whatever you're trying to

teach the child is probably lost when you blow up, it may help keep you calmer. And worse—it isn't just lost for the child who is I the target of the anger, but probably for his co-twin as well.

I think of myself in the lecture hall. The speaker wasn't furious with me, but with his assistant; however, the emotional climate between the two of them affected every single person in the auditorium in some way.

If you grew up in a family that saw fear or anger as a way to teach a lesson, remember that the emotional overlay of a situation is taken in along with the instruction.

For example, my first day as a community college teacher, I was quite nervous. I sat down to memorize my telephone extension and my office number. The numbers were similar; and in my confused and fearful state of mind, I never got them straight. After five years at that college, I was still looking up those numbers. When I tried to remember them, the feelings came back and got in the way.

So if you're trying to get your toddlers to remember to hang up their coats, don't put an emotional overlay on the situation that brings fear or confusion. They may look at the hook, forget the coat, and recall only the feelings. At that moment, the lesson you intended to teach is lost. ♥

When Twins Learn to Talk

Listening to your twins . . . and applying these practical procedures can prevent, detect and treat their language development problems.

By Pat Fasanella

ultiple birth organizations report that language development is one of the most frequent concerns of parents of young twins. Statistics vary widely, however, on just how common it is for twins to have problems in this area.

"I get about one letter a month from parents about language development," says Sheryl McInnes, of Canada's Parents of Multiple Birth Association (POMBA). "Most have their kids in speech therapy . . . I think we can assume there

is a problem, or parents wouldn't be asking so often."

Australia's LaTrobe Twin Study, an ongoing research project, finds language development the most common parental concern they address. Their conclusions show it is not unusual for twins to be at least one month behind singletons in saying their first word. Between the ages of 3 and 5, they report twins are, on the average, six months behind their single-born peers.

Research done in the United States shows that twins tend to use fewer words per sentence than singletons—5-year-old twins and 3-year-old singletons are at the same level in their sentence lengths.

CAUSES OF DELAY

At the age when singleton children are learning to speak by imitating their mother, father or older siblings, twins often spend much of their time talking to each other. Since they are learning many of the same words at the same time, they tend to reinforce each others' immature speech patterns and mispronunciations.

In addition, parents often have little time left from taking care of their twins' physical needs for the verbal stimulation that is basic to early speech development.

Many parents also report that their twins have little contact with other children during their toddler years. Again, they end up talking with each other and delaying the need to develop the language skills to communicate with others.

Twins sometimes develop special names for each other that seem to be a unique expression of the twin relationship. One identical boy who was constantly being confused with his brother said matter-of-factly one day, "I'm Chris, but my whole name is Tony/Chris." A set of twin girls could not pronounce one of their names, so they called each other Phaedra and "not Phaedra."

According to Twinline, a research based organization in California, "New evidence suggests that some twins may be more advanced with language than single children, and other research has found that some twins change standard language (such as using 'me' for the two of them together) which may seem to be difficulties with language, but which is really very appropriate expressions of the twin experience."

Let's look at a special condition, idioglossia, often called twin talk or twin language, because this rare development of a language or communication is known only to the two people who use it and is found most often in twins.

Consider the following example: When iden-

Guidelines to Determine Communication Disorders

Following are 20 rough guidelines as outlined in the Pediatrician's Handbook of Communication Disorders to aid in determining whether the child has a referable problem. If any of the following conditions exist, the child should be referred to a speech professional.

1. If the child is not talking at all by age 2.

2. If speech is largely unintelligible after age 3.

3. If there are many omissions of initial consonants after age 3.

4. If there are no sentences by age 3.

5. If sounds are more than a year late in appearing according to development sequence.

6. If there is an excessive amount of indiscriminate irrelevant verbalizing after 18 months.

7. If there is consistent and frequent omission of initial consonants.

8. If there are many substitutions of easy sounds for difficult ones after age 5.

9. If the amount of vocalizing decreases rather than steadily increases at any period up to age 7.

10. If the child uses mostly vowel sounds in his speech at any age after 1 year.

11. If word endings are consistently dropped after age 5.

12. If sentence structure is consistently faulty after age 5.

13. If the child is embarrassed and disturbed by his speech at any age.

14. If the child is noticeably nonfluent (stuttering) after age 5.

15. If the child is distorting, omitting, or substituting any sounds after age 7.

16. If the voice is a monotone, extremely loud, largely inaudible, or of poor quality.

17. If the pitch is not appropriate to the child's age and sex.

18. If there is noticeable hypernasality or lack of nasal resonance.

19. If there are unusual confusions, reversals, or telescoping in connected speech.

20. If there is abnormal rhythm, rate, and inflection after age 5.

Infant & Toddler Language Development

Ages 0–1 child should be able to:
• Repeat sound made by others;
• combine 2 different syllables in vocal play;
• vocalize in response to speech;
• repeat same syllable 2–3 times (ma, ma, ma);
• use single word meaningfully to label object or person.

Ages 1–2 child should be able to:
• Say five different words;
• say own name on request;
• answer yes/no questions;
• point to 3–5 pictures in a book when named;
• ask for "more";
• combine use of words and gestures to make wants known;
• ask for some common food items by name when shown (milk, cookie).

Ages 2–3 child should be able to:
• Combine two-word phrases;
• hold up fingers to tell age;
• give more than one object when asked using plural form (blocks);
• use no or not in speech;
• ask the question, "What's this (that)?";
• say me, mine rather than own name.

Ages 3–4 child should be able to:
• Imitate sounds M and N;
• understand meaning of backwards;
• understand basic weight concept;

• identify three geometric forms;
• interpret pictures;
• identify sex when asked;
• use plurals;
• count to 3;
• match primary colors;
• give his name in full;
• name objects from memory;
• repeat nursery rhymes;
• name colors.

Ages 4–5 child should be able to:
• Sing simple songs;
• understand between, beside, behind, above, toward;
• tell what familiar animals do;
• communicate thought and feelings;
• color a circle and stay inside the lines;
• categorize;
• differentiate night and day;
• compare textures;
• tell stories;
• know opposites;
• count to 10;
• name coins;
• rhyme words;
• identify objects by use;
• imitate drawing a triangle;
• understand concept of many, some, more;
• grasp concept of length.

tical twin boys, Scott and Todd, were adopted at 3 years of age, they spoke only to each other, only in their own private language. "Not one word they used was like the English language," said Norma Klein, their adoptive mother. "I could not teach them to talk English. As long as they understood each other, they didn't care to learn. It wasn't like Pig Latin or a word turned around; it just wasn't like anything."

If the twins wanted something, they would pull on their mother and point or show her what it was. At first, the Kleins found this secret language amusing. As Scott and Todd grew older and still could not be understood though, it became a serious problem

For two frustrating and baffling years, Klein tried to teach her sons. Still, they entered kindergarten with no language other than their own. By the end of the year, no progress had been made, and the Kleins were frantic.

A decision was made to switch the boys to a different school for first grade. According to Klein, "A special little nun made up her mind she was going to make them talk." With her help and two years of speech therapy, Scott and Todd finally broke through their communication barrier and idioglossia.

Idioglossia cases as severe as the Kleins' are extremely rare, usually involving twins who have grown up relatively isolated. These twins usually have an especially close relationship with each other and spend most of their time together without the benefit of regular contact with other children.

Studies on intelligence and language in twins by the French researcher, Zazzo, state that nearly all identical and up to half of fraternal twins develop some degree of special communication in their early years. Studies done by multiple birth organizations in Canada, Australia, and the United States show that twins may be prone to other speech and language difficulties, as well.

Not all twins, of course, have speech and language difficulties. The Australian study shows a number of factors that help pinpoint those who may be at risk. Boys are more likely than girls to have speech problems in the singleton and twin populations. Identical twins outnumber fraternals in needing speech therapy. Also at risk are premature, low birthweight, and undiagnosed twins. Finally, twins who are part of a large family, where parents have little individual time to spend with them, are often prone to speech and language problems.

There is an encouraging highlight to these studies however. By 6 years of age, most twins have completely "caught up" with singletons in speech and language proficiency.

Researchers have yet to explain this occurrence. They surmise though, that starting school may force twins to expand their communication skills. They now have a definite need to be understood by playmates and others beyond their immediate family. Also, twins who experienced premature or complicated births have caught up physically with the rest of their age group by this time.

"Our own experience with families of twins," state researchers with the LaTrobe Study, "is that we spend much more time reassuring parents that any language delay in their twins is not going to have profound consequences for the children's lives, than we do with the less fortunate families where there really are severe problems."

Parents do need to be alert to their twins' speech development, though. Many outgrow minor problems, but some do not. A deficit in language development can and often does lead to a poor self-concept and academic failures.

Understanding oral language is also basic to learning reading and math. Researchers are now beginning to link early language problems with later learning difficulties.

Much can be done by parents to help stimulate language development in their children. The following parenting techniques have been suggested by Linda Christ, speech pathologist and coordinator of speech and language therapy in the Racine, Wisconsin Unified School District; and twin-specific studies done by Parents of Multiple Birth Association (POMBA) of Canada, Australia's LaTrobe Twin Study and the National Organization of Mothers of Twins Clubs in the United States:

- Continually talk to your children. Instead of just pouring milk quietly, say, "Mommy's pouring milk into the cup." Everyday life is filled with language experiences. Don't just do something. Talk about what you are doing and why you are doing it.

- Reading to children is important. Don't only read the story, but talk about the story, using different vocabulary and sentence structure. Ask questions about the story to see whether the child is understanding it.

- Encourage children to talk and give them a lot of praise for doing so. Don't allow pointing and grunting. Any attempt at verbalization should be reinforced.

- Listen attentively to each child's speech and show an interest in what each has to say.

- Help young twins be members of the family group and to interact with each other and the group.

- Do things separately with each twin as often as possible. Take advantage of this time to enjoy each other's company and carry on uninterrupted conversations.

- Provide opportunities for twins to play and communicate with other children separately and together before school age.

- Take a walk or ride to the gas station, grocery store, library, Grandma's house, or around the block. Talk to each child individually about the trip. Stop and examine things. Encourage questions and answer them. Take time to listen.

- Avoid using baby talk or special words the twins have "invented." If a child says a word

Gibberish

Reprinted from *The National Organization of Mothers of Twins Clubs Newsletter, Notebook*, Winter, 1977.

Idioglossia. What is it? Some call it twin talk or twins' jargon. Others call it gibberish or a form of communication known only to the two involved. Whatever the terminology, idioglossia is said to be very rare and is usually found in twins who have grown up in an extremely close relationship without benefit of the influence of other children.

Recent articles appearing in publications across the country explored the subject of idioglossia while bringing 6-year-old Virginia and Grace Kennedy of San Diego to the attention of America. Victims of idioglossia, Virginia and Grace were thought to be mentally retarded. After enrollment in a school for retarded children, they were found to be mentally alert and quick to learn. The girls' plight revolves around their inability or refusal to speak in anything but what appears to be their own language. Now undergoing speech therapy, Virginia and Grace are the subjects of intensive studies being conducted on idioglossia.

While the Kennedy twins continue their verbal struggles in California, yet another "victim" has revealed a similar plight of twenty years ago. In an interview in New Orleans recently, Claudia Vasilovik recalled the days when she and her identical twin Claire were unable to communicate with others.

Many similarities were noted between the Kennedys and the Vasiloviks. While the Kennedys spoke English and German in their home, the Vasilovik family spoke English and Italian.

The Kennedy girls had physical problems shortly after birth, but Claudia and Claire were physically healthy. However, they were the result of a complicated pregnancy. Mrs. Vasilovik had severe toxemia, among other complications, and spent five months in bed. The girls were delivered two weeks after due date and arrived 55 minutes apart.

Like the Kennedys, the Vasilovik girls had very few playmates in their Chicago neighborhood. Those few became even fewer after neighbors called to complain that their children were mimicking the twins' gibberish.

Claudia and Claire had virtually no language until almost 4 years of age. By 4 1/2, the girls had developed their own private language that even their parents could not penetrate. It was at that age the girls were enrolled in speech therapy where they remained for approximately two years.

During the therapy years, "Claire" became "Sair" and Claudia became "Yoy" to each other. The names stuck down through the years, but the girls allow no one else to use these "very special and private" names.

Frustration crept in often when the girls wanted desperately to be understood. "Don't you understand?" would be blurted out in perfect English in the midst of a temper tantrum, whereupon they immediately reverted to their gibberish.

Their first distinguishable word during therapy was "umbrella," a three-syllable accomplishment. By first grade, the girls had progressed to normal speech patterns while kindergarten had been limited to a tug on the teacher's sleeve for attention, followed by their usual gibberish and subsequent tantrum with "Don't you understand?"

While in speech therapy, the Vasolivik girls were the subjects of a research study on the behavior of twins. This study was conducted at the University of Chicago and the findings on Claudia and Claire were included within the subsequent report.

Although Claudia and Claire cannot remember many of their escapades, their mother refreshes their memories occasionally. Mrs. Vasilovik still guards her old copper tapes as she would a treasure. On these tapes, the girls can be heard babbling and singing in their unique gibberish. At one point in these tapes, Claudia is asked, "Why don't you let Claire sing now?" whereupon she replies, "No, indeed!" in perfect English.

One of Mrs. Vasilovik's more embarrassing memories is the time a policeman stopped her for speeding. While trying in vain to explain her actions by playing the "I don't know what came over me" bit, the twins chose that particular moment to become linguistic. From the rear seat came two tiny voices in unison and in perfect English, "Oh, my mommy does this all the time."

Although very close as young children, Claudia recalls she and Claire seldom dressed alike, never double-dated after a single disastrous evening, and resented anyone's asking, "Are you twins?"

Ironically, after their speech plight of youth, Claudia received her BA in Drama and Speech from Loyola University of New Orleans. She is now a freelance actress and appeared as an interviewer in *Countdown to Super Bowl*, an ABC movie of the week.

Claire received her M.A. in Education from National Teachers' College in Illinois and now teaches math at a school in Chicago.

Claudia sees herself today as having a superiority complex while she labels Claire "normal." The 23-year-old girls are both single and "doing their own thing" many miles apart.

incorrectly, repeat it in a short sentence saying it correctly. (If the child says, "I want cookie," you say, "You want a cookie.") Don't force the child to repeat your example.

- Don't expect perfect speech. Accept and praise each child for his efforts.
- Try making any sounds your child is having difficulty with while you both watch your face in a mirror.
- If there is concern about a child's speech, language, or hearing ability, check with a professional immediately. A certified speech and language pathologist is the expert in this area and should be consulted. One can be found through a local pediatrician, school district, hospital, university, or telephone directory.

Speech professionals feel that all children who are experiencing difficulties in language acquisition or the understanding of language should be evaluated. Parents should consider their children for testing if they are more than six months behind the norm.

Early evaluation and therapy are two of the most important resources available to children with speech and language problems. Parental awareness is the third.

Knowing what to expect of children at each age and stage of development can reassure parents of those with minor language delays and alert those who have serious problems. ♥

Special Language for a Special Relationship

By Alice M. Vollmar

"Umah, doodee, beedah." It may sound like nonsensical gibberish to the rest of the world, but to a particular pair of twins, those made-up words may make perfect sense.

"This private language—called idioglossia—is a communication system shared by two that may be unintelligible to others," Nancy Carter, a speech and language pathologist in Minnesota's Early Childhood Education program, said. It consists of twisted or made-up words, sounds or gestures sometimes very elaborate—and reduces the need or desire to communicate with outsiders."

Identical twins Alex and Garrett, 4, rarely use their private lingo now, said their mother, Patty Nolan. Like many twins, her boys used a private language to communicate with each other until they became fluent in English. Often, they used it to plot mischievous antics, like simultaneously dumping their food on the floor.

Fraternal twins Kimberly and Scott, 6, also abandoned their twin talk when they became adept at English. Their mother, Julie Aasgaard, recounts a particularly vivid memory of an unintelligible exchange between her twins, followed by the gleeful overturning of their milk cups.

"Our twins babbled to each other from the beginning, so it's hard to know when they started to understand each other," said Aasgaard. "In fact, they turned out to be language delayed: They could say words, but didn't put them together to make sentences."

The Aasgaard twins went to a language therapist for two years, following testing at age 2 1/2.

"I realized that because it's harder to take two along, sometimes twins are deprived of exposure to language on outings to do shopping, for instance," said their mother. "And with two very young kids, one-on-one talking time is sometimes cut to a third of what it would be with one."

So, Aasgaard encouraged her twins to use correct English by involving them in activities with other children, placing them in separate preschool classes, taking them on individual outings and talking to each child. Those strategies, along with speech therapy, paid off. Soon, Kimberly and Scott started to converse in

Strengthening Speaking Skills

Educational speech pathologist Nancy Carter offers the following suggestions to parents:

• Speak clearly and not too fast. Look each of your children in the eye when talking to him.

• Sometimes repeat what each of your children says, expanding on the sentence. (Child: "I see an airplane." Parent: "Yes! I see the big silver airplane, too.")

• Try to include all family members in conversations.

• Point out surrounding sights and sounds, such as wind, cars and planes; things that are the same and different; larger/smaller, shorter/longer, first/last things.

• Talk about the way you see things in the community, such as how cold it is or that the sidewalk is slippery.

• Explain words you use. Encourage questions. Compare opposites, such as happy and sad.

• Plan events ahead; talk about them before, during and after.

• Talk about what is heard on radio or seen on TV, what happened and why.

• If one of your children is interested in something, look at it with him. Name it. Describe it. Compare it to something else. Encourage your child to talk about it.

• Provide opportunities for play with same-age friends other than those at preschool or elementary school.

• Practice learning telephone numbers, your address, days of the week, short poems and rhymes.

• Make a game of rhyming words. For example, "Cat sounds like bat."

• Have each of your children reach into a bag of different sizes, shapes and textures, picking one to describe to you; select and name an unseen object yourself, and describe it to your children.

• Help each of your children learn to follow directions. First give one direction; then, after he has mastered that, give two. After you see that he can follow two directions in order, give three at a time. (For example: 1. Close the door. 2. Open the door and hang up your coat. 3. Put this on the table, close the door, and get the book.)

English and discontinued their private lingo.

Sometimes twins switch back and forth from English to "twin talk," as in the case of fraternal twins Amanda and Thomas, almost 5. "It's their own way to communicate, especially when they don't want anyone else to know what they are talking about," said their mother, Nancy Herman. "At first, they used the twin language all the time; then, they started to pick up English. Now, they just use the twin lingo occasionally; it certainly didn't deter them from learning to speak English."

Parents need not be alarmed if their twins speak both English and their private language, according to Cynthia Jacobsen, Ph.D., Director of Children's Mercy Hospital Hearing and Speech Department in Kansas City, Missouri.

"It's as if they are bilingual, and in some ways, those twins who speak both 'languages' are more versatile," said Jacobsen. "What matters is: Can your twins use language to get along in the world? Language is the foundation for reading, math, problem-solving and social interchange."

A private language can develop as a primitive means of communicating with the constant companion co-twin. "It is not really a different language, but a child's mispronunciation of the adult form," said Jacobsen. "Because there is another peer readily available to receive the message and a strong opportunity to share objects and nonverbal clues, the likelihood of that imperfect word being reinforced is high. If twins are left to themselves, more words may be learned this way."

As parents of twins know, it's difficult to pay attention to two children at once. In their book, *Twins From Conception to Five Years*, Averil Clegg and Anne Woollett note that you may, "feel you can't attend adequately to either child, and perhaps become less involved with either child's activities than you would if there were only one. Twins may become their own best audiences. But of course, in these very early years, they are not proficient at speech yet themselves, so they don't provide good models of how language is used."

LANGUAGE AND TWINS

Identical twins Jacob and Joshua, now 1 1/2 years old, "jabber at each other and laugh and we don't know what they are saying," said their mother, Roseanne Hooper. "The boys were born 3 1/2 months premature; now, Joshua says five words in English, but Jacob only says 'Mama'. Due to their prematurity, they've been closely followed and will start speech therapy."

Researcher Svenka Savic has conducted studies that illustrate the fact that, generally speaking, speech development is different for twins than it is for singletons. "If a twin wants to respond, he has to find a way of getting in quickly," Savic noted. "He has to develop special strategies for listening to speech and for joining and staying in conversation. These needs will take precedence over grammar and will also affect the length of his sentence. He has to find 'short, efficient ways' of using language." Thus, twins' speech may seem less sophisticated than that of their singleton peers.

REINFORCING PROPER SPEECH

Verbal interaction with his parents and other adults, older siblings, and playmates is critical to a child's learning language, note the experts.

"Parents can provide an environment where the child is likely to learn understandable speech," said Jacobsen. "For example, it's been found that children whose parents read to them a lot have better language skills. It's also important to initiate incidental language by talking to a child about what you are doing, such as saying, 'I'm washing your toes.' This influences the rate at which children talk. If you do these things, you may avoid having to undo practiced errors of speech.

"If the 'twin language' persists for more than six months, contact a pediatric speech-language pathologist," advised Jacobsen. "Usually, if parents provide other playmates, so the twins are not solely by themselves, and model correct word usage, the 'twin' words will decrease in frequency." ❤

Chapter 8

EMOTIONAL DEVELOPMENT

Two at Two

By Janet Gonzalez-Mena

Parenting is a dynamic, ever-changing process. Each new stage of a child's life involves rapid developmental changes, and parents need to be able to respond behaviorally and environmentally to these changes. That means parents must constantly readjust, not only to their twins as individuals, but to the way each child displays the characteristics of the developmental stage.

The biggest readjustment period for all concerned comes when infants get up on their feet and become walking, talking toddlers. And, of course, that event doesn't necessarily occur for both twins at the same time.

As the developmental stage of the child changes, so do the parents' primary responsibilities. Even rewards for the job are different.

For example, pity the parent who used to take pride in her infants' appetites. Suddenly she discovers that the son who used to gobble up a whole bowl of strained peas has become a toddler who argues about eating the two little peas served up to him, then sneaks them onto his co-twin's plate. The decline in appetite experienced by most young toddlers occurs at about the same time they start exerting their independence in other ways and exploring their power in relation to their mother. This mother is faced with finding ways other than feeding to feel good about herself as a parent.

Keeping children safe becomes a major concern for parents of all toddlers, but to parents of twins, it's an enormous issue. One mother explained, "It puts your heart in your throat to suddenly watch your children going in two different directions and worry about how you're going to keep them safe."

Child-proofing the house becomes a priority—a development evoking mixed emotions on the part of parents who had hoped that they could leave things the way they liked them, rather than rearranging furniture, putting locks on cupboards and hiding favorite but fragile knickknacks.

Even more difficult than the safety issue is the problem of civilizing toddler twins!

No one expects much from babies. They are naturally uncivilized. They cry, laugh, mess, bang and clutter as the spirit moves them. But the upright children who replace them must learn to be social, civilized people. This expectation from the outside comes at the same time that children get very involved with the issues of independence, possession, power and control. Suddenly parents are forced to deal with the conflicting behavior that arises as a result.

WHY THE "TERRIBLE TWOS"?

This situation is what gave rise to the term "the terrible twos." However, by thinking of the toddler stage in such a negative light, parents sometimes make it harder on themselves and their children by girding up in order to remain in control. What they really need to do is to become aware of the twins' changing needs and learn to deal with the behaviors that accompany a child's learning to stand on her own feet, explore the world and herself, and discover her power both as an individual and as a twin.

For example, possession is an issue for toddlers. As they learn to see themselves as individuals who can possess objects (and people), they also encounter pressures to "share." This creates turmoil.

One mother of twins, Ginger Gregory of Napa, California, explained how careful she is to introduce only toys that can't be used as weapons. "No way was I going to buy two push toys with handles or even two magic wands," she said. "Nothing 'sticklike' ever came into my house until I was sure that my children had the ability to work out their conflicts over objects and control themselves at the same time. It's different with just one child who has no one to whack."

Feeling powerful and independent are two other issues for toddlers, who need to sense that they can make things happen in the world—that they have some control. At the same time, they need restrictions, as their capacity for getting into trouble is greater than their self-control, as any parent of 2-year-old twins knows.

One such mother reported that when one of her toddlers found he was too weak to move a chair over to get on top of the dresser, he called for help from his co-twin and the two of them together accomplished the feat. Luckily, their mother was right behind them; she took the chair and put it in a closet, explaining the restriction.

Toddlers need restrictions, yet along with them come the "acting out" of frustrations and also the interesting phenomenon of "testing." Both the expression of frustration and testing may appear as misbehavior; yet in reality, both serve important purposes. Children learn to express their feelings and also get the chance to

Empowering your toddler twins

Many parents have discovered positive methods of acting, interacting and coping that empower toddler twins, while still permitting them a feeling of being on top of things. Here's a sampling of their discoveries:

• **Avoid issuing challenges.** When you make out-and-out demands, you can almost guarantee a rebellious response. Learn to state what you want in a positive, matter-of-fact, non-provocative way. Say, "Feet belong on the floor" instead of "Get down off that couch!"—It's just a simple rewording, but it works!

• **Let the environment provide limits whenever possible.** You don't have to make a rule about staying out of the garage if the garage door is kept locked. You don't have to warn about the fireplace if there's a gate across the opening to the living room. You can change your role from police officer and protector to supporter and facilitator whenever the environment sets the limits.

• **Instead of simply saying "no," give choices.** "I won't let you bite your brother, but you can bite this teething ring or this wash cloth." By avoiding the word "no," you model a more positive approach, one that is less likely to be challenged. When you offer two alternatives, your children may get so caught up in making a choice that they'll forget to continue the forbidden behavior.

• **Avoid questions with "yes" or "no" answers.** Instead of asking, "Are you ready for lunch?", ask, "Do you want to eat lunch in the kitchen or out on the porch?" The more ways you can think of to give choices, the more powerful your toddler twins will feel. The more powerful they feel, the less they will have to defy you.

• **Let your children know the effect of their behavior on others.** "He doesn't like it when you take his toy away." "It hurts when you hit me!" "I feel upset when you pour juice over your head." This is part of the civilization process. They won't necessarily be guided by the feelings of others yet, but you're laying the groundwork for later. As they learn more about the effect they have on their world, this knowledge will eventually help lead to greater control on their part.

• **Allow anger; teach appropriate expression of feelings.** Some toddlers have short fuses as they deal with the numerous frustrations of the physical and social world. Give the message that all feelings are acceptable, but only some behaviors are. Teach them that it is okay to be angry, but they must learn which angry expressions are allowed and which are not. "You can hit the pillow, but not your sister."

• **Provide for independence.** Allow your toddler twins to try things for themselves, within limits and under your watchful protection. They need to see themselves as capable people, and to reach that point through active exploration of their world with your support behind them.

• **Be patient—it takes toddlers a long time to learn to share.** Toddlers are just coming to understand the concept of possession. They must learn to hang on before they can let go.

check out the restrictions or limits you have imposed on them.

The physical limits—the gate across the top of the stairs, the chair in the closet—are no problem. Children can see and feel these limits. They are simultaneously expressing frustration and testing the limits when they are pushing, banging and shaking the barriers, physically discovering that the limits are solid. Once they make that discovery, they eventually go about their business.

However, the limits that are verbalized by a parent are not as clear as a strong physical barricade. Children will spend more time testing these verbal limits than they will spend turning the handle of a locked door.

"THIS IS ONLY A TEST!"

Here's an example of the ways toddlers test parental limits: Kasey throws a plastic toy across the room. Her mother explains firmly but gently that it's not okay to throw toys because people get hurt when that happens. Kasey decides to find out if her mother really means what she's saying. Is this a real limit that holds, or just a whim? She tosses another toy and turns to her mother to see what will happen. Her mother takes her by the hand and explains again that it's not OK.

In the meantime, Kasey's co-twin, Megan, decides to see if the limit applies to her. She runs over to the toy Kasey threw the first time, picks it up and tosses it at her sister. Her mother, understanding the importance of consistency, explains to Megan just what she told Kasey. As she does so, she holds both girls firmly in order to prevent them from repeating the action.

It may end there, but it is conceivable that one or both will continue testing by looking for the answers to such questions as: "Can I throw some toys but not others? How about a bean bag? Is dropping the same as throwing? What if I just drop a toy on the floor—will Mom stop me?" Of course, they don't verbalize these questions; instead, they ask them through their behavior.

Just because one twin has already tested a limitation, that doesn't mean her co-twin does-n't have to try everything out all over again for herself. It's hard for parents to be patient with the second child after having just gone through a testing routine with the first. It may not seem fair that there should be twice the testing with twins, but that's the way it often works.

Testing is an important learning tool for toddlers because to them, parental limits surround them like an invisible fence. The only way that the children can learn what these limits are—and how strong they are—is by checking. They test by continually bumping into this fence until they are thoroughly acquainted with the size, shape and strength of it. Once they discover just how far they can go, or where the boundaries are, they don't need to keep checking anymore.

Of course, that's only a temporary solution, since as they grow and develop, their world expands, and parental limits change to accommodate their children's new abilities.

Toddlers seem to fare best when they are not restricted unnecessarily. Parents should permit limits broad enough to allow for plenty of room inside the invisible fence.

POWER TO THE TODDLERS?

The greatest challenge to parents of toddlers at this stage of development is keeping out of power struggles. That means making the limits as broad as possible, while still keeping children safe and civilizing them. It's important to grant toddlers their power and still provide the control they need.

Children's push for independence nearly always brings out unfinished business with which parents haven't dealt thoroughly in their own lives. When they first encounter defiant or rebellious behaviors, most parents find their own emotions triggered. It helps for parents to take time out from dealing with the behavior of their children to clarify their own feelings. Most people feel powerless and out of control when faced with one, let alone two, defiant 2 year olds. It helps to have some strategies in mind.

Ginger Gregory explained her strategies for dealing with tantrums: "If just one of my children is having one, I immediately begin to pay attention to the one who is not kicking and

The moment they entered the terrible twos!

I remember very clearly the moment when I realized that my toddler twins, Samantha and Gretchen, had entered the "terrible twos." You see, I had long forsaken wearing earrings during my twins' infancy because any mother knows that a darling little 6 month old will coo and gurgle her way into your heart and then, when you least expect it, wrap her pudgy fingers around a dangling earring and yank with the strength of a Sumo wrestler. But I thought I'd give them another try. After all, I reasoned, I couldn't remember being yanked on in weeks, and our twins were just weeks away from that watershed of maturity, their second birthday.

I swear I was only upstairs for a second, locating my favorite pair, putting them on and taking a glance in the mirror for good measure. As I had expected, when I came downstairs, my twins barely gave them a second look. Unfortunately, the reason for their disinterest was immediately evident. While I was upstairs, they had toddled into the dining room and were gnawing on a dusty pair of red candles that had been in my hutch since last Christmas. Caught red-handed (in more ways than one), they smiled at me sweetly, rose-colored wax covering their once-white teeth, dripping down their chins and hardening on my Oriental rug. This singular incident marked our passage into the terrible twos."

I have talked with other shell-shocked mothers who have endured this stage of their children's development. In spite of every attempt made by said children to overthrow the ruling party. Eventually, the coup was disbanded and order was restored, but only after months of terrorist exploits at the hands of people only 27 inches tall. I was sure that the war stories recounted by these women were exaggerated. Either that, or they just didn't know how to control their children. Anyway, what's a little mischief among friends? This would not happen when my turn came. But happen it did.

I treated the candle caper as an isolated incident. Maybe they were having an off day. Nonetheless, I decided that for the safety and welfare of all concerned, childproof locks would be installed on every cabinet and drawer.

Unfortunately, this did little to deter their curiosity and left me with a kitchen that looked more like Fort Knox than French Country. In fact, the locks only seemed to pique their interest. The locks became a challenge— a barrier to overcome. The twins figured out how to dismantle them in record time, while I, on the other hand, pulled my shoulder out of its socket every time I absentmindedly went to open a locked door or drawer.

The "terrible twos" brought with them an independence I had never before witnessed. Our twins were no longer content to sit and watch Mommy fold laundry. On the contrary, as soon as my hands were full and my back was turned, they set off on their escapades. One day, as I threw a load of wash in the dryer, I came back to find food coloring squirted all over the brocade paper on the dining room walls. Red, blue, yellow and green arched, swirled and streamed down the panels like so much graffiti on a city subway.

Despite my attempts to remove the mess with myriad cleaning supplies, the stains remained. I'm thinking of incorporating them into a mural someday, but until then, the "graffiti" serves in my home as a visual aid to every childless couple considering starting a family.

A similar incident occurred when I was up to my elbows in soapy scrubbing pads while cleaning the bathroom tub. Our twins were merrily dismembering a Mr. Potato Head when I suddenly noticed the sound of their laughter growing more and more distant. This was not a good sign. I heard the microwave go on, followed by what sounded like a sonic boom and then—what was that?— a fresh, minty smell. I raced to the kitchen, but the damage was done. Pink liquid spewed from my microwave like lava from a volcano. I wrote down Pepto-Bismol on my grocery list—I had a feeling I'd be needing it.

A double dose of the terrible twos has not only produced physical effects, but has changed our family's entire lifestyle. I can live with the wallpaper, I can buy more candles, but I can no longer enter card shops, gift stores, bulk departments or major supermarkets with the twins in tow. They have left previously content sales clerks searching for a career change. They have been banned from our public library until the children's room proctor returns from therapy or until they reach the age of 5—whichever comes first. They have shut off the power at our post office, bringing to a halt that bastion of efficiency.

The twins have turned our once enjoyable dinners out into search and destroy combat cuisine; consequently, we no longer frequent restaurants beginning with the word Chez. I found my meat thermometer in the vegetable garden and, in what may be a related incident, our cat has suddenly developed a nervous twitch. Although my hair has grown back, my nerves have worn thin. Most days leave me feeling as though my life is nothing more than a parody of Homer's famous observation: "She came, she saw, she dialed 911."

When I think I can take no more—when I am positive that someone switched babies in the hospital and my real children are alive, well behaved and living in Iowa—I remind myself of a time when they had uncomplicated smiles, when they required and requested only the most basic of creature comforts. Now I see them grinning like Cheshire cats and I can only hope they didn't diaper the neighbor's dog again.

And yet, I am left feeling envious of their oblivion, their innocent ability to blatantly break the rules. They are pint-sized Picasso's and the world is their blank canvas. They are the best kind of dreamers unafraid to grasp, to clasp. I am in the middle of this bittersweet haze, confused and amazed by them, praying that this phase will pass while aching at the memory of the heartbreaks that growing up will bring.

For now, however, I have a few more antics to endure. I recently found them, for example, cow-eyed and docile in the corner of their room. It became apparent that they had ingested an entire 16-stick pack of chewing gum; foil wrappers lay at their feet like so many tokens from a Las Vegas blowout. My only consolation was that it was sugarless gum!

In the end, I told myself, this too shall pass—literally. It always does. I sighed and shrugged my shoulders. What's a little mischief among friends anyway?

by Patricia Hawley, Batavia, New York

screaming and throwing herself around. It often works like a charm. In this case, it's a real advantage having twins."

However, she went on to talk about the phenomenon of the double tantrum. "When both my girls are in the midst of a screaming tantrum, it's all I can do to remain calm. When I feel myself getting sucked in emotionally, I just leave the room until I can get a grip on myself again. It's good to have a strategy or two tucked up your sleeve for dealing with defiance and tantrums when you have twins."

Gregory has discovered how she can feel powerful, or at least calm, in the face of her dynamic duo's behavior. All parents need to develop similar methods so they can make good decisions about limits and controls. Then they won't need to spend extra energy unnecessarily limiting their children's behavior because of their own control issues.

Parents' baby-caregiving jobs are to feed, change, hold and comfort them in ways that teach their infants to trust the world and the people in it. Parents' toddler-caregiving job becomes a matter of encouraging exploration while keeping toddlers safe and helping them become civilized.

Parents naturally bump heads with their toddlers occasionally—parents have their jobs to do, toddlers have theirs. Therefore, parents of toddlers need to become aware of their multiples' changing needs and learn to deal with the behaviors to which those needs give rise as their children get up on their own two feet and work at becoming independent. ♥

Smooth Moves!

By Linda Baraban

Change! Even the mere mention of the word upsets many families. That is why one category of change, childhood transitions, is so dreaded by and stressful for some parents and their children.

When changes are made in children's routines, the youngsters often signal that they are uncomfortable by acting inappropriately or sleeping and eating in unusual patterns. To make matters worse, well-meaning friends often goad supertwin parents with their just-you-wait until-the-next-change type comments: "Just you wait until the triplets start walking, learn to climb out of their cribs, quit taking a nap, start driving, start dating or go to college." The survival secret for parents of higher multiples is to contemplate only one transition or change with their supertwins at a time!

Planning is fundamental to reducing the anxiety that accompanies change. It helps to project what potential problems, as well as what possible solutions, might result from the forthcoming change. Timing is also a critical element in the planning process.

Besides assessing each child's developmental readiness, both parents need to weigh whether they have the extra time needed to promote a change, such as beginning toilet training.

Parents of supertwins also need to trust their own sense of timing when it comes to instigating changes in their supertwins' routines, and resist outside pressure from family or friends to act according to some external timetable. Because there are more variables to consider with supertwins, some transitions may not be appropriate to introduce at the time that it would be typical to do so with singletons.

Lastly, even if parents dread or are ambivalent about a forthcoming change, their children's cooperation can be maximized if they can "market" the positive aspects of each transition.

FROM BREAST TO BOTTLE TO CUP

One of the first transitions parents encounter is weaning infants from breast or bottlefeeding to cup drinking. They need to plan to gradually introduce this change by individually teaching each baby to drink from a cup. A good way to start is by giving each child some juice out of a cup once a day. (Using formula or milk to teach cup-drinking often leads to frustration and resistance by babies.)

Parents need to anticipate that early cup drinking will be messy, and plan to use lidded cups with easy-grip handles, serve clear juices and put a plastic drop cloth on the floor. During this learning phase, they may also choose to wear old clothes or cover up with an oversized shirt. Use the bathtub or outdoors for early practice sessions, and remove cups that are intentionally thrown or shaken to teach babies that this behavior is not permitted.

Timing choices vary. Some parents recommend starting use of the cup as soon as juices are introduced. However, many parents of supertwins don't have the extra time or energy during early infancy to teach cup drinking. An appropriate time to introduce cups might be when the babies can sit up comfortably in their own high chairs and are holding their own bottles without much frustration.

Breaking the bottle habit entirely is the next step. Many parents of higher multiples keep their infants on the bottle longer than singletons. This may be due to developmental delays, but also because parents enjoy the closeness during feeding time that they were too exhausted to enjoy during the newborn days.

On a "good" day, during a fairly lightly scheduled week, parents may want to start their multiples drinking their daily quota of milk from the cup. It will probably go smoother if all the children switch simultaneously, thus avoiding fights over a co-twin's bottle(s). Some ideas to help the process include praising the successful drinkers, telling the toddlers how big they are getting to be and how they're drinking out of cups just like Mom and Dad. Buying each child his own brightly colored cup may also make the change more exciting. If the babies resist drinking the milk from the cup, they may enjoy trying to use a drinking straw as an intermediate step.

When switching from formula to milk, parents need to plan to introduce the new taste of milk gradually. Every few days, they can try decreasing the formula in the bottle by one ounce and making up the difference by adding milk to the bottle.

"GIVING UP" NAPS

By 1 year of age, most children show signs of giving up their morning nap. By age 3, most children don't need one in the afternoon either. Parents should plan for these transitions by gradually implementing a new schedule. When multiples start staying up all morning long, their parents may have to work hard to keep the youngsters awake through lunch time. Therefore, they should plan to serve lunch earlier than usual for a while, to start the afternoon nap early, and to provide a late afternoon snack to carry multiples through until supper. Parents will also need to plan how their own activities will have to be rescheduled during lost nap time.

Tired, cranky kids should be anticipated for a while during the adjustment process. Late morning and early evening activities should be interesting but not too frustrating to help tired children stretch out the hours until rest time. It would be wise, perhaps, to avoid shopping or outings during the late morning or early evening until the adjustment is made to avoid having to drag reluctant travelers along the way.

The time to eliminate naps is when the struggle to get multiples to nap lasts longer than the nap itself. Of course, each child is an individual and may have different sleep requirements. This is why flexibility is essential during this transition. Although it is often hard for parents to have a positive attitude about this loss of uninterrupted time for them, a "quiet time" can be established each day, during which the children go to their rooms to read or play on their bed with a quiet toy, while the parent has a chance to replenish her own energy and collect her thoughts. This also allows a tired toddler to nap without his co-twins interference.

FROM CRIBS TO "BIG BEDS"

When moving toddlers from cribs to beds, parents can help them look forward to the change by involving each child in the choice of new linens or a favorite soft toy he may keep with him in his new bed.

Part of the parent's role is to tell his toddlers

how big they are getting and that they will soon be able to sleep in a "big boy" bed or "big girl" bed like an older sibling or one of their friends. In addition, parents must anticipate that their children may miss their cribs, climb out of beds and tend to wander at bedtime. Therefore, they should help to teach positive bedtime habits by setting consistent rules about and consequences for getting out of bed, as well as establishing an enjoyable bedtime routine.

It is time to move multiples out of their cribs when they regularly climb out of them, creating a safety hazard. This may be a change to approach with each child individually; the first child to go in a big bed can help parents anticipate bedtime problems and re-think rules and consequences. One piece of advice: Avoid changing from cribs to beds during a disrupted period in the household, such as the birth of a new baby. Faulty timing can result in a difficult transition and result in poor sleeping habits.

MOVING TO SEPARATE BEDROOMS

Another transition that often occurs during the toddler years is moving the triplets or quadruplets from sleeping together in one bedroom to individual bedrooms. Once again, parents need to involve their children in the process by allowing them to each help decorate his room in some way, such as with a bulletin board featuring his favorite pictures and little treasures. Parents are best advised to anticipate that each child will miss his co-triplets or quadruplets and decide how to handle the situation should they want to sleep in a sibling's room some nights.

To encourage positive reactions to the change, parents can point out the benefits of having individual rooms and constantly reassure each child that he is safe. Certainly it is time to make this change when one or more co-twins has clearly different sleep patterns, or when opposite-sex children begin having friends sleeping over who want to just have "the boys" or "the girls" together.

Admittedly, even with the best planning, transitions with triplets and quadruplets can be challenging and complex. As parents encourage these changes toward autonomy, they can share their multiples' feelings of accomplishment. ♥

Keeping Cool in the Chaos

By Janet Gonzalez-Mena

Feeding, diapering, holding and putting them to sleep when they need it . . . these are just a few of the ways parents of multiples can help their young children experience a sense of satisfaction. Allowing them plenty of latitude to safely explore their environment creates a sense of satisfaction, as well. It's a matter of reading toddlers' signals and meeting their needs promptly and responsively.

As any parent of multiples knows, that's harder to accomplish than it sounds because parent needs and individual toddler needs often collide. Parents know the scene very well: They want to lie down just when one (or more) of their children wake up; or parents are ready to go out when one (or more) of their children starts fussing because she needs a nap.

There's no simple solution to this problem of colliding needs. In fact, resolving this dilemma of how to get same age children's and parents' needs met is at the heart of parenting multiples.

Four of the most common ways parents can address this issue successfully are:

1. Avoiding substituting one need for another, such as food for attention. Substitutions don't leave the same satisfied feeling that need-fulfillment does. In later life, people find themselves eating and eating, but never feeling full, for example. Because of early misguided parental responses, some children just don't experience as much satisfaction as they might.

2. Helping children experience the exhilaration of hard-won success. Sometimes parents stop their children from trying something difficult because they want to protect them from stress or danger. Protection is an important parental function, of course, but it should be used wisely.

3. Setting priorities for how parents fill their children's time. It is easier sometimes for parents to fill their children's time with what they think is important, rather than what the children think is important. The parents, not the children, need to choose the activities—within reason, of course.

However, children have a way of getting around parental priorities. I remember the son I sent off to nursery school to learn something. Well, he did; he learned a lot of things. But his most triumphant moment, which came at the end of his first school year, had little to do with the staff's careful curriculum planning or my personal agenda for him.

It was at an open house that he inadvertently shared his moment of triumph with me. We were watching a slide show of the year in review. My son sat on the floor in front with the rest of the children. Picture after picture clicked onto the screen, each being replaced by another.

From where I sat in the back, I could see my son lounging on a cushion, silently staring. Suddenly I saw him sit up straight, his face alive with feeling. "That's the best thing I ever did," he announced in a loud voice to no one in particular. I looked from his face to the picture on the screen. There he stood, projected bigger than life, covered with dirt, shovel in hand, knee deep in a hole. The look of satisfaction spread across his sweaty face on the screen matched the face I was watching, as he remarked loudly, "I digged that hole all by myself!"

4. Avoiding handing out "easy entertainment" in the name of "fun." Don't get me wrong, I believe that there's nothing wrong with fun. We all need it. It's not a matter of helping children experience either "fun" or "satisfaction," but rather a balance of fun and satisfaction.

Personally, I find "fun" just what it claims to be—an amusing diversion. Fun distracts me, but doesn't bring a sense of fulfillment. Satisfaction, on the other hand, provides a lingering effect. Satisfaction can come from something fun, but it derives from a much broader range of sources.

Can you tune into what it feels like to be entirely satisfied? I can. It's a feeling I sometimes get after a wonderful meal or when I fall into bed truly tired out. I also get a feeling of satisfaction after I've put a lot of effort into something and finally accomplished my goal.

A friend who climbed Popocatepetl in Mexico recently, showed me his slides. In one, he stood triumphantly at the top, 17,000 feet about sea level. He had both arms high in the air. Everything about his victorious stance said, "I made it!" He obviously felt great satisfaction at the moment that slide was taken. It wasn't a "fun" hike he took—it was tough. He didn't get his satisfaction handed to him—he had to work for it.

Although I've never climbed a volcano, I know the feeling. It's like being full—satisfied. It's a feeling that comes after great effort.

Meeting needs is what satisfaction is all about. I can get satisfaction in all sorts of ways even without climbing volcanos. My favorite kind of satisfaction is what I can only describe as peaceful contentment that comes when I manage to appreciate life as it is. ♥

Why Toddlers and Their Parents Want Power

By Janet Gonzalez-Mena

 y girls are very determined, very into testing the limits. We bump heads a lot," Loretta Cronk said about her twin girls who attend the toddler program at Napa Valley College's Child Care Center. Cronk's confidence shows as she explains how she handles the situation. "I'm very flexible. I don't make an issue unless it's a real issue—like running into the street. Then I become as determined as the girls are."

Another parent, who isn't so clear or confident, asks, "Why do toddlers do that—run the other way, fight and resist all the time. What's going on anyway?"

What's going on is the toddlers are expressing their need to feel powerful. They want to be capable and independent. Problems arise when the toddlers' push for power is stronger than their ability to control themselves and accept limits. When adults provide the control and thus restrict them, confrontations result.

Restrictions are necessary if children are to be both safe and civilized, of course, but it is necessary for children to have a sense of power, too. They need to develop their ability to act effectively, to control and to influence.

Cronk talked about the different approaches her twin girls take in earning about the world and increasing their sense of power. "Rachel always questions me. She has to have a reason for everything," Loretta said "Rebekah, on the other hand, questions by action—she unscrews the light switches on the lamps to see what will happen."

The girls' teachers, Lynn Wyman and Kathy Cizek say Rebekah and Rachel, who can play independently from each other, approach power issues much as other children in the toddler program do. "They resist the routine now and then—like making a game out of hiding when approached to go to the bathroom. On the positive side, they both gain a real sense of power from being given responsibility—like when given the task of wiping the table, putting games away, or being in charge of filling the water table with the hose," Wyman commented.

Cizek remarked that Rebekah and Rachel differ from another set of twins in the program in one important respect. "The Cronk twins don't have a big 'twin power trip'. They don't put up a united defense against the other children or guard their own territory. But the other set of twins (boys) seem to derive a sense of power from being a team. They share with each other, but not with other children."

Toddlers derive power in a variety of ways. If parents deprive children of their sense of power, the youngsters often are hampered in their development. They use their energy to make themselves feel powerful—usually in ways that are troublesome to both their parents and themselves. An out-of-control child has a great deal of power over the adult who is helplessly trying to stop a tantrum or other form of misbehavior. Biting often falls in the power-play category, too, because it gets such a strong reaction. Eating and toileting problems often have power issues behind them as well.

So what can parents do when their job of keeping their toddler twins safe and civilized constantly conflicts with the power needs of their children? The following suggestions are designed to reduce conflict by granting the toddlers their power, but controlling them when necessary:

1) State desirable behaviors in a matter-of-fact way as a positive suggestion, thus avoiding a challenge. For example, instead of saying, "Get down," point to the floor and say, "You can put your feet right here." Or instead of saying, "Don't hit the dog'" try telling your twins, "You can pet the dog gently." It helps if you sound confident that your twins will do as you suggest.

2) Give your twins choices. Ask them to choose between two desirable alternatives by saying things like, "Do you want to take your bath now or after dinner?" or "Do you want half a glass of milk or a full glass?"

Another way to give choices is to say what the children cannot do and then give two alternatives. "You can't throw the blocks, but you can throw the Nerf ball or your teddy bears," is an example of this method of offering choices.

3) Become aware of how twins attract adult attention. Children need to be responded to as individuals, and have close and intense interactions with the important adults in their lives. If they don't get this kind of attention normally, they'll get it by misbehaving. Make a conscious effort to give your twins attention during the pleasant times and do what you can to ignore the unpleasant ones. Then children learn they can control your behavior by "acting good" rather than by misbehaving.

4) Look at your own power and control issues. As a parent of twins you may feel even more powerless than the average parent. If your own power needs are not being met, you may be trying to exert more control over your children than is necessary.

Decide which parenting issues are important enough to really take a stand on and which ones you can let go. Is it worth a fight over what your children want to wear to the neighbor's to play? Can running through the sprinklers take the place of a bath just this once? Adults who feel powerless have a harder time seeing what is truly important than those who are confident in their sense of power.

For child-rearing to be the most satisfying, both parents and children should feel powerful. Parents—who are bigger, stronger, wiser, and more experienced—should feel in control most of the time. However, that control should not be at the expense of the children's sense of power. Control should be shared with the children as they are able to handle it. Little by little, parents relinquish control to the children until the children are guided by their own self-control. When the empowerment process is complete the parents' job is finished. ❦

Paying Attention to Twins

By Janet Gonzalez-Mena

Parents need to pay attention to what they pay attention to. Confusing? Not really.

Although children's personality traits may be inborn, they are reinforced or modified by parental attention. In other words, the traits parents notice and acknowledge tend to stick around, while those that are ignored take a back seat or fade away altogether.

Once a parent, day care teacher or other important person in a twin's life decides to pay attention to and label a certain trait, she often creates a self-fulfilling prophecy that causes that child to feel bound to live up to the label.

When does this self-fulfilling prophecy begin? It starts early—in toddlerhood—when children fall into patterns of attention-seeking. One child, for example, learns that he gets parental attention by acting kind and sweet, while his co-twin finds that he gets it by misbehaving. It is important to recognize these patterns and work to broaden children's ideas of who they are by noticing the "misbehaving" child when he is acting kind and sweet, and giving positive attention to the "kind and sweet" child when he is exploring, experimenting, asserting himself and pushing a little.

This patterning seems to manifest itself in two ways: 1) each twin differentiating himself by some trait or set of traits (such as aggressive vs. passive or people pleaser vs. rebel or even "good" vs. "bad" twin) or 2) each twin switching roles.

Parents solidify their children's pattern of behavior (see number 1 above) by viewing each child in a limited way, by paying differential attention to each when he is exhibiting familiar behaviors, and by ignoring each child at times when he is manifesting behaviors that don't neatly fit their perception of him.

Parents reinforce the second behavior pattern previously discussed in this article when they see particular sets of behaviors as belonging to their children, but not always to the same child. They may comment, for example, "Sam is passive, and Jessica is the aggressive one." Periodically, sometimes to the surprise of the people around them, the children switch roles, and their Sam becomes the aggressive one in response to Jessica's now-passive stance. However, this still presents a problem because both children continue to be stuck in narrow roles. They can only act in response to each other, not as individuals. They are playing out their parents' idea that twins are two-part sets.

Neither the first pattern (the permanent role) nor the second pattern (role switching) allows children to grow into who they really are or allows them to develop to their full potential.

How can you avoid falling into parenting according to these two patterns? Try these suggestions:

• **Be alert.** Look for patterns in your multiples' behavior and become aware of how you respond to them with your attention. Make clear decisions about what behaviors or traits you will acknowledge and which ones you won't. Think of your parental attention as something as vital as food—it is what all children need to grow into fully functioning, healthy, effective human beings.

• **Resist labeling your multiples.** If you are tempted to use labels to describe your children, for example, put extra time and effort into noticing when each child's behavior varies from that which is expected. Then pay attention to that behavior!

• **Regard each twin as an individual, not as a member of a set.** If you find yourself saying, "This child behaves in a certain way, and his co-twin behaves in another way," is a tip that you perceive them as a set rather than as two individual people.

• **Find ways other than praise to pay attention to your multiples.** Praise is fine in limited amounts, but constant or overblown praise becomes insincere and is disregarded as such by the recipients. Sometimes a pat, a smile or just eye contact says, "I noticed!" even better than praise does.

• **Avoid getting your multiples so hooked on your attention that they no longer respond to their own inner needs and satisfactions.** If your children always depend on a

Paying Attention to Self-Esteem

What is the relationship between personality traits and self-esteem? Since low self-esteem can be a result of labeling and carelessly placed attention, it may seem logical to assume that it is possible to raise self-esteem by the way parents pay attention to each of their children.

However, just because parents pay the right amount of individual attention to their twins at the proper times doesn't mean that each of their multiples will automatically develop high self-esteem.

Self-esteem develops as each child responds to a multitude of experiences, some positive and some negative. Although parents can control some of the experiences their children have, they can't possibly control them all. For example, they can't prevent prematurity, a condition which may have long-lasting effects. And even though both twins may have been premature, one may have been born smaller and in more critical condition than the other, a situation which will affect that child differently, but not necessarily in predictable ways.

Parents not only lack the power to control all circumstances, they also lack the power to control their children's perception of those circumstances. Whether the child regards a given experience as positive or negative is up to the child. For example, the child who was born larger and in better condition may not see this as a positive in his life. Parents can love their children greatly, but what counts is whether the children perceive themselves as loved. One doesn't automatically follow the other.

In addition to parents lacking control over their children's perceptions, they also lack control over their children's responses to any given situation. They can arrange circumstances so that their children are likely to respond in positive ways, but they can't guarantee that that will happen.

They can, however, guarantee that they express clearly and frequently the degree of esteem in which they hold their children and can pay attention to the behaviors they are trying to promote.

response from you, they are cheated out of learning to reward themselves. There is a fine line between using attention consciously and effectively, and overusing it in a manipulative way. ♥

Kid Frights

When twins develop intense fears.

By Tina W. Zimmerman

While raising twins carries numerous challenges, nothing has been as disconcerting as dealing with our girls' fears. Our identical twins, Anne and Joy, now age 6, developed intense fears at 18 months of age: fear of everything from loud noises to water. For the next two years, we were on an emotional roller coaster as I repeatedly tried and failed to "cure" them. In addition, I knew of no one else going through this, which left me feeling terribly isolated. These days, I have a much better perspective about the whole ordeal and the girls seem to have outgrown most of their fears. I hope our story will give encouragement to those going through the same experience.

I noticed it first when a very loud garbage truck came driving by our house one day. They both listened for a few seconds, and then simultaneously began crying and desperately grabbing any part of me they could. Each child was climbing upward as if to fight for the safest spot—which was apparently on top of my head! I tried soothing words, but they could not hear me over their own screams. The truck was long gone, but they continued to look as though they truly feared for their own lives. Finally, I just had to yell, "Stop it. It's gone!" After yelling this out a few times, they finally quieted down, but the fear in their eyes remained.

THE FIRST OF MANY INCIDENTS

Soon after, the girls became terrified of bathing in the tub. It wasn't long before fear of insects, wind, cars, loud children, rain, and of course, thunder, appeared. Even the squeak of a door or the hum of a fluorescent light could send them into a panic. We were literally prisoners in our own home at times, because they were too afraid to go outside where all the noises were.

Common fears of childhood

The fears of an infant or toddler are generally reactions to real events. As your child enters the preschool stage, fearfulness usually stems from something he imagines. A study in *The Harvard Medical School Mental Health Letter* (August 1998) reported that in a survey of 1,000 children, 90 percent of kids between the ages of 2 and 14 had some specific phobia.

Additionally, fears seem to change with age. There is some belief that fears are part of a natural survival instinct, so as infants grow into toddlers fears change in accordance with their survival needs. Newborns fear loud noises and a loss of support, while fear of strangers begins at 6 months to 1 year and generally lasts until the age of 2 or 3. Also starting at age 1 and persisting until 7 or 8 is a fear of separation from parents. Preschoolers often fear the dark, animals, large objects, changes in the environment, masks, supernatural creatures and sleeping alone. Older kids often worry about death, physical exams and news stories such as kidnapping and war. Other common phobias of childhood include dread of water, the bath, heights, and fear of bodily harm.

It's important to remember that fear is not a bad thing; it often serves to prevent toddlers from getting into potentially harmful situations. Here are some tips for navigating your way through your children's fears:

Acknowledge the fear. Whatever scares your children is very real to them, regardless of how irrational it may seem to you. Let your child know that you understand her fear. Ignoring a fear can intensify it and cause other fears to mushroom.

Avoid confrontations. Don't force your child to confront his fear directly. Gently, step by step, help him through the fear.

Don't tease.

Offer reassurance. Be supportive and positive. Explain that you will help him deal with scary things and then make good on that promise. Every stride should be encouraged and rewarded.

—The Editors

And, as you might expect, when one saw the other become frightened, she too began crying.

It pains me to remember their genuine agony and my sometimes insensitive reactions to their pai. Initially, I was sympathetic but, at times, after the day-in and day-out turmoil, I began yelling, crying or begging them to be reasonable, while longing for them to be "normal."

It became clear there was nothing I could do to get rid of their fears, but it was my job to help them cope and realize they would not always feel this way. Counseling was suggested when lifestyles had to be dramatically altered. Looking back, this probably would have been in our best interest, but I first wanted to try the desensitization techniques at home. These helped for temporary periods of time, until the next bout of fearfulness popped up. This pattern of waxing and waning is apparently common until around age 6, when fears tend to disappear.

With regard to the tub, I first made sure they saw me frequently enjoying a tub bath. I invited them to come sit by the tub and play, bathe their baby dolls. When it was their turn, they were each given a sponge bath while sitting next to the tub. This lasted about two weeks, with gradual encouragement for them to play with the bath water. Next, they were invited to sit on the side of the tub with their feet dangling in the water, a few days later to sit in the tub with me.

And so the progression went. When a move met with resistance, it was back to the previous level until they felt a little braver.

Just as important was the praise they received after the bath. They were told how brave they were, and that pretty soon they wouldn't be afraid at all. They were so encouraged and relieved to know that they wouldn't always feel this way!

COMING TO TERMS WITH REALITY

It was the process taking place within me, however, that helped the most—my acceptance of who my little girls were. No, they weren't like all the other kids, but they were precious and they needed my help. This finally hit home one day

A Bibliography for Parents

These books provide excellent information on the positive management of childhood phobias, according to Herbert L. Collier, Ph.D., of Scottsdale, Arizona, who is a clinical psychologist and the father of grown twins.

• *Bear Hugs for Being Afraid: Activities for Easing Common Childhood Fears*, by Patty Claycomb and Gayle Bittinger.

• *Monsters Under the Bed and Other Childhood Fears*, by Stephen W. Garber, Ph.D., Marianne Daniels Garber, Ph.D., and Robin F. Spizman.

• *Taming Monsters, Slaying Dragons: The Revolutionary Family Approach to Overcoming Childhood Fears and Anxiety*, by Joel Feiner and Graham Yost.

• *The Gessell Institute of Human Development Series, Ages 1–14*, by Louise Bates Ames et al.

Michael Kaplan, M.D., a child psychiatrist at the Yale Child Study Center in New Haven, Connecticut, suggests using some of the excellent parenting books you have on your own bookshelf to gather information and tips on how to deal with fears in young children.

• *Your Baby and Child From Birth to Age Five*, by Penelope Leach.

• *Caring for Your Baby and Young Child*, from the American Academy of Pediatrics.

• *What to Expect the First Year*, by Arelene Eisenberg, Heidi E. Murkoff and Sandee E. Hathaway, B.S.N.

when at a fast food restaurant, I suggested they play in the ball pit. They timidly refused, probably because of the other rambunctious kids there. Instead, they began playing with their toys at the table. I could feel the familiar surge of disappointment welling up inside me. But trying not to give in to it, I just sat there, watching them play at the table. They were having a great time pretending with their toys. Suddenly, I had a sense they would indeed outgrow this fear too, one day. And there would be plenty of time for more lessons in bravery. But for now, they needed to enjoy the moment; they were happy, carefree . . . fearless. ♥

The Feelings Behind Their Tantrums

By Janet Gonzalez-Mena

Toddlers are renowned for their tantrums, and it's no coincidence that tantrums typically start during this stage of their development. Imagine yourself about 18 months old. You have a need to make things happen and you're bursting with energy—energy harnessed and guided by mighty willpower. All your systems are go. But can you go? No. You are blocked at every turn.

Sometimes the impediment is your own small size; you can't quite reach the gate latch, for example. Other times it's your limited muscle power; you can't turn the door handle. Or immature physical skills stop you; you can't get your shoes off when they're double-tied!

Sometimes what blocks your intentions are the physical properties of things. No matter how hard you try, you can't carry water in the flour sifter. Then, of course, there are the social obstacles. When you are ready to play, somebody puts you down for a nap. When you want a lap, it stands up and walks away. When you want the teddy bear, it leaves in somebody else's arms.

If your feelings of frustration are strong enough and your temperament warrants it, you're likely to throw a tantrum. Whether you develop the habit of throwing tantrums depends, to some extent, on what happens after the first one. Three factors help determine whether tantrums become an ongoing pattern or not. These factors are: labeling, storing anger and finding tantrums rewarding.

LABELING

Sometimes toddler twins hear statements like, "He's the one with his grandmother's temper!" or "She's my little redhead," or "He's the feisty one." Anytime children hear labels applied to themselves by adults, there is the danger that they will come to believe them. It's important to avoid all labeling.

STORING ANGER

If children are not allowed to express their anger, they tend to store it up—keep it in a sealed jar. As the jar fills, the pressure builds. When the pressure is high enough, the seal breaks and the contents spill out all over. This pattern of dealing with anger is apt to continue until the person either outgrows tantrums (if ever), or else learns to keep a lid on the jar. In the latter case, the suppressed anger creates an unhealthy situation. The best way to get over tantrums is to learn to keep the jar empty by expressing anger as it arises.

FINDING TANTRUMS REWARDING

The most important factor in whether tantrums continue is whether the child gets something out of them.

If the child throws a tantrum in the grocery store and finds himself with the toy he was begging for when the tantrum began, he's learned a lesson in manipulating adults. Once a child learns to control his environment in this way, the tantrum habit will be hard to break. And when his co-twin observes the rewards, he, too, may well give it a shot, even though tantrums aren't part of his usual way of dealing with the world.

Another way tantrums become rewarding is when they turn into attention getters. Parents can prevent this by staying calm, and resisting the urge to try to control the tantrum by making a big fuss about it.

The best way to deal with tantrums is to avoid them. The actions of one mother of 2-year-old twins who were constantly doing things they shouldn't was much like a dance. Things would be going along fine, the dance smooth and rhythmic, when suddenly something would pop up to disrupt the flow. She would then take a series of avoidance steps. For example, when one child wanted to empty the wastebasket onto the floor, she would skillfully redirect his energy to his bucket of blocks. "Not the wastebasket; empty this instead," she suggested, without getting either pushy or mad.

His sister then started throwing toys, and the

mother stopped her, giving her the choice of a foam ball or a bean bag, and saying, "You can throw this or this if you want." She avoided numerous tantrums with this technique, and did an incredible job of sidestepping potentially volatile situations.

But of course, parents can't avoid all tantrums. So what do they do when one or both of their toddlers is screaming and flailing out of control?

Anger-Free Power Plays!

So how do you keep your toddler twins from stirring things up—from manipulating your feelings with their own, and turning their disappointments into power plays?

It's a simple answer: Help them feel powerful without using anger. Here are some ways you can empower toddlers:

• Give your children, individually and together, your focused attention sometimes. If they get their attention needs met, they can do without your presence for periods. Also, as they start feeling more powerful in other areas, they won't need so much of your attention.

• Set up the environment so that children can feel independent. Put things they need within their reach.

• Think about size and scale when you set up the environment for toddlers. Little people who live in a big world get messages about their size. You can change that with some small furniture, some personal private space.

• Give individual choices. Having the ability to decide such things as what to wear, how much to eat and what to play with gives a person a sense of power. It's important that twins not be responded to as a pair, but as individuals. You don't have to offer a world of choices, just several options ("Do you want to wear shorts or long pants?"), and let them make individual choices.

• Encourage problem-solving. There's nothing like tackling a tough problem and solving it, without being rescued by someone, to give one a sense of power.

• Cut down on the number of times you overpower them, even if it's for their own good. Dominated people feel powerless.

• Give them as much consistency as possible so they can learn to predict. Living in an unpredictable world creates feelings of powerlessness.

The secret to handling toddlers' tantrums is to let them express their feelings with as little parental involvement as possible. Of course, parents have to protect them from hurting themselves or each other, and from destroying anything. But it is most effective if parents can perform this protective function while staying emotionally detached—disengaged.

It might help to think in terms of gears. In a highly charged situation like a tantrum, it's easy to engage and grind gears or go hopelessly around in circles. It's very handy at these times to understand the value of remaining disengaged.

Some parents engage because they feel it's their responsibility to somehow make their child happy once more. That doesn't work. The more the parent tries, the more the child sees she has a puppet on a string. The tantrums increase rather than decrease as a result of the parent's engagement.

Some toddler twins know how to disengage when their co-twin is throwing a tantrum. For example, when Chelsea is throwing a fit because she can't make her pillow do what she wants it to, her co-twin, Briana, sits by calmly, waiting in a supportive kind of way until Chelsea pulls herself back together. Briana doesn't try to make her sister happy, nor does she get mad herself. Instead, she remains disengaged the whole time, but still close by. Her presence has a soothing effect.

Instead of staying calm and letting it pass, parents can find themselves in a confrontation with the screaming child. At that point, it becomes a win-lose situation. The parent becomes more and more determined to impose her will on the child, and ends up as angry as the child in her need to control the tantrum.

When that happens, the management of the tantrum quits being about feelings and starts being about power.

It doesn't take much for a child to discover that some furious screams and a little rolling around on the ground can make things happen. Her busy mom drops what she is doing and gets to her in a hurry. The child learns that she can turn a preoccupied parent who isn't paying much attention to her into a bundle of emotional energy—all focused in one direction. What power! This little person, who can't reach the sink to get her own drink of water, learns that she has the ability to turn a grown woman into an angry, blathering blob of quivering flesh.

There are a number of ways to avoid tantrums. For example, when you help children experience their personal power, you take away their need to feel powerful by controlling your emotions through tantrums. Also, when you allow them to express anger appropriately each time the occasion arises, they are less likely to store up feelings that can come spilling out as a tantrum.

If by chance a tantrum occurs despite your efforts to avoid it, remember Briana's example. Don't get hooked into the feeling, but rather provide a good solid anchoring point by remaining present and supportive, but uninvolved. ♥

The Natural Push Toward Independence

By Janet Gonzalez-Mena

The goal of parenting is to raise independent, self-sufficient individuals, whether those individuals are singletons or multiples. Although it may seem as though children will reach this goal automatically, there are no guarantees. There are, however, some steps parents can take that will make the goal of independence more attainable for their multiples.

As toddlers, multiples will naturally begin to assert their independence. Therefore, this is a perfect time for their parents to pick up on their cues and provide them with separate experiences. Here's one mother's story:

"Caleb is acting peculiar," reports Georgy Charland, mother of twins Caleb and Zachary. "He's pushing his father away, and he's never done that before. He's saying 'no' a lot, too. It seems as though he is suddenly trying to be independent."

"How old is he?" I ask.

"He turned 2 years old last Friday," she answers.

"Aha!" we say simultaneously.

Of course, some children don't wait until 2 years of age before they assert their independence; in fact, some begin as early as 18 months of age. But sometime before the age of 3, most children show the kind of rebellion that marks the beginning of the push for individuality. Through their temper tantrums, power struggles, constant "nos" and other assertive behaviors, they are saying, "Hey! I'm a separate person! I can stand on my own two feet. I have opinions. I can disagree. I have a will." In the example above, Caleb is starting now; and Zachary will probably begin soon, though perhaps not in the same way nor as strongly.

In order to form their own identities separate from their parents, all children have the task of becoming individuals separate from their parents.

Multiples face this task, plus the perhaps even more difficult task of becoming individuals separate from each other. Parents can help this natural, normal process progress by regarding their twins as two separate people rather than as a unit. Besides giving them constant, simple, separate experiences, it is a good idea for parents to physically separate their twins from each other periodically so that they have the opportunity to relate one-on-one to other people.

With this in mind, Georgy is consciously using physical separation as a way of responding to Caleb's new behavior. She is taking his cue that the time is right to begin to let Caleb and Zachary lead slightly different lives. She has asked her husband to include their sons, individually, in activities he does in the course of the week. Her mother is helping, too; she takes one twin shopping and then takes his co-twin out to dinner the next day.

All is not perfect, however; Caleb cried incessantly when Zachary went to dinner. This kind of reaction can be painful to all involved, and some parents might give up at this point, thinking that their multiples are not yet ready to be separated.

However, if parents don't take advantage of their twins' first years to let them experience being apart from each other, they may face larger difficulties in the years to come. Even a preschool experience can be painful if twins who have been treated as a unit instead of as individuals are plunked into a different environment to interact with other children and teachers.

By the time their twins are toddlers, parents may be accustomed to having the general public treat them as a matched set or as one person with two parts. At times, it may be tempting for parents to see their twins that way, too, especially when being parents of twins demands so much of their attention. But just as it is healthy for an adult singleton to be close to another person, so it is healthy to see adult twins who have experienced themselves outside of their twinship.

Therefore, although parents may not be comfortable with the idea of separating their twins, it is a positive step forward. It is part of learning to be an individual who stands on his own two feet, thinks his own thoughts, and knows his own desires and feelings. ♥

Sowing Seeds of Independence

By Janet Gonzalez-Mena

As they strive toward independence in the second year of life, many toddlers begin to assert themselves by defying their parents. But not all toddler co-twins do so in the same way.

According to Marsha Miller of Fairfield, California, mother of 3 year-old twins, "Sarah is openly defiant—very verbal about it. But Bonnie quietly goes behind my back to assert her independence."

Although Bonnie was born first, she was the smaller twin, and still is, according to her mother. Her small size and the slower rate of her development (compared to her sister) may have influenced her parents to do more things for her so that she is not as independent as her sister. Perhaps this explains, at least in part, why it is Sarah who shouts "no!" while Bonnie's defiance is less dramatic.

This drama of defiance is hard to ignore, even when parents know that it is a normal stage related to the development of independence. Perhaps the defiant stage is easier to live through if parents recognize the fact that their children are developing minds of their own, minds that they will need to have when they quit looking to their parents as the authorities, and therefore, the ones to defy.

Eventually, her peer group will become each twin's authority. If she's had some practice at saying "no!" to her parents, a twin may be better equipped to say a strong "no!" to peer pressure to avoid improper, dangerous or illegal behavior.

Of course, while parents like Miller are recognizing the long term benefits of defiant behavior, they can't allow their defiant twins to run into the street or pull the cans off the grocery store shelves. So they have the tricky task of remaining in charge and controlling their behavior while helping their children develop will power. This is one of the most challenging paradoxes of parenting.

Here are more hints that are not paradoxical about promoting growing independence:

1) Don't do for your toddlers what they can do for themselves. Ask them to take off their own jackets instead of doing it for them, let them climb up into car seats instead of lifting them, and let them dish up their own food instead of serving it to them, for example. Recognize, however, that everyone needs someone to take care of him sometimes, even when he has the skills to take care of himself. Sometimes children ask to be fed, for example, even when they know they can feed themselves.

2) Provide a safe environment in which toddlers can explore and experiment. Children can best develop independence in an environment where the risks are challenging but not dangerous. For example, physical skills are encouraged when children can run, climb, roll, tumble around and not get hurt. When children can explore and experiment without danger, they are more likely to do so.

3) Work toward establishing a good attachment between you and each of your twins.

Going Their Separate Ways

Here are some tips for using your toddler twins' push for independence as a starting point for helping them become unique individuals within their twinship:

• Let your children get used to making decisions on their own, so that they can recognize that they are unique individuals with their own thoughts and desires. For example, by asking your children, "Who wants what kind of cereal this morning?" they will realize that they can make their own choices and have separate experiences without destroying their twinship.

• Be sensitive to your twins' differences by appreciating and accepting their individuality. Your expectations will influence their perceptions of themselves, which in turn affects their behavior.

• Encourage individual space, possessions, choices and experiences.

• Appreciate your twins' rebellious behaviors for what they are—the push to become independent, self-sufficient individuals. Although it's not easy when both of your toddlers are shouting "no" and running in opposite directions, realize that this stage will eventually pass. With your guidance and teaching skills, your children, by the age of 3, will find other, less rebellious ways to express their individuality.

• Respect your children's twinship, but also let each of them know that he is a special and unique individual.

Children who feel they have a sound "home" base, have more freedom to move toward independence, even though this principle, too, seems like a paradox. Having a secure base from which to move seems to encourage exploration and risk taking, both important aspects of independence. Twins often have the advantage over singletons because of their attachment to each other as well as to their parents. One way to promote attachment is by spending time together in which parents are available to each child, focusing on what each needs, and being attentive and responsive.

4) Model independent behavior. Children need to see adults acting independently, taking a stand, exploring, experimenting, and approaching a problem with a problem-solving rather than a defeatist attitude. They imitate adults who are important in their lives.

5) Encourage individuality in expressions of independence. At the same time be careful that, in the name of individuality, you don't encourage independence in one twin and overly cater to the dependent behavior of the other. This caution is especially warranted in the case of boy/girl twins as it is so easy to fall into the pattern of reinforcing old sex-role stereotypes.

6) Be aware of varying rates of development. Although the toddler years are the ones most noted for behavior that marks a push for independence, a premature birth can influence when this starts. Don't push your children to catch up to the charts (almost no parent pushes for children to be defiant even when the charts say it should start at a certain age).

In spite of all these ideas about how to appreciate, and indeed encourage independence, you may still find your toddler twins incredibly messy, unruly, and hard to live with. Rest assured that, just as your children are normal, so are your reactions to them. 💗

Avoiding the Boredom Trap

By Janet Gonzalez-Mena

Bored teens are a problem in this country. Talk to any group of folks concerned with adolescents, and you'll hear that a lot of the bad things happen because many teens have nothing to do. They're bored so they get into trouble.

So, what do bored teenagers have to do with toddler twins? Boredom prevention starts early. It begins when parents clearly distinguish their own needs and perceptions from those of their children.

BOREDOM BREEDS EARLY

Here's an all too common scenario. A new parent peers over the side of the crib and sees a baby lying there unable to walk, talk or even lift its head. The parent imagines how it must feel to be so helpless. If the adult had just to lie there, he or she would feel bored. Therefore, the adult figures, the baby must—feel the same.

The solution seems simple enough: Entertain the baby. At the slightest whimper parents pick up their babies and carry them around. Or they may buy bunches of crib toys designed to entertain. They dangle things in front of their babies things that make noise and move. And they prop their babies up in front of the TV.

What these parents don't realize is that babies have keen senses and a whole new world to explore. They don't need to do much except lie around and take everything in. Boredom is not a problem for babies. It's a problem for adults.

CREATING WHINERS

Multiples especially have an infinite variety of things to observe because they have each other. And it's not just human life that's interesting to them. The whisper of a breeze and the flutter of a curtain at a window provide a world of wonder.

When adults entertain babies rather than appreciating their need for lying around, they teach babies to be dissatisfied with life's little pleasures. Children learn in a hurry that just a little whimper can summon mom or dad to liven things up.

When this happens, babies stop observing curtains and listening to the wind. They forget that they have the capability of creating their own activity. They get hooked on more sophisticated entertainment. Then, when this enter-

Battling boredom

What can you do to keep from falling in the trap of being your toddlers' number one source of entertainment?

Learn to separate your feelings from those of your children. Develop your powers of observation. Read behavioral clues. Are the behaviors you're reading as boredom really boredom, or are they signs of some other need?

Avoid fixing every problem for them. If your children are truly bored, don't rush in too fast to fill the void. Give them time to think up something to do on their own before giving them a change of scenery, new toys or turning on the TV.

Consider the environment. The way you set up the surroundings can make a difference in whether your children are easily bored. Having enough choices of things to do and freedom to do them helps.

Toddlers need space and encouragement to explore their world. They need to manipulate things. They need to be able to move freely and practice their growing skills of walking, running, climbing, rolling and more.

Watch out for over-stimulation. Just having each other around is stimulating enough for toddler multiples. Be careful about how much more you add to their worlds. A few simple toys are all that is necessary, not a warehouse of sophisticated gadgets.

Be aware of how you play with your children. Join their play down on their level in an interactive way rather than always as an entertainer. Follow their lead. Again, watch out for over-stimulation. If they get so wild they can't settle down when you're tired of playing, probably they have too much of a good thing.

tainment stops, they whine and fuss, validating their parents' original assumption.

This problem creeps right into toddlerhood. Some parents are so used to keeping their babies entertained that they don't let up when the little ones get up on their feet.

Instead, they liven up their entertainment acts, provide more sophisticated toys, turn the TV on more often, adding video tapes and finally computer and video games. None of these things: toys, TV, computer or video games, are problems in themselves. The problems come from adult perception that children don't have the ability to find self-satisfying ways to spend their time.

I've noticed that children who can easily create their own activities are those who watch little or no TV, have a reasonable number of toys, an environment set up for them to play and parents who assume their kids can figure out things to do on their own.

LET KIDS ENTERTAIN THEMSELVES

It's not that those children who think up their own activities don't ever get bored. All children get bored sometimes, but boredom serves a function.

It provides an incentive for children to pursue new interests and create new activities. When parents see that their children are truly bored (not just bored in the mind of the parent), it's better to give them space and time to think up something to do rather than jumping in and fixing the problem for them.

I'm not trying to make parents feel guilty. Instead, I'm trying to look at a widespread problem that seems to worsen every year. It isn't anybody's fault. After all, we want the best for our children. However, most of us were influenced by the push for early stimulation.

We bought into the message that it's a parent's job to be sure children have plenty to do. I'm no exception. I know firsthand about the tendencies we all have to entertain our children and keep them happy. Part of the problem is that, as a society, we see childhood as a period that should be free from burdens, so we don't require youngsters to take part in any of the work of creating and maintaining the home or the community beyond.

As a result they spend their childhood seeking entertainment. But when they run out of entertainment, they complain or get into trouble.

Toddlerhood is the perfect time to start teaching children to help out around the house. Two-year-olds like to do "grown-up things" if given the chance.

Of course, they don't have adult skills, but can learn them through seeing that their involvement is part of keeping the house in order. Now, we don't want to overburden toddlers with too much responsibility. Childhood should be fun. It's fine to play with toddlers and buy them toys.

The issue is overindulgence. You can tell you've gone too far when children come to expect to be entertained and forget how to keep themselves occupied. ♥

Comforting Solutions to Pacifier Problems

By Janet Gonzalez-Mena

When I was a new mother, my pediatrician told me that pacifiers were important because of babies' sucking needs. "Often their tummies get full before they satisfy those sucking needs," he said. He was adamant about getting babies in his care started on the pacifier, but he never told me about the problem waiting down the road.

Two years later, I wasn't a new mother anymore, and I was sick and tired of the pacifier. My son Bruce was hooked on the thing.

Looking back, I see that the way I used the pacifier was the problem, not the pacifier itself. Although it started as a means of giving him more sucking time, I eventually over-used the device. I was frantic to comfort him whenever he cried. I couldn't stand the thought of his experiencing a moment of discomfort, so I "fixed" his every problem.

Once his mouth was full of latex, he forgot what was bothering him. It worked, but if I had it to do over, I'd do it differently. Perhaps if I had tried more often to figure out what he really needed instead of automatically "pacifying" him, he wouldn't have become such a sucking addict by the age of 2.

I tried several times during those two years to slowly wean him off his pacifier, but each episode just led to power struggles. Then came a whole row of sleepless nights, which finally brought the situation to a head. Bruce would wake up every time the pacifier dropped out of his mouth, and call for me. I reached the end of my patience. That pacifier had to go!

WORDS OF WISDOM

I asked friends for advice. "Make a ceremony of cutting it up and putting it in the garbage," was one suggestion.

"Just get rid of it—and be assured that your decision is for the best," said another advice-giver. "He doesn't really need it, you know," she added.

She was wrong; he did need that pacifier.

He'd never in his life gone to sleep without it. How would he manage? I worried myself into a frenzy.

In spite of my anxiety, I was determined to get rid of the pacifier. I woke up the morning of the designated day with a feeling of dread. At breakfast, I talked to Bruce about my decision. I explained that he didn't need the pacifier anymore and that it wasn't good for him to keep sucking on it. I skipped the proposed cutting-up ceremony, because I wasn't so sure about that approach.

After breakfast I sneaked into his room, recovered the pacifier from his bed, then hid it in the top of the cupboard. The morning went smoothly and he never mentioned the pacifier. A little friend came over to play and kept him busy enough to keep his mind off his sucking habit.

"Fine," I said to myself. "But wait till naptime. After lunch, Bruce played while I cleared the table. I was just getting ready to put him down for his nap when he tripped and banged his knee. I was in the midst of comforting him when his baby brother cried out from the other room, so I left Bruce briefly. When I returned, he was sound asleep on the floor where he had fallen. I picked him up and gently put him to bed. He didn't waken. "Well," I thought, "we got through naptime."

We got through the afternoon too. No mention of the pacifier. Then came dreaded bedtime.

We had our snuggle and story; I was ready to turn out the light when he started to whimper. I held him and stroked his head. "Mommy . . ." he said, looking up with tear-filled eyes.

"Yes, Bruce?" I said, wondering if I could hold to my resolve in the face of his obvious agony.

"Mommy?" He took a big breath and continued. "Can I have a vitamin?"

"Sure, Bruce," I said, grinning. I rushed from the room to fill his request.

He took the vitamin gratefully, laid his head down on his pillow, chewed, swallowed, closed his eyes and went to sleep. Never again did he ask for anything to put in his mouth at bedtime. It was as though he had never even heard of a pacifier.

None of my other children ever got too dependent on the pacifier. Two refused it from day one, and two sucked for a few months and spit it out for good. So I never had to unhook another toddler.

IT'S NOT ALWAYS A BIG DEAL

I discovered years later that my experience wasn't unusual. It happens that many toddlers need the pacifier far less than their parents believe. I was surprised at the number of stories that were similar to mine. The funniest one came from a mother whose preschooler willingly sold his pacifier to his uncle for two dollars. At bedtime he shrieked with anger when he discovered that the sale was final. He felt he had been deceived and was so upset that his mother took him to the store the next day so he could buy a new one with his two dollars. Strangely enough, he never sucked on the new one; he just put it in his nightstand and kept it there.

It's hard to give advice on how to break the pacifier habit, because each child is different. In Bruce's case, I could have ended up with a huge power struggle on my hands; instead, I became my son's ally in helping him take a step he needed to take.

But there are some general rules regarding the use of pacifiers that parents might want to keep in mind. First, don't run frantically for it at every peep but try instead to determine what the real needs are; instead of the pacifier, does your child really need a hug, or food, or a drink, for example? Second, realize that crying is a normal way of expressing feelings. You want your children to express their feelings, not just be "pacified."

Moreover, don't let sucking become a moral issue instead of merely a need and comfort device. I once asked my mother if I ever sucked my thumb, and her eyes widened in horror. "Oh no, Janet," she said. "You were a good baby!" I was astonished that she had connected my thumb to morals.

The use of pacifiers, like thumb-sucking, isn't a moral issue at all. If there is a "good" or "bad" to it, it's as a habit—which pacifiers become if used after the need for additional sucking wanes, but the desire for comfort and security continues. Help your child break the pacifier habit when you think he's using it more to satisfy the latter than the former.

In the meantime, teach him alternate means of achieving comfort and security, so that when the time comes, giving up the pacifier won't be such a sacrifice after all. ♥

Cross-Country Toddlers

By J. Cameron Tew

Sometimes I think we should have named our boys North, South and East—seems like those are the three directions in which they always wander off! Even with both parents present, triplets and quadruplets instinctively know they have the advantage. It's as though they were trained by General Patton himself in tactical maneuvers.

The first time I saw multiples take off in different directions was in the shopping mall. Identical twin boys were sitting in a stroller, with their mom pushing them. She stopped to loosen their seat belts, but before she could get them safely strapped back in, one jumped out and fled toward a toy store, and the other raced around the corner into another store. Being alone, the mother had little choice but to go after one child and then search quickly for the other. Luckily, a kind woman caught the second escapee and brought him back.

Like this caring lady, we parents have nothing but the safety of our children in mind. That is why my wife, Angela, and I always follow these important steps whenever possible to make sure we know everyone's whereabouts:

• When we go shopping, we always use a stroller. I know that children eventually outgrow them, but we suggest prolonging getting rid of this godsend for as long as possible. While it might be heavy and bulky to use with three or four children, think of the alternative. A stroller is a surefire way to make sure multiples all stay together. I'm sure you have seen children in harnesses being walked around by their mother or father.Next to the stroller, we've learned it is the only safe way one parent can transport several children from one place to another.

• Don't be hesitant to buy harnesses for your multiples. Ignore the stares and frowns you might get from strangers. They probably don't have multiples. Remember that your children's safety is the most important thing, and harnesses make sure they are never more than an arm's length away.

• If you feel like taking a walk without your stroller, plan it when both parents can go. Then give the children a choice—they can wear the harnesses or hold your hands. We've found that holding hands is a great way to give our children some freedom but still ensure that they cannot get into danger.

I realize, however, that these ideas will not work for all occasions. Sooner or later, you will want to let your children out in the back yard or take them to a park to play. In such spacious areas, it may be just too tempting for your children not to run off in different directions. So here are some solutions we've found to the childhood "wanderlust" challenge:

• When looking for a park, find one that has a fence around it.

• Consider forming a play group with some other parents of multiples for such outings. With several parents around to watch, even a larger number of children can be safely contained in an open area.

• Angela and I just recently built a fence in our back yard to keep the boys from getting into too much trouble. I cannot count the number of times we have pulled Jason out of the woods while Nathan ran up our driveway to play with the older neighborhood kids in the cul-de-sac. And at the same time, we could be sure that Brandon was hopping off somewhere to find a bug or twig to stick in his mouth. A fence is the best solution for us, but it may not be for others.

• Set firm ground rules. Explain to the children where they are going to play for the day. If a child doesn't follow the rules, place him in time-out. Before he resumes play, explain to him and his siblings that they must all follow the rules in order to be able to play outside, for everyone's safety. With this number of children of the same age, one person must watch all of them in a safe, limited space.

Then, if someone breaks the rule, be sure to follow through with the consequences. You can be sure that there will be some temper tantrums, but it's amazing how peer pressure from siblings can have the desired effect. ♥

Encouraging Personal Responsibility

By Janet Gonzalez-Mena

Encouraging your twin toddlers to take responsibility for themselves requires a good deal of your patience.

As their little fingers fumble with zippers, sleeves and straps while attempting to dress themselves, for example, you may think that would be much faster if you assisted them. Though it may be difficult to stand by, hands at your sides, while they struggle to accomplish something solely on their own, your patience will pay off as they gain confidence, self-help skills and competence in caring for themselves.

Teaching your twins responsibility can actually begin when they are infants. By encouraging each to get involved in his own care at a very young age, they will actually be well down the road to accepting responsibility by the time they are toddlers.

But how can you involve twins in their own care? Consider each as a member of a team. This perception will pay off—you'll eventually get teamwork. Thinking of the babies as members of a team means that you will be focusing on them as people, rather than as recipients of actions such as dressing or diapering.

In taking a teamwork approach, you will be discussing what you are doing with your children rather than distracting them from what's actually happening. When you engage your children in the process of their own actions, you are making them more than just recipients of your actions.

There are many activities that lend themselves to a teamwork approach, enabling the cultivation of self-help skills. Such simple devices as your halfway removing a sock and offering each baby his own foot to finish the task gives the message that he can help.

Giving each of your babies a spoon when he first grabs for the one you're feeding him with, will, for example, show him that you appreciate the fact that he wants to do things for himself.

PLAYING MOTIVATION GAMES

Although acts such as self-feeding and clothes removal usually need no motivation, difficulties may arise when the toddlers' sense of independence conflicts with what you want them to do: You want them to put clothes on, and they want to take them off. You want them to brush their teeth, and they run the other way. How can you effectively handle a situation which they are attempting to resist? Follow these tips:

1) The most important factor in gaining the cooperation you need is the avoidance of power struggles. As soon as your twins perceive that they are in a win-lose situation, their resistance will increase. However, the more you can make it appear that what you want them to do is not a big deal and that you do not have a giant stake in it, the better chance you have for success.

Be matter-of-fact and calm—even cheerful—when you approach a situation that involves personal responsibility. Make a game out of picking up toys. Make tooth brushing a regular routine that becomes a habit instead of a fight.

2) Offer a desirable activity as a reward for finishing an undesirable one. For example, saying, "When you both finish getting dressed, we'll go to the park" is likely to motivate; while saying, "Hurry up and get dressed, we have to go to the doctor" is not.

3) Give consequences for delays. For example, saying, "When you put on your pajamas before the timer rings, we will have time for two stories instead of just one" may be a motivator. (Set the kitchen timer for 5 minutes.) It is, of course, important to follow through and not give the reward of the second story if the child does not "beat the clock."

4) Don't do something for a child that he can do for himself. Understand, however, that sometimes a child may need extra nurturing; it doesn't hurt to do something for him once in a while if it's something that he can do for himself. Just be careful that you don't get into a pattern of always doing for one and letting his co-twin do for himself.

5) Avoid comparing their performances. This method may seem to encourage a child to do what you want him to do, but it also teaches him to compare himself to his co-twin, not to just compare his behavior. In such a situation, one twin often decides to define himself as the loser; and a self-fulfilling pattern may evolve. As a result of prior comparisons, one twin may label himself as "lazy," "no good" or "incapable," and then spend years living up to that label. ❦

It's the Little Things That Count

By Janet Gonzalez-Mena

Some parents use the phrase "quality time" to mean those special occasions when they do something out of the ordinary with their children (either separately or together). That's certainly one definition. But if that's the only time they spend giving their offspring undivided attention, parents are limiting the opportunities they have to share experiences as a family.

Special occasions don't influence one's life as much as more ordinary day-to-day experiences do. Parents can use the numerous exchanges between themselves and their multiples that occur in daily living to build relationships between the two generations—an important aspect of parenting.

I define these exchanges as "quality time"—a chance to use ordinary time together in a way that makes it special. One example of this phenomenon is what my husband calls a visiting." This is an old fashioned concept lost in the whirl of modern life when "together time" is apt to center around television.

Every day my husband "visits" his father, who lives with us, by going into his room and plopping down in a chair. His goal is just to be there. That isn't the only time he spends with his father; he also sees him at meals, when he needs help with something and periodically throughout the course of each day in the give and take of family living. But "visits" are different because there are no goals and no expectations connected with them—they simply listen to music, pore over a letter from far-away relatives or look at pictures.

RESPONDING TO ACTION

Parents can "visit" their toddlers by sitting down on the floor and joining them in their play. By "joining" I don't mean taking over. Under these circumstances, most parents feel the need to teach or to entertain so they make their children recipients rather than partners. To overcome this tendency to conduct an adult-directed experience, I suggest that parents put their children in charge of the action for the period of the "visits."

In the kind of child-directed, shared experience that I'm advocating, the adult sits at the children's level, fully alert and receptive, responsive to what they initiate without guiding or entertaining. The adult is responsive rather than directive.

Because adults are used to taking charge and initiating things when around children, this kind of shared experience may feel very strange—yet it is one of the most beneficial ways to pay attention to toddlers.

DIRECTING THE ACTION

A parent doesn't have to just "visit" in this open, playful way to have quality time. Some quality time is task-oriented. With a goal in mind, the adult takes charge—directing the action.

Diapering is an example of goal-oriented quality time. To make this a truly shared experience, the parent must focus fully on the child being diapered. That means she must be "all there," mentally and emotionally. The child doesn't have to cooperate or even be happy; but if the parent manages to engage him in the process, it counts as quality time. A parent focused on the bottom half of a child, while that child's top half is engrossed in a television commercial doesn't count. Both the whole child and the whole parent must be fully present at the occasion.

Once parents come to see that diapering and other must-do chores can become regular periods of quality time, they benefit from "found" time that doesn't put extra demands on them. Parents who work outside their home, in particular, can profit from this "found" time. They know how hard it is to fit everything, including quality time, into the few evening hours sandwiched between the end of their work outside the home and their children's bedtime.

Quality time can arise spontaneously as the 2 year olds arrive at Dad's knee with a book to read. In contrast, it can also be built in to a trip to the grocery store when one twin goes with Mom and his co-twin stays with Grandma.

KEEPING INVOLVED

Although these special times together and incidental quiet conversations are wonderful, quality time doesn't have to be pleasant to be valuable. In fact, some of the best quality time comes as parents become involved in conflicts with their children.

Disagreements can provide a good deal of undivided attention. Focused person-to-person contact is what quality time is all about.

Actually, the intensity of a dispute is often a bonus when it comes to relationship-building, because the focus during that experience is stronger.

Sometimes, disputes center more on trying to create intense interactions than on trying to work out the details of a particular issue. In fact, some children create this occasion for intense focus because they need to hear their parent's message, "What you do matters to me."

Should parents plan separate alone-time with each of their multiples on a regular basis and, if so, for how long and how often? Many factors must be considered before answering these questions. If parents regularly pay individual attention to their twins when they change them, feed them, or when one co-twin approaches them for something, they probably don't have to schedule much "separate" time. However, it does help each twin learn to identify himself as an individual and gives parents a chance to focus on one child alone if occasionally one twin visits his grandparents or a friend, while his co-twin remains at home, for example.

The way to discover whether twins need more individual quality time is to notice their behavior. If they constantly compete for attention, usually operate as a unit, or seem to need more separateness, then planning for special time alone with each parent or another special caregiver can be a way to meet both of their needs. ❤

Toddler-Made Gifts

By Janet Gonzalez-Mena

One of the primary lessons of holiday times—that "giving" feels as good as "receiving"—is a lesson that even toddlers can begin to understand. Of course, it takes years for this lesson to be taught completely, but toddlerhood isn't too young an age at which to introduce the message.

Though toddler-age children are not able to participate in every part of the making of the following gifts, with tissue, tape and lots of patience, they can at least get involved in the wrapping of them!

KID-SIZE IDEAS

1) Give framed pictures of your twins.

2) Make a videotape of your twins talking to their siblings or parents (with another adult supervising the creation of the tape).

3) Create hand prints in various media. A clever variation on the plaster of Paris hand print that hangs on the wall is a handprint pillow. Trace around little hands on iron-on fabric, cut the "hand" out, iron it onto contrasting fabric, sew and stuff.

4) Make crayon melt pictures. Protect a warming tray (not turned on yet) with aluminum foil; put paper on top of the foil and let children draw on the paper. When the drawings are complete, plug in the tray and watch the crayons melt into rich, luscious colors. What looks like a scribble with plain crayons looks like an abstract piece of art with melted ones. Add mats or frames for a finished look. This particular activity needs lots of adult supervision because of the warming trays' heat.

5) Construct a contact paper collage. Gather attractive bits of things—wrapping paper, ribbon, small pieces of fabric, cut-out pictures, pieces of evergreen. Offer an assortment so that each work of art will be an individual creation—each twin choosing his favorites. Let your children stick what they choose on the sticky side of the contact paper, arranging and rearranging their masterpiece as they choose. Encourage

Creating Positive Experiences

When you sit down to do arts or crafts with your twins, keep these guidelines in mind so that they get the most benefit from the experience:

• Let them enjoy the experience. Toddlers concentrate much more on the process than on the product. They will explore the media, experiment with the process, and make it into a positive sensory experience. Expect this and try not to limit it unnecessarily. If possible, try the art activities numerous times, then pick the best products to use for gifts. If you have only enough materials for each child to make one item, or you have to limit the experience to only one session, you'll be under stress to produce a "perfect" gift the first time, which may prevent your children from getting the most out of the activity.

• Give the children freedom to create. Don't give pre-drawn pictures to color, for example. Let the pictures be their own artwork by allowing them to make their own decisions about what to stick where in the collage. It may not "look like anything," but the fact that it is nonrepresentational doesn't detract from its artistic qualities.

• Don't ask children to name what they draw. Later they will do this on their own, but during the early years they should feel free to scribble, squirt, dribble or glue at will without any pressure to "make something." Symbolic representation is beyond toddler ability.

• If things don't turn out as lovely or as interesting as you would like, comment to the children about the process not the product, with words like, "You really worked hard on that" or, "It seemed as though you really enjoyed doing that." The more positive your toddlers feel about early art experiences, the more likely they will be to produce later works which you can really appreciate.

• Educate the recipient of the gifts, if needed, so that the gifts are received in a way that promotes your children's understanding of the benefits of giving.

the process, which to them is more important than the product anyway. When the collages are finished, cover the top with another piece of clear contact paper. Matted and framed, these pictures are worthy of hanging on a wall!

6) Create pictures with squirt bottles filled with a thin salt paste. Mix equal parts of salt and flour, adding water colored with food coloring until the paste is runny enough to come out the end of an empty detergent bottle. You can either give children individual pieces of paper, or you can tape a large piece of sturdy paper (butcher paper works well, or a piece of poster board) to a table top, and let them squeeze to their hearts' content. Later, when dry, you can cut out the "pictures" from the most attractive or interesting parts, mat them and/or frame them. Or, instead of using paste in squirt bottles, you can use paint (water soluble, nontoxic, of course) in roll-on deodorant containers to make the pictures. Use the same technique as the salt paste to end up with pictures without hampering the children's creativity.

7) Homemade cards or books can be created by starting with a selection of stickers and felt pens. If they are old enough to talk, toddlers' words can be captured in the book or card.

8) A scented Christmas tree ornament, which can later be hung in the closet, can be made by sticking whole cloves into an orange or other citrus fruit and hanging it with a ribbon. (The smaller the better—little hands get tired of sticking the cloves in.)

9) A Hanukkah menorah can be made from a strip of wood and walnut shell halves. You can create half-shells by inserting a sturdy knife in the little hole in the rounded end of the walnut and twisting to pop the nut open. Remove the nutmeat and you'll have two perfect shell halves. Give an appropriate number of shells to each child, along with a strip of wood already sticky with glue. Let the children attach the shells to the glue on the wood as they see fit. It doesn't really matter whether the shells are all evenly spaced or facing the same direction. When glue dries, put a candle in each shell. ♥

Putting Multiples in the Classifieds!

By Janet Gonzalez-Mena

Some children are "object-focused," while some are more interested in people than they are in things. The latter category of human beings uses objects, of course, but they use them to enhance the social world they love so much. In a nursery school or day care center, for example, you'll find these children offering pretend cups of coffee to playmates, or singing to dolls. Or they may have turned the playhouse area into a spaceship, and be busy practicing people skills on their way to Mars.

Children use things, but it's people and human relations that most intrigue them. They show an intense interest in learning about others, in interpreting messages, in reading feelings. They practice these skills every day.

OBJECT ORIENTED

The "object-oriented" child in exactly the same environment ignores the cups of coffee, the dolls and the spaceship relationships; instead, he is under the table with some kind of tool, trying to unbolt the legs. One "object-oriented" child was given a jumble of padlocks and keys that had been collecting in the preschool cupboard for years; the child, who seldom sat still for five minutes during circle time, spent an entire hour matching up locks and keys—an enormous task that no teacher at the center had been willing to tackle.

A year or two later, when I was trying to take the training wheels off his bike, the same child told me that I needed to turn the nuts in the opposite direction of how I was turning them.

SELF-ORIENTED

Not all individuals focus mainly on people or object. A third group is "self-oriented." They have an inward focus. They are their own central interest. The "self-oriented" child is the one you see in the nursery school or day care center off by herself, swinging dreamily on the hammock or painting for long periods at the easel. These children often worry preschool teachers. They seem preoccupied, disengaged; and parents and teachers often feel an urgency to get them involved—to busy them with either people or objects.

How does any of this relate to toddler twins? A survey sent out to adult twins and parents of twins revealed some interesting information. Most parents said that they could see how both they and their children fit into these categories. Several cautioned, however, that one must not compare, nor group, children.

One parent said that twins with different orientations can puzzle or concern parents, especially if they have a "self-oriented" child who is in startling contrast to a very outgoing co-twin. She went on to explain: "One of my daughters is very people oriented and the other isn't. I worry about the latter being left out. I feel responsible for giving (her) some strategies for helping in social encounters. It's hard to let less 'people-oriented' people just be!"

Letting children be themselves is hard for most of us. Social skills are so valuable that many of us encourage them over the skills related to "self" or "object" orientation.

This categorizing scheme is merely one more way to celebrate the differences between twins and a way to help parents support their individuality. There is a need, however, to provide each child with a variety of experiences, and to improve the balance of the different aspects of each personality. Parents should definitely allow the dreamer to dream, the dancer to dance and the artist to paint, but they also need to encourage relationships with other people, as well as some experience with objects in the environment. Allow the budding mechanic to practice her skills, but get her involved with people as well. Help her get in touch with herself. Encourage the "relationships expert" to at least take a look at the broken tricycle and do some speculating about how to fix it.

Of course, no child is all one way or the other—most are a combination. But think about the adult population and early orientation: Can you see that engineers, mechanics and physicists were probably "object-oriented" children? Those people you know in the service professions were probably "people-oriented" as far back as toddlerhood.

Then there are the artists, dancers and writer types. The tendency for self-absorption comes early on in some. Sometimes you can tell one type from the others even in infancy; some babies are focused inwardly and others focus more outside themselves.

Ask yourself these questions: Where do I fit in the "object," "other people," and "self-oriented" categories? Am I more one type than the other? Where do my children fit? Do my differences complement or conflict with each other?

Obviously, children should not be boxed into these simplistic categories. Still, recognizing a child's natural inclinations can help parents understand how orientation affects perceptions, interests and skills. ❤

The Problem-Solving Protection Trap

By Janet Gonzalez-Mena

Problem-solving is a valuable process that consumes a good deal of a toddler twin's time and energy. All day, every day, he deals with little problems, like how to get the lace out of every single hole in his shoes. He also deals with big ongoing problems, like how to cope with the feelings of fear and loneliness when separated from his parents or his co-twin.

The variety of problems each toddler twin encounters is enormous. Many are physical problems, like how to get that interesting toy that is just out of reach on the shelf, or how to turn the knobs on the television so that something happens. Some of his problems are social—like how to get someone to play with him, or how to not get caught while turning the knobs on the television!

A toddler twin also faces emotional problem solving, such as how to cope with the feelings of anger and frustration after being caught turning television knobs and stopped. His other emotional problem solving includes what to do when the big dog next door runs up, jumps on him, and scares him, or how to handle his feelings when he's alone in the day care center because his twin is in the group that went on the field trip.

Many of the problems twin toddlers work to solve are ones that their parents wish they had never thought of. (They also create problems on a regular basis, which gives their parents a chance to practice their own problem-solving skills!) It may help to remember that practice at problem solving develops intellectual skills.

BUILDING SELF-ESTEEM

What happens during the toddler, period may later affect the individual's perception of himself as a competent problem solver. When toddlers see themselves as doers—capable people—they are more apt to try to solve problems rather than run away from them or give up. Some adults who give up or retreat when challenged were once toddlers who were discouraged from solving their own problems by the adults in their lives.

One common way adults discourage problem solving in toddlers is by keeping them from encountering problems, or rescuing them when they do encounter them. Children who have problems solved for them don't get the practice needed to perfect the problem-solving process. They also get the message that they could never do it by themselves—that they need an adult.

Rescuing has its place. Toddlers in deep water or heading into the street need to be rescued. But most cases are not so dramatic; yet, adults may treat them as if they were. The toddler who trips and falls may not need help at all, but the natural inclination seems to be to rush over and lift the child back to his feet. When adults pause to assess the situation before acting, they are less likely to rescue. It is a strain to watch a child working on a difficult task—wiggling and squirming to get his foot into a shoe that keeps bending down at the back. Most adults need to practically sit on their hands to keep from doing it for the child—or at least from reaching over and holding the back of the shoe. But the child who persists will learn to do it without adult help and will gain the reward of having conquered a challenge.

Some adults go the other direction. They watch a child who is pretty sure to fall on his face but who refuses all help. Then when the obvious happens, the adult conveys an "I told you so" message that may be incorporated into the self-image as "I'm not a good problem solver." Adults need to make decisions about which risks are worth taking and which are not, and prevent their children from taking on the ones that are too big.

WHEN TO INTERVENE

To facilitate problem solving in toddlers, parents need, first, to be aware of when problem solving is occurring. Next, they need to refrain from offering assistance until they see that the child is on the verge of giving up. However, stopping them from failure may not always be beneficial—failure is often good feedback. Children come to accept failure as feedback when they are ultimately successful most of the time—and that is where a parent can help.

Parents need to develop a sensitive awareness of each child's threshold by asking themselves the following questions: At what point will my twins' frustration get in the way of their actually dealing with their problems? (Frustration is not necessarily bad—it can be a powerful motivator.) And, when are my twins on the verge of quitting?

After answering these questions, parents can then step in with a tiny hint about what to do next. The trick is to intervene at just the right time—not too early and not too late. Provide the very smallest bit of help possible, then step back again. Sometimes, just calmly saying, "Try it another way," is all that is needed.

Twins may have an advantage over the rest of the population when it comes to problem solving because they often work as a team. Doyleen McMurtry, director of the Child Development Laboratory School Solano Community College, Suisun, California, explained, "Sometimes twins even develop separate areas of expertise in problem solving. I have seen twins who worked as a team—one was the shoe buckling expert, the other was the climbing expert (like when the ball gets stuck on the roof). This teamwork may be both an advantage and a disadvantage. Once one twin learns a skill the other may not apply himself because he can always turn to his brother to 'fix' it."

McMurtry also said twins may support each other in problem-solving in the social realm. "I've seen circumstances when one twin wanted to change the direction of the play and didn't get any response from the other children involved; the support of the other twin swayed the group toward the change of direction."

It is probably a good idea for parents to be aware of whether or not their twins work as a unit at problem solving and how this is serving them. Parents can appreciate their children's team approach while encouraging both children to eventually develop a full set of skills.

Problem solving is a valuable part of children's early experience and contributes to their overall development. The world needs competent problem solvers; you can provide the greatest amount of support by observing your toddler twins busily working toward that end. ♥

Resolving Conflicts Without Creating Victims

By Janet Gonzalez-Mena

Consider the following scene: "Mommy, Jesse hit me!" With her eyes scrunched up and her face streaked with tears, Amber, Jesse's co-twin, appeared to be the epitome of misery as she held out her arm to show her mother a small red mark on it.

Amber's mother scooped her up, patted her head and brushed away her tears. "Let me see, Amber, you poor darling. Mommy's going to put some cold water on this nasty hurt," she told her gently. "Don't cry. How about a Popsicle?"

This mother made these comments with her back to Jesse, thinking that by ignoring his aggressive behavior, it would go away. This may have been true; however, while trying to eliminate Jesse's aggressive behavior, she was reinforcing Amber's victim behavior.

"Me, Mommy . . ." Jesse protested.

She replied, "No, Jesse, you hurt your sister. You can't have anything." Patting her still sobbing child, she and Amber left the room.

Although this scene may be a bit exaggerated, similar situations occur in homes and day care programs throughout the country in which children are taught that being a victim is rewarding.

ROUND #2:

What can you do to help your twins learn to get along without inadvertently rewarding their undesirable behavior? To answer this question, look at how Jesse and Amber's mother could have handled this situation:

"Mommy, Jesse hit me!" Amber runs to her mother and holds out her arm to show her mother the small red mark. Instead of scooping her up, her mother takes her hand gently and leads her over to where her co-twin stands with a defiant look on his face and a teddy bear in his arms.

Crouching down to her children's eye level, the mother takes Jesse's hand in hers. She turns and says gently to Amber, "Tell Jesse you don't like to be hit." She has maneuvered the two so that they are facing each other.

"No hit!" says Amber to her co-twin, as her mother instructed.

"That's right!" Her mother nods at her, indicating approval of her choice of words. She looks immediately to Jesse, who is holding the teddy bear behind his back.

"Mine!" he screams.

His mother expands his sentence for him, saying, "You want the teddy bear . . ." and immediately looks back to Amber.

"No, mine!" Amber angrily reaches for the bear but then hesitates, remembering Jesse's slap she just received.

This is the point at which most adults jump in with some version of grownup justice. But, by doing that, the lesson moves from "how not to be a victim" to "what's fair."

Instead of focusing on "what's fair," the purpose of an adult presence in a situation like this one is to ensure that no hitting occurs and to encourage both children to stand up for themselves. In other words, the outcome—the winning or losing—is not nearly as important as the processes of self-assertion and conflict management.

Rather than taking the bear away or giving it to Amber, this mother has tried an alternative method—encouraging her children to talk about the situation in order to solve the problem.

ROUND #3:

Here's how this situation would be replayed with Amber's mother encouraging Amber to stand up for herself:

"Mine!" Amber would say emphatically, forgetting the pain from the slap in her desire to get the bear.

"You really want the bear," her mother would say, reflecting her sensitivity to the intensity of her child's feeling. She then would turn to see how Jesse had received Amber's statement.

Jesse would most likely scream, "No!" one more time, but he may also get bored with this face-to-face "arguing." If so, he would drop the bear, remove his hand from his mother's grasp and run off to become involved in another activity.

As in this latter scenario, most toddler arguments often die out if an adult is nearby to help both children express their feelings and stop the hitting before it starts.

However, what if Amber had lost interest and left the scene or had given in and let Jesse keep the bear? Would she have been considered a "victim" in either case? Not necessarily. It is important to note that there will be times that, in spite of standing up for herself (with her parent's gentle, persistent support), a child won't always come out on top. When that happens, she needs to learn how to cope with her feelings of disappointment.

This coping is easier if a parent or other adult is there to put a child's feelings into words by saying things such as, "You're unhappy that you don't have the toy you wanted." This can be said matter-of-factly and without the gushing sympathy that rewards victim behavior. ♥

Providing Sensory Play Experiences

By Janet Gonzalez-Mena

When you and your toddlers are cooped up inside the house due to inclement weather, illness or an impending visit by the washing machine repair person, for example, "cabin fever" may strike. Your toddlers may drag out all of their toys, color on every available sheet of paper, work every puzzle and read a million stories.

But on some days, keeping your children entertained demands creative, unconventional activities. To stimulate their senses of touch and vision, as well as keep them entertained, try these ideas:

• Give your twins trays of sand, salt or corn meal, and small figures, cars, dolls, action figures or plastic creatures with which to play. (Editor's note: To ensure the safety of play objects, keep those that are small enough to be swallowed or that have sharp edges away from young children.) Since their own world is restricted when they have to stay indoors, with these additions, toddlers can create their own small worlds.

Those figures listed above are also fine play toys by themselves or when added to block play; however, the additions of sand or salt serve as additional sensory stimulation.

• Water play is another fun activity for toddlers confined indoors. Pour a small amount of water in a dish pan. (The dish pan could be put in a plastic wading pool to further confine the potential mess!) Put a thick bath mat or pad under it to absorb drips and to prevent the children from getting too wet. Add some pouring utensils, containers, small dolls, action figures or floating objects.

Cooking projects, such as corn meal sifting and making bread dough, can keep twins entertained for a long time. Other cooking projects that can engross toddlers if they aren't hurried through them include mashing bananas and snapping spaghetti.

Play dough also works well as a soother. The children can be involved both in creating it and playing with it. The simplest recipe is two parts flour to one part salt and enough water to make a doughy consistency; color by adding food coloring to the water. ❤

Sanity Savers for "Cabin Fever"

1) Deliberately slow down your pace. If you are frantic, irritated, nervous or harried, your children will pick up on your emotions and react in a similar manner. If you are calm, you may influence them just by your quiet presence.

2) Have plenty to do. When children have a choice of engaging toys, materials and activities available to them, they are less likely to get wild and more likely to get involved. Knowing that toddlers tire of playing with the same toys over and over, it's smart to have a set put away on a top shelf somewhere that you can take down, especially on rainy days.

3) Take a walk. Sometimes the simplest activities are the most fun. An old Swedish saying goes, "There's no such thing as bad weather, just inadequate clothing."

4) Go on outings. Some parents plan little trips on rainy days just for the purpose of getting out of the house. When you and your children return from an outing, whether you walked to a neighbor's or drove to the grocery store, home often seems interesting once again.

5) Exercise. If you can't go outside to exercise, find some way for you and your children to exercise indoors. It is important that they jump, run, roll, climb, bend and stretch regularly. If you're willing, pull the cushions off the couch and let the children tumble around on them. Allow them to dance in the living room; do calisthenics in the family room; or ride tot trikes in the garage.

6) Provide get-away spots. Children love to have places in which to be alone or to hide together. Cardboard boxes, tents and card tables with bedspreads draped over them all.

7) Provide small retreats. Even pulling the couch out from the wall and letting your children hide behind it can give your toddlers a sense of having their own special place.

Stubbornness: Parents' Friend or Foe?

By Janet Gonzalez-Mena

Although it may be easier and more desirable to parent twins who follow their parents' every wish, parents need to encourage children to question, think, make their own decisions and take a stand on things in which they believe. In fact, parents need to know that a certain amount of this so-called "stubbornness" is a normal and desirable behavior that will serve children well, once they learn to combine it with affection and reason.

"IT'S A LIFELONG TRAIT!"

Some parents label their twins who behave stubbornly as "obstinate," "determined" or "strong-willed," thinking that these character traits may persist beyond the toddler years.

Ann Dutson, a Sonoma, California, mother of 16-month-old twins, Devon and Diane, is one of these parents who applaud her twins' stubborn behavior and doesn't mind putting the labels of "strong-willed" on her children.

"I think being strong-willed is a good character trait, both in normal amounts and when it persists beyond toddlerhood," Ann remarked. "With minds of their own, children have a better chance to grow up to be leaders and not followers.

"Therefore, I actually encourage stubbornness in my children because I'm anxious to produce secure, rational adults who know what they want and how to get it. Although it's easier to raise children who obey you instead of resisting you, I'm not interested in raising robots who do what they are told to do!"

As Ann is well aware, some of the greatest achievements of humankind have come from people with minds of their own who dared to be different. However, she is also aware that living with two obstinate toddlers can be difficult sometimes.

"It's not as hard as it could be," continued Ann, "because my twins aren't both stubborn at the same time. It's tempting to label them and say that my son is the stubborn child and his co-twin is the more easygoing one. However, I avoid making comparisons like that. Besides, when I really think about it, they often flip-flop. There are times when Devon has finished something and is ready to move on, and Diane is the one who resists being made to stop.

"I know from experience that the peak of their stubborn stage is still to come. At 16 months of age, my son is showing his developing willpower by becoming rigid as a board when it's time to put him in the car seat. My daughter resists being diapered, and they both protest when it's time to get out of the bathtub. But this is just the beginning. When they learn to say 'No, I won't!' then their stubbornness will be in full bloom."

"IT'S JUST A STAGE!"

Christine King of Santa Rosa, California, has watched her identical twins, Camille and Rebecca, move through this normal toddler "stage" of being resistant. "It was strong when they were about 18 months old, and now, at 2 1/2 years of age, it has begun to diminish," she acknowledged.

Refusing to label their behavior as stubbornness, she believes her toddlers' current rebellious nature is just a hallmark of their passing through a predictable stage of child development. "I think stubborn children are those who really hold their ground. Truly strong-willed children persist much longer than most other children."

Christine also said she's more stubborn than her children, but she has made a conscious effort to model "letting go" by changing her mind sometimes. "I think it's important for children to see parents who are flexible and not so worried about 'losing face' that they can't ever apologize or adapt," she added. ♥

Super-Two! Times Two

By Allison Berryhill

Faster than a speeding Big Wheel, more determined than the Little Engine That Could, able to leap tall crib rails, church pews, and playground fences in a single bound. Two-year-olds are, indeed, super. When mild-mannered babies crawl into their proverbial phone booths and come bounding out as fullfledged toddlers, your Daily Planet is in for a whirl.

Two-year-olds tread exciting developmental territory, explains Jane Nelsen, marriage, family and child therapist and author of *Positive Discipline for Preschoolers* (Prima Publishing, revised edition). It is their nature to be curious and assert their independence. So discipline at this age should guide children toward respectful, safe behavior while bolstering their budding self-confidence.

That sounds good on paper, but even one 2 year old can deplete parents' reserves of energy and patience. Twins drain the pool at twice the rate. A particular episode with 2-year-old twins is lodged in my memory. My boys dumped cereal, threw silverware, drew on themselves, and peeled off a chunk of living-room wallpaper. Among the three of us, we sustained a 40-minute crying jag. With each intake of breath, I prayed for patience.

> Kim, mother of Alex and Andi (now 8): "They're each different. Just because something worked with one didn't mean it would work with the other. At 2, ownership was important to my girls. I had to have two of everything."
>
> Michelle, mother of Derek and Kayla (now 2): "Trying to divert their attention is a never-ending battle. I try to stay a step, even a half-step, ahead of them. I've had to adjust what I can live with. They want my mop and brooms and some water for the mop. This used to drive me nuts, but I figure they're not hurting anything."
>
> Pam, mother of Sam and Aaron (now 5): "I felt like I had to repeat myself constantly. One would try something, then the other. I always kept certain objects in my purse: little cars, pencils and pads of paper, a calculator. The calculator was a great distractor; still is."

With each exhalation I lost ground. I thought, "Surely tomorrow will be better," then looked at the clock and gasped: It was only 9:15 a.m. "No one said it would be easy," says Nelsen. "Twins require double supervising, double redirection." But with understanding of toddlers' emotional development, and advice from other parents of multiples, the SuperTwos can be, "if not a piece of cake," at least a little sweeter.

THE WORLD OF 2-YEAR-OLDS

Two-year-olds' notorious squalls and commotion are evidence of awakening autonomy, child psychologists explain. Around 18 months of age, little tykes begin marching for independence—therefore, the refusal to hold your hand, stay in car-seats, and eat their peas. They are driven to explore and experiment—hence the compulsion to unlace shoes, dump cat food, and poke paper clips into the VCR.

These biological forces exceed children's limited physical skills (witness the tot who wants to pour his own milk), leading to frustration. And because these urges often bulldoze the boundaries of acceptable behavior (tossing those peas she's refusing to eat), parents feel overwhelmed. "Get into your children's world," Nelsen encourages. Try to see situations from their perspective. Me-do-it stubbornness and deliberate mess-making are not necessarily "naughty." Rather, they are ill-equipped attempts to explore and declare independence. Positive discipline involves supervising and redirecting children so that their developmental urges are satisfied but in appropriate, safe ways. Imagine the toddler as a plumber's apprentice facing his first leaky faucet. If the only tool he has is a hammer, all he can do is pound, and we're in for a mess.

The parent, in turn, is the master plumber. It's her job to introduce more suitable tools, help the apprentice feel useful and capable ("Hold this pipe, please"), while teaching him better ways to fix leaks. Whacking the apprentice, scolding him, or shooing him off to consider how wrong it was to use the hammer might stop the pounding, but does little to improve his plumbing skills.

KIND AND FIRM

Discipline, says Nelsen, should not be confused with punishment. Where punishment is "payment" for past mistakes, discipline is kind and firm guidance for future behavior.

For example: It is not acceptable for Junior and Juniorette to club the dog with the vacuum cleaner wand. But a parent who can redirect firmly and kindly ("Let's brush Scruffy gently, together"), can transform the episode into a learning experience. The children feel helpful and better understand how to care for their pet. Repeating "kind and firm" under one's breath in trying situations can keep a parent grounded with these cornerstones of discipline.

What about the next time you turn around, and the twins have moved on to clubbing the cat with a stapler? Guiding 2-year-olds is not a one-time quick fix, but a day-in-day-out process of supervising, distracting, and redirecting.

Locking horns with 2-year-olds is a lose-lose proposition. As parents firmly stop inappropriate behavior, an explosion of will and temper is likely. Parents must think faster than those speeding Big Wheels to distract and redirect children to acceptable alternatives.

Instead of yanking the stapler from the toddlers' hands (a reflex reaction), try holding open a pocket and inviting him to "poke it in." Better yet, supervise a bit of stapling (on paper!) then lock the stapler away when the interest wanes.

KEEP IT SIMPLE

Margo Magill, kindergarten teacher and mother of twin daughters, recalls the toddler years: "I tried to set loving limits with simple rules, such as 'Hands are for helping, not hurting.' And use kind words."

Magill stresses the importance of parents modeling positive behavior while setting clear boundaries. "You can't expect young children just to know how to behave." If you want children to be respectful and polite, you must treat them respectfully and politely, she explains.

And just because it's normal for 2-year-olds

Who's the Boss?

Unfortunately, when stubbornness occurs during toddlerhood, children aren't able to understand what is best for them, nor are they able to sort out important issues from minor ones. Therefore, the following suggestions may help you and your twins get along when they act in resistant ways:

1) Offer choices. When given choices, children are less likely to be stubborn. For example, ask, "Do you want to wear your sneakers or your sandals?" instead of saying, "You have to wear shoes."

2) Change commands into positive statements whenever possible. This takes some practice, but it works. You can influence your twins' behavior more effectively by saying, "The dog likes it when you pet her like this . . ." than you can be demanding, "Stop pulling the dog's tail." Demands, which are often viewed as challenges, create resistance instead of cooperation.

3) Explain to your twins the reasons you want them to do, or not do, something. If you automatically say, "no" to their request without explaining why, you teach your children to do the same thing. Ann Dutson, the mother of 16-month-old boy/girl twins, said, "When I'm asked 'why?' I seriously consider my answer. If I can't offer a good reason for it, I may decide to change it."

4) Give warnings before transition times. For example, when it's almost time to leave the park, say, "Five more minutes before it's time to go." Right before you leave, signal to your twins another warning, such as, "Two more times down the slide and then it will be time to go."

5) Be firm when making demands that are in your children's best interests. Let your children know what you expect from them and then stand firm on those expectations.

6) Don't try to rule through intimidation. When children are threatened, they often become even more obstinate. Therefore, gentle, persistent firmness usually is more effective.

to want to climb furniture doesn't mean it's appropriate for them to tromp on Aunt Edith's antique settee. When possible, plan ahead to avoid situations that pit children's urges against adults' expectations. "We put children in inappropriate places," notes Nelsen, "then we blame them for inappropriate behavior."

THE "N" WORD

Isn't there a time for parents to just say no? Yes and no. Frequent nos may deter mess, noise, or inconvenience in the short run, but in the long run frustrate children's developing self-confidence. Furthermore, Nelsen reminds parents that young children do not comprehend the abstract concept of no the way adults do. "Why else would a child look at you, grin, and do it anyway?" she comments.

Try saying yes more often. With assistance, 2-year-olds can vacuum, crack eggs, plant flowers, pour milk, use scissors. Save no for times when safety or respect for others is at stake.

Say it kindly and firmly, and be ready with creative alternatives to fill the gap it creates. "By babyproofing your home, you can say no less often, which keeps the word more meaningful," says Magill.

TIME OUT

My twins were cranky and tired. Dinnertime had dissolved into a war of wills. Both boys wanted to put glasses of milk in the freezer—an idea too ridiculous and messy for me to sanction at this late point in the day. My firm and kind "No" was met with howling and kicking. I felt ready to join in. Instead, I hoisted a boy to each hip, and we headed to the carpeted landing of our stairs.

"The Stairs" is where we compose ourselves and calm down. While time alone can help older children cool off, 2- and 3-year-olds derive more benefit from "time out" spent with a comforting adult. "Kids need to feel better to behave better," explains Nelsen. Children want to belong and feel loved. When weariness and hunger combine with "my way" urges, small children feel woeful.

Instead of using "time out" as punishment, let it be a positive way to shake misery. Nelsen suggests using a special pillow or cozy blanket. Both twins can participate, even if only one is out of sorts: "Your sister is having a hard time. Let's help her feel better." After a few quiet moments in mom's arms, and a verse of "Baa-baa Black Sheep," little lambs are usually ready to return to the fold.

Two-year-olds are super little people: supercharged with emotion and energy, superpacked with curiosity and determination. As twins establish autonomy from their parents as well as from each other, they will no doubt shake up Metropolis. But the learning and growth that fuel these super-heroes will give you a year both comical and marvelous. Or wait—make that a *Marvel Comic*. ♥

Tell Me What You're Thinking!

By Michael K. Meyerhoff, EdD.

I once read a magazine article that reported the results of a survey in which people were asked what supernatural power they would most like to have. Some mentioned the ability to fly, others said invisibility, and a few chose the power to move objects with thoughts (telekinesis). But the majority chose the ability to read other people's minds.

If all of those being asked were parents of infants and toddlers, I think that choice would have been unanimous. How many times have parents of twins watched their newborns gazing up at them and wondered what was going on in their little heads? How many times have they seen their 2-year-olds do something crazy or heard them say something outlandish, and wondered what on earth they were thinking about?

It is clear that the minds of infants and toddlers do not work like those of adults. It is equally clear that what is going on in the minds of newborns is not the same as what is going on in the minds of 2 year olds. Parents sometimes find these differences to be charming and amusing. Sometimes they find them to be alarming and exasperating. But almost always, parents find them puzzling. They feel that interacting with their infants and toddlers would be a lot more stimulating, and things would go a lot more smoothly, if they had a better understanding of how their children's minds were developing during the first years of life.

Thanks to a Swiss psychologist named Jean Piaget, researchers now have a pretty good picture of the process. Incredibly, the original descriptions produced by Piaget were based solely on observations of his own three children. However, they have proven to be largely accurate through studies of thousands of children by hundreds of researchers over the years. Although parents still won't be able to read exactly what's going on in their babies' minds a little knowledge of Piaget's notions can go a long way toward increasing their fascination, and decreasing their frustration, when dealing with the minds of their infants and toddlers.

BASIC PIAGETIAN PRINCIPLES

According to Piaget, babies are born with virtually no ability to "think" at all. Moreover, they are locked in "egocentrism," unable to distinguish themselves from the world around them, because they know nothing about it. They have no conception of time or space, and they're not even familiar with their own hands and feet, much less their mothers and fathers.

What they do have at birth is what Piaget calls the "ready-made schemata" or reflexes. These include sucking, swallowing, grasping, crying, responding to sounds, looking at sources of light, and gazing at human faces (especially the eyes), among others. These behaviors are rather primitive and uncoordinated, but they are the building blocks of intelligence. They allow babies to begin the process of adapting to their environments, and adaptation to the environment is what intelligence is all about.

As Piaget sees it, the ability to adapt grows through the continuous interaction of two major functions—assimilation and accommodation. On one hand, babies are constantly taking in or assimilating various elements of their environments through their existing mental structures. On the other hand, they are constantly adjusting or accommodating those structures so as to improve their capacity to assimilate.

He calls the first two years of life the "sensory-motor" period because intellectual and physical growth are so closely interrelated in the beginning. Babies begin to learn about the world through their senses and the motor activities of their bodies. Gradually, they achieve greater control and mastery of their bodies and they gain greater experience with more aspect of their surroundings through exploration and experimentation.

Eventually, they come to the realization that they are only a small part of a much larger world. The practical intelligence they acquire, which is limited to getting direct information and results from their immediate surroundings, slowly but surely forms the foundations for the distinctly "intellectual" functions of memory, language, and imagination. By the age of 2, they have moved into the period of "representation," and now can deal with things through strictly mental manipulations even if those things are not present to their senses.

THE STAGES OF SENSORY-MOTOR DEVELOPMENT

Piaget noticed that all children develop this early intelligence through an invariant series of stages, with each level of mental functioning building logically upon the preceding one. During Stage 1, which occupies the first month of life, babies simply exercise their ready-made schemata, those basic structures they were born with. This enables them to take in what is necessary for their survival. For example, the sucking reflex allows an infant to assimilate nourishment from his mother's breast.

At the same time, as the infant gets more and more experience, he begins to refine those structures into more effective and efficient forms. Whereas a newborn often has difficulty finding the nipple— sometimes sucking the skin of his mother's breast in the wrong place—once he is a few days old, he has learned to adjust his body, head, and lips in ways that will best accommodate the size and shape of his mother's breast and her position during nursing.

However, at this point, his behaviors remain essentially reflexive in nature. He will suck not only on his mother's breast, but also on anything else that happens to come into contact with his mouth, such as his father's little finger. Moreover, his various behaviors remain largely independent of one another. For instance, he will look at a rattle that is placed in his field of vision, and he will grasp a rattle that is placed in his hand; but he will not grasp a rattle he sees, nor will he look at a rattle he is grasping.

During Stage 2, which goes roughly from 1 to 4 months of age, babies begin to coordinate basic motor activities and sensory experiences to form simple skills and perceptions. As they exercise their bodies, they gain greater control over their movements and they gain more and more information about the results of those movements. Eventually, their activities become more varied, they start to discriminate among different aspects of their environments, and they learn to combine previously unrelated activities in ways that produce more beneficial results.

It is during this period of life that a baby will make the remarkable discovery that she is connected to her own hand. Previously, the soothing (if not nourishing) activity of sucking on her hand when it happened to reach her mouth, as well as the interesting spectacle of seeing her hand when it happened to pass through her field of vision, were merely the results of lucky accidents. Having enjoyed these fortuitous events she now moves around in an effort to make them happen again. Gradually, she learns to control her hand and her head so that the act of bringing one into visual or tactile contact with the other becomes a smooth, regular pattern of behavior.

The crowning achievement in the coordination of these basic behaviors is the development of "prehension" or visually-directed reaching. Now, for example, when a baby hears a rattle, she will look at it as well. Having seen it, she will move her hand toward it and grasp it. Having grasped it, she will bring it to her mouth and suck on it. This indicates that she has

become reasonably familiar with the limits of her own body and therefore is ready to start exploring the world of things "out there."

During Stage 3, which goes from 4 months to approximately 8 months of age, babies start applying the simple strategies they've developed to a whole new world of objects. At first, they simply take a more active interest in their immediate surroundings. Eventually, as they achieve the ability to crawl around, they develop a seemingly insatiable appetite for exploring every area they have access to and thoroughly investigating everything they encounter.

As they go about their activities, they discover that they can create rather interesting events, and they continually strive to make those events last longer or happen again. Early on, they merely apply their simple skills at random. For instance, a baby will first suck on anything he finds, then shake it, then throw it. Later, as his various actions produce different results or different degrees of the same result, he begins to develop a crude classification system.

By hearing a toy make a rattling sound, watching a ball roll and feeling the soothing effect of a teething ring, he learns that some objects are "things to be shaken," others are "things to be thrown," and still others are "things to be sucked." He also learns some basic principles about the relationship between actions and things, such as harder, faster, and louder, for example.

However, he still has no real understanding of cause and effect. He just knows that his behavior seems to have some magical power. Thus, for instance, he may notice that banging on his crib rails will make a mobile suspended above him move about. Then, when he sees a window curtain flutter in the breeze, he may bang his crib rails in the expectation that the curtain will move again.

During Stage 4, which occupies the balance of the first year of life, children develop a better sense of the relationship between means and ends. For the first time, they begin to exhibit truly intentional behavior. As a result of the many experiences they've had in using their simple strategies on different objects in different situations, they've learned a great deal that now enables them to coordinate these strategies to cope with more complex challenges.

For instance, during the previous stage, if a child saw an interesting toy on a table but couldn't reach it, she would be stymied. She might have waved her arms or kicked her feet, but all to no avail. Now, she knows that if she pulls the tablecloth, everything on the table will tumble down to the floor where she can get to it. By using one object to reach another, or by moving aside one object to reach another, she shows not only that she is capable of purposeful goal-directed actions, but also that she is abandoning "magical" repetitive strategies in favor of realistic behaviors adapted to specific situations.

Unfortunately, her ability to keep a goal in mind as she works to achieve it remains at a rudimentary level during this period. The child still cannot perceive of things existing independently of her actions upon them. In other words, as long as she can see the object of her desire, she can pursue it. But for the most part, once it is out of sight, it also is out of mind.

During Stage 5, which is roughly from 12 to 18 months of age, children become a lot more adept at getting around using their hands, and various other means. They continue to explore and investigate, but now experimentation becomes a strong interest as well Previously, they used their skills only to learn about specific things they encountered and to get specific things they wanted. At this point, they also use those ever-improving skills to find out what will happen "if."

Whereas their behavior was primarily "repetitive" during Stage 3, and mainly "purposeful" during Stage 4, during this period, it can best be described as "systematic." For instance, a toddler may take his rubber ducky out of the bathtub and drop it in the toilet. Enjoying the splash this makes, he will reach in, take it out, and drop it in again—only this time from a greater height. Soon, he will take a bar of soap and drop that in to see what kind of splash that will make. Eventually, he will manage to drop anything and everything else he can get his hands on into the toilet as well.

By bringing new objects into the game and creating new events, the child has demonstrated that he is beginning to understand the distinction between himself and the world around him. He now knows that things exist even though he can't see them, and he realizes that they have properties that are independent of his actions upon them. However, he is still largely tied to the "here and now," so his explorations and investigations of possibilities remain on the level of "groping," or "trial and error."

During Stage 6, which occupies the remainder of the second year, children finally achieve "representation," the capacity to retain mental images and to work out new strategies through strictly internal mechanisms. When presented with a novel problem, they now can take all they have learned from their experiences with different things in different situations, test the possibilities mentally, and then pursue a directly appropriate course of action.

For instance, a child may want to move a pile of blocks from one room to another. She collects the blocks, and walks to the door. Since she needs her hands to open the door, she then puts the blocks down in a neat stack on the floor. However, as she starts to open the door, she realizes that the stack of blocks will be in its path; so she stops, and carefully moves the blocks aside. In other words, she now can create a picture in her mind of what will happen, and then use this picture to readily figure out a new and better way to achieve her goal.

Having achieved the ability to "use her head" at last, it is clear that the child has come a long way. Nevertheless, the growth of intelligence is far from finished at this point. While she is now capable of true "thinking," that thinking is still rather crude. In much the same way that she learned how to use her body and her senses in an increasingly appropriate fashion, she will spend the next several years learning how to use her head more efficiently and effectively.

I once observed a 2-year-old girl named Tina sitting at the kitchen table with her mother and father. As she was playing with various utensils, she knocked over a glass of milk. While her mother was cleaning up the spill, her father playfully asked her, "Who did that? Did Tina do that?" The child thought for a moment, and then said "No, Lisa (her older sister) did that."

It was obvious that this little girl had envisioned a potentially unpleasant event (punishment for making mess), and thus had conjured up what she figured would be a successful strategy for avoiding it (blaming her sister). Unfortunately, as impressive as this thinking was for one so young, it was clear that she still did not have the capacity to realize that there was no way she could "beat the rap."

THE QUICK OVERVIEW

This has been a rather brief discussion of the early stages of intellectual development, but already you may be able to see how a little knowledge of the process and some awareness of where one's children are on the continuum can be quite enlightening and can have tremendous practical consequences. Now, when your twins sit in their high chairs and plop spoonfuls of Jello all over the linoleum, you may realize that they're not little monsters who are out to get you, but simply determined little scientists who are testing the various qualities of some very strange materials.

Of course, a more complete knowledge of Piaget's notions will produce an even greater awareness. Unfortunately, Piaget's original writings are in complicated, highly technical French. Furthermore, most of the translations and interpretations produced by university scholars over the years are almost as unfathomable, even for graduate students in psychology and education.

Fortunately, the book *Your Baby's Mind and How It Grows: Piaget's Theory for Parents*, written by Mary Ann Spencer Pulaski (Harper & Row, 1978), beautifully outlines the interests and abilities of children at each of Piaget's stages and explains in great detail how they proceed from one stage to the next. Pulaski also provides a lot of sound advice regarding what parents can do to feed and encourage the growth of their children's intelligence in ways that are appropriate to each step along the way.

It is important to remember that, although all children proceed through these steps in the same sequence, they may take them at slightly different speeds. You may notice that even your twins will not have precisely parallel rates of progress. Therefore, be sure that you use any age indications provided only as a general guide rather than an exact prediction of where each of your children will be at any given time. ♥

Creating Thinking Lessons

By Janet Gonzalez-Mena

Is spending time learning academics an appropriate activity for toddlers? It depends on how one defines "academics." If it means looking at flash cards, doing worksheets, having structured lessons, or memorizing drills, I have to answer "no."

My definition of academics is different from the one above. I see academics as the developmentally appropriate parts of the process of learning to read and as the tools needed for intellectual development—for thought. According to this definition, academics are appropriate activities in which to engage toddlers, as long as these activities are, I repeat, developmentally appropriate.

Here's how the developmental progression advances: First, children learn to talk by adopting a set of sound symbols that allows them to label the concrete world and eventually begin to think about and communicate ideas, feelings, wishes, and needs.

That first set of symbols must be well established before children learn the next set—written numbers, letters, and words. This second set of symbols, which are more abstract than the first, are symbols of symbols. They all involve the manipulation of concepts—both in the mind and on paper.

But toddlers aren't ready for the second set. They are too busy incorporating the first set of symbols—the sound symbols of oral language, and the concepts behind those sound symbols. They are well-equipped to learn about the concrete world and the world of communication. They are not yet developmentally ready to understand the secondary symbols which represent the concepts they are just beginning to incorporate.

Now I'm not opposed to toddlers learning to say their ABCs or count to 10 (or higher). Those two skills are on the same level as learning to wave "bye-bye." They're performance skills that make the people around them happy just as when a dog shakes hands or rolls over on command.

The problem is that some adults elevate the ABC-performance to more than just a cute trick or spend far too much time and effort in training along these lines. This becomes a serious problem if the child resists the training. It's also a problem when the child becomes merely a tool for adult satisfaction.

INTELLECTUAL DEVELOPMENT

The theory of intellectual development described above—the progression to using more and more complex symbols—comes from a Swiss researcher named Jean Piaget, who spent a lifetime showing how children learn to think and reason. According to this theory, cute tricks which are rewarded by parent attention have little or no part in the intellectual development of children, which is a far more complex process than the training involved in a stimulus and response mechanism.

It's even possible that training children using a stimulus-response approach (which is what flash cards and reciting the ABCs are) actually delays more complex learning. With the emphasis on performance, children may not get the kind of experiences they really need to fully develop intellectually.

Furthermore, the training of isolated skills teaches children to look as through they're thinking when they're not. They seem to understand concepts that they don't know anything about, giving the impression that they can use processes that they are unaware even exist.

So what is my message? Am I telling parents

to stop teaching their children anything? No! What I'm asking is that parents see the difference between true intellectual development and simple rote memorization.

ROTE MEMORIZATION

Rote memorization is what children have accomplished in order to recite rhymes and the alphabet, or respond to flash cards. Rote means they don't understand what they are saying, they merely repeat or give a standard, predetermined response. They can't manipulate the thoughts or symbols they gain through rote memorization—they can only spit them back out.

What can parents do instead of training their children in this mode? They can understand and promote real learning. Let's take as an example the process of learning to read. Instead of boxing the skills involved in learning to read into a simple stimulus-response mode, parents can broaden their view to see the enormity and complexity of a process that begins at

Pointers in Promoting Learning

As described in article above, learning to read is a complicated process that starts early. It can be very satisfying for parents to see their children gain knowledge in concepts, abilities and skills. Parents who recognize this process of emergent literacy can promote it in the following ways:

• Provide numerous experiences that encourage children to use all their senses, including visual and auditory.

• Encourage whole-body physical involvement. Physical explorations are the basis for later mental explorations.

• Surround children with print and demonstrate its uses.

• Encourage symbolization of all sorts—pretend play with toys, drawing, "writing."

• Encourage oral language development. Reading and writing are simply written expressions of language.

• Give children a wide variety of real-life experiences so when they do start reading, they'll have firsthand knowledge of the things about which they are reading.

birth and continues until the child becomes a proficient reader. This process has been labeled "emergent literacy."

Children are born into a world of print. They must develop the capabilities, skills, understanding, and desire to use it. All this starts with babies responding to sounds and focusing on the face of the person feeding them. These two senses—hearing and sight—are obviously related to later reading. The other senses are also related, but not so obviously.

As babies grow, their parents help the unfolding of their abilities by providing a variety of seeing and hearing experiences, as well as other kinds of sensory and physical experiences. In the early years, physical development is linked to intellectual development. In other words, the explorations that later are done in the head are the business of the body for the first years.

Parents also provide the love and attachment that are the foundation for motivation behind learning of all sorts, so it is impossible to separate the various areas of development in a toddler. All-around development is vital to emergent literacy—one cannot educate the mind alone. The feelings and the body are tied in to intellectual development and are inseparable in the early years.

SEEING IT IN PRINT

While children are working on total development with the help and support of their parents, their parents can also be getting them used to print conventions. For most parents who read magazines like this, what I am talking about is a rather automatic process. It has to do with exposing children to print and to all the ways that people use print in their lives.

The most obvious way to start is to read to children. At first, they will point and look at pictures. They may even take the book in their own hand, insist on turning the pages back and forth, and demand to read in their own way. But eventually, if book time is a regular part of their lives, they will begin to understand that the words they hear have a relation to the black squiggles they will begin to notice on each page.

Perceiving this relationship may be a long time in coming, but that doesn't matter. They are gaining experiences in other kinds of symbols as they learn to interpret pictures and see the relationship of those pictures to stories. Besides, reading times provide pleasurable associations as children feel closeness to their parents, and get a feeling for books that is all mixed up with a sense of satisfaction and warmth.

If the parent's aim is to produce a reader—one who is not only able to read, but chooses to read, providing opportunities for developing the good feelings about reading are as important as the skill-building. Children who are read to regularly come to understand what reading is and its purpose. Parents augment this interest in print and place a value on it by reading books and magazines for their own enjoyment. That is, they model the behaviors they are trying to encourage in their children.

Parents who are interested in promoting emergent literacy can also point out how useful print is. They can draw their children's attention to the times they use print for various purposes, such as reading the directions for hooking up an appliance or assembling a piece of furniture. When cooking, they can show their children the recipe they are following. These experiences give children further clues about the value of reading.

Another way that children learn reading is by writing. Encourage toddlers to "write" by making crayons, felt pens and paper available. Let them explore and experiment to their heart's content (but supervise them so they stay on the paper). At first, they'll scribble, which is neither art nor writing, but rather an effort to produce an effect. Later, they'll name their scribbled productions which will eventually become differentiated.

Some children announce spontaneously that they are "writing" rather than "drawing." They'll only do this early "writing" if they live in a print-filled world and see adults using writing as a tool in their own lives. (For example, a mother can make it a point to let her children watch her write a note which she puts on the front door telling the washing machine repairman to come around to the back of the house.) ❤

Want Tight Security? Try Bunnies and Blankies!

By Janet Gonzalez-Mena

Two-year-old Jason sits in the waiting room of the doctor's office clutching a bedraggled piece of cloth that was once a blanket. He strokes what's left of a silky binding while sucking his thumb.

Sarah hugs "Beary," a furry stuffed teddy bear, close to her as she snuggles under the covers in her crib and hums a song in preparation to going to sleep.

Jessica stands by the window at the babysitter's home, watching her mother drive away. In her hand, she clutches a silky nightgown. Periodically she puts it to her face—first smelling it, then rubbing it against her cheek.

These children are using what are called "transition objects," in conjunction with "self-calming devices," to make themselves feel better. Jason is more able to cope with his fears of the doctor when he has his familiar "blankie" in his hand and is able to suck his thumb. Sarah eases the transition from wakefulness to sleep with the company of her soft bear and the sound of her own voice. Jessica finds her mother's nightgown a source of comfort—a bit of home away from home—while coping with the transition to day care.

Although the general public may regard children who use these devices as "insecure," child development experts and psychologists see self-calming as a desired skill. Rather than being insecure, these children are, according to the experts, coping in perfectly normal ways. Transitional objects and the self-calming that goes with them are useful devices for easing fears and helping children through anxious moments.

How do ordinary objects, such as blankets, stuffed animals and pieces of clothing, become transitional objects? Children develop attachments to objects, just as they develop attachments to people. Sometimes it's hard to tell why a child picks the particular object he does; other times it's easy to see why a certain item may be the chosen one.

For example, a blanket may be associated with the warmth and comfort of infancy. The child may have fond memories of lying in bed, being tucked in by parents. The feelings that go with that experience become a part of the blanket—the object itself.

Or the chosen object may belong to a parent and remind the child of him or her. For example, Jessica's silky nightgown not only comforts her with its smooth texture, but also with its look and smell which evoke memories of her mother—giving her further comfort.

The use of transitional objects by toddlers is by no means uncommon. Attachment to a transitional object is only abnormal when it goes beyond the preschool years with the same strength it had when the child was a toddler, or if the child clings to the object so strongly that he or she is hampered in doing other activities.

These instances do indicate cause for concern, not about the object itself, but about what kinds of stress or difficulties are creating the need for such long-term or frantic clinging. The source of the problem needs to be "treated," not the comforting device. So if one of your twins or both become attached to security objects, accept that fact. Don't push them to give them up; they will eventually outgrow them.

My 4-year-old son, Bret, illustrated this point well when he walked into the room where I was trying to comfort his screaming 3-day-old brother many years ago. In Bret's arms, folded in his very best fashion, was the colorless, binding-less blob of a blanket he had used during most of his four years of life, expressly for those times when life was just too hard to handle. "Here," he said, "this is for the baby—I don't need it any more."

Surprised, I took his gift, with a tear in my eye for the sacrifice he was making. But he was right; he never needed that old "blankie" again.

If your children don't give up their transitional objects on their own, and they get to be a true problem because of the age of the children or because the attachment interferes in daily activities, let each child help develop ways to gradually let go. One child was willing to go off to kindergarten with just a small patch of his old blanket in his pocket—not enough to attract notice. Another child asked that his blanket be made into a toss pillow and put on his bed.

Allow ownership of security objects, says Susan Anderson, the mother of 3-year-old twins, Maia and Adrian. "Maia's flower blankie and Adrian's bunny blankie were their first personal possessions. All their other toys were joint property; their blankies were the one thing they never had to share."

Be clever in finding ways to keep the objects clean—or at least sanitary. When they see their child forming a strong attachment to an object, some parents purchase a duplicate of the item, so they can wash one without making the child give it up during that cleaning process.

Many parents cut a security blanket in half in order to be able to wash "one" and keep "one"

available for their child.

This latter idea only works for some children; it may be considered "mutilation" to others. If you haven't solved the problem any other way, and your child won't "let go" long enough for a washing, let him or her help give the object a "bath."

Your twins may or may not use transitional objects to comfort themselves. If they do, perhaps they have similar objects—like Maia and Adrian, though that isn't always the case. Some twins become attached to very different objects. Sometimes only one twin has need for an attachment object, while the other finds another means of self-comfort. Whatever the pattern, all of these means of self-comfort are normal toddler behavior.

Be glad your children have ways of soothing their own feelings. That's one of the advantages of being a child. Don't you wish you could get half the satisfaction from a security blanket as toddlers? I do. ♥

Chapter 9

PLAY AND CREATIVITY

Should You Buy Two of Every Toy?

By Janet Gonzalez-Mena

Christopher and Nicole struggle over a teddy bear. Each twin grips the bear's arms, desperate to pull it away from the other.

How can parents solve this problem? Should they buy two identical bears? Will that take care of it? Maybe. Does this mean parents of toddler twins should buy two of everything?

THE YES SIDE

There are two answers to this question: yes and no. It simply depends on your point of view.

At first, it's a good idea to have double of everything. Toddlers aren't old enough to be able to share, so if there is only one toy and two toddlers, there are bound to be squabbles. Until children get a sense of possession, they can't understand the concept of sharing. One way they get a sense of possession is by owning things. Once they are clear about ownership, they can be taught to share. Children also get a sense of individuality when they learn to say, "This one is mine and that one is yours."

Teachers in early childhood programs understand how important it is to have lots of the same kind of toys to cut down on frustrations. At the beginning of the year, most centers put out many duplicates and even triplicates. As the children get older the variety of toys increases, but it's not necessary to duplicate everything. By the time children are 3 and 4 years old they can handle not having exactly the same thing as other children, but toddler multiples aren't as adept at that.

THE NO SIDE

Toddler twins are going to squabble. That's a given. It doesn't matter how many little motorcycles you have, they'll both want to ride the same one. Those squabbles aren't about toys anyway, they're about rivalry. The way to solve the problem is not to buy more toys, but to deal with the rivalry, primarily by checking to be sure you aren't feeding into it.

When parents compare their children, they intensify their childrens' feelings of rivalry. Using competition to motivate does the same thing. It may seem expeditious to say, "Let's see who can get her shoes off the fastest!" or "Which one is going to finish her dinner first?"

Competition creates winners and losers. It affects children to lose, and if the "loser" is usually the same child, she may eventually develop a self-esteem problem.

CREATIVE SOLUTIONS

Squabbling really doesn't hurt anything—it teaches children how to get along. They can even develop problem-solving skills by working out difficulties with each other. Even toddlers can come up with creative solutions if they are given the opportunity.

When Shelby trotted off on the one stick horse, Amanda was brokenhearted. She wanted to ride it. But then she found a broom propped in a corner on the deck. She climbed on and rode away. It didn't take long for Shelby to be holding out the stick horse to see if Amanda would trade. She suddenly perceived the broom as the more desirable riding toy.

If parents adhere to the rule of buying duplicates of everything for their twins, they may end up teaching them consumerism. Many parents end up overdoing it on the toys anyway.

Children who are used to having everything they want may grow up to see owning objects as a primary goal of life. Let children be inventive and creative when it comes to finding things to play with. They may surprise you.

THINK ABOUT IT

The two views are presented in the extreme to give you more to think about. Both sides of this issue have good points. Perhaps you haven't thought about the issue of buying toys in quite this way before. Obviously there is a middle ground. Give it some thought. You may find the best answer is to combine both points of views. ♥

Having Fun Being Alone Together

By Janet Gonzalez-Mena

Molly holds a block to her ear and says in as grown-up a voice as she can muster, "Hello?" She stares into space, expressionless, then frowns, stamps her foot and slams the block down on the floor, hanging up on her imaginary caller.

Next to her sits Sarah, her co-twin, who is holding a doll wrapped loosely in a blanket. Sarah clutches the doll to her chest and murmurs nonsense in a singsong voice.

Molly and Sarah are engaged in pretend play. Through this kind of play, children create mental images and learn to deal with the world in a symbolic way. They try on different roles and, in this way, come to view the world from perspectives other than their own. Pretend play also provides opportunities for toddlers to transform reality and practice mastery over it. Finally, this form of play gives children the chance to recreate and reconstruct what has happened in the past in order to release pent-up emotions.

Most toddlers engage in parallel play, play in which each is off in her own pretend world

Creating A World of Make-Believe

Considering how worthwhile pretend play is for your toddlers, what can you do to encourage it? Here are some suggestions:

1) Provide experiences that your children can replay. A trip to the store, fire station or your office gives your children ideas for their pretend play.

2) Provide props. For young toddlers, a couple of hats and scarves will stimulate pretend play. Older toddlers can use slightly more complex props. For example, a few hand stamps, an old adding machine, and some paper and pens suggest office play; on the other hand, a wagon, hose and two firefighters' hats give an impetus for firefighter play.

3) Give your twins plenty of uninterrupted time and space for pretend play. If your children are always involved in some kind of structured activity, they may not have enough free time in which to give free rein to their imaginations.

4) Reduce your twins' television-viewing time. Although it may seem as though your children are using their imaginations while watching television, they are passively—not actively—engaged. "Couch potatoes" have less energy and need for creating worlds of their own through imaginative play.

5) Allow free expression. Children often work through their anger symbolically. If, for example, your twins are spanking dolls, you may be worried about the aggression they are exhibiting. However, this is symbolic aggression. Many child development experts believe that the best way to curtail aggression is to "get it out of your system" symbolically. Therefore, pretend play allows children to act out their true feelings.

6) Appreciate the way your children play out past and future events.

Through experiencing something symbolically in pretend play, children can actually change the way they feel about it. For example, a child who replays a hospital stay is coming to terms with the fears that are a part of this experience.

while being physically close to each other. Their conversations may even run parallel, each talking to herself rather than to her playmate. One may influence the other's pretense, but they don't actually interact.

The majority of toddlers engage in parallel play more often than they do in interactive play. Parents may find that their twins have a tendency to move beyond parallel play sooner than their singletons, mainly because each has had a constant play partner since birth.

"I notice that my boys give each other ideas that keep them going," said Georgy Charland of Napa, California, mother of 18-month-old twins, Caleb and Zachary. They don't talk much about what they are doing, but they don't have to because they are so in tune with each other. It's hard for me to tell just what game they are playing when they both put hats on and run around the house chasing each other, for example; but they know."

Sometimes toddler co-twins give more clues as to what their play is about when they "pretend" interactively. Two-year-old Julie stands large foam blocks on end, creating an enclosure. She enters through a space she has left and announces to her co-twin, Nick, "House!" Nick jumps off the block that he has been riding as a horse, grabs a doll and enters the "house," knocking all the foam blocks down. He carefully lays the doll down in the middle of the tumbled blocks, then methodically helps his co-twin rebuild the house around the two of them. The game switches from builder to doctor as Julie and Nick take the clothes off the doll, and Julie looks for something to use as a thermometer.

Though few words are exchanged, various facial expressions, exaggerated gestures and body movements give each co-twin clues about what is happening. The children not only know what the pretense is, but both have obviously agreed to play along with it and have developed mutually meaningful representations of objects, events and even identities. Through interactive pretend play, they are learning to negotiate and cooperate. ❦

Capture Enriching Play Experiences
Create your own neighborhood playgroup for the under school-age set.

By Cheryle Levitt

Where will your 2-year-old twins be going to nursery school?" several parents asked me as our children, Aliza and Yonatan, approached 18 months of age.

This question took me by surprise because the thought of sending my children to nursery school had not yet crossed my mind. I was just grateful that at 18 months of age, my children were finally sleeping soundly through the night, beginning to verbalize intelligibly, learning some independence and beginning interactive play with other neighborhood children.

But their question encouraged me to do some research. And after considering the formal nursery school possibilities for the coming year in our community and in our family's current financial status, I soon concluded that our family was not emotionally or financially prepared to enroll Aliza or Yonatan in a formal nursery school program. But I did feel comfortable organizing a cooperative playgroup together with other parents in which our children would play together at specified times and rotate going to each other's homes.

Based on my experiences in organizing that playgroup, I now believe that a cooperative playgroup is one low-cost way to provide secure, happy, enriching play experiences for toddlers. I also found that one of the extra rewards of this enrichment experience for children is that it is also enriching for parents because it allows for their involvement in their children's growth and development.

BENEFITS

One wonderful benefit of a playgroup is that it provides children with a social/play/learning experience among a limited number of peers in

Playgroup vs. Nursery School

Here are some of my other suggestions to help those who are considering a cooperative playgroup as a substitute (as in our family's case) or a supplement for 2-, 3- and 4-year-old preschool education:

1) A playgroup works best when the children involved are close in age—within a range of about six months of each other. The play experience, designed by the parents, is most effective when it is geared to the developmental level of the group and has a basic framework within which there is much flexibility.

2) In general, the children are most stimulated when provided with a variety of experiences, balancing free play with some structured activities.

3) The length and number of these structured activities (see #2 above) need to be short and few in the beginning for 2 year olds and can gradually increase as the children age.

4) Once the children are accustomed to the different playgroup environments, their parents can leave them in the care of the host parent. Sometimes parents may decide to have co-hosts share the responsibility, or the host parent may want to obtain a helper.

5) Four to six is usually the average number of children that is both manageable and conducive to productive group activity.

6) Each setting needs to provide socialization opportunities for children with their peers by including time for free play, songs, stories, arts and crafts, music, exercise, snack/lunch and outdoor play. Field trips may be a part of both a nursery school and a playgroup. The basic daily schedule with a flexible format ensures the smooth operation of both the nursery school and playgroup.

7) Two to 2 1/2 hour sessions (commonly in the morning) give toddlers enough time to play, yet still nap after lunch or in mid-afternoon. This time frame may increase as the children grow older.

environments that are cozy and safe with a high ratio of adults to children. Since the parents have input into planning the play experiences, they are not passive bystanders but rather active participants in their children's play.

In a playgroup, the children have the opportunity to get accustomed to different home environments, as well as make new friends and develop these peer relationships during the group's time together. Many continue these friendships after playgroup and attend school together. Because of their having to adopt to such a variety of settings, many children become more flexible, in general, to new situations after being involved in a playgroup of this type.

The group's inherent flexibility is yet another benefit. Its design is based on the needs of a small number of parents and children; therefore, changes in scheduling, structure or activities can be made easily on an ongoing basis. There are very few administrative tasks to do, once the group is organized.

An extra bonus: Because some members may actually consider the program cost-free, they may want to purchase larger play equipment that can provide years of enjoyment—play kitchens, swing sets, sandboxes, slides and clubhouses—with the money they would have spent on preschool tuition.

DISADVANTAGES

A possible disadvantage to beginning a cooperative playgroup is that it requires parents to invest some of their time. The host parent must devote a small amount of time to pre-planning that day's activities, including setting up for the group prior to its arrival. The morning of playgroup at my house was completely devoted to the children; leading playgroup took precedence over making telephone calls, or doing laundry, dishes, home repairs and anything else.

Some busy parents may be unable or unwilling to make this ongoing commitment. Others may not want four to six children traipsing through their house or may be involved in home repairs or redecorating and thus be unable to accommodate the group.

A Sample Playgroup Day

SUNNY DAY

9:30–10:00 Arrival and free play (active)

10:00–10:15 Circle time (songs and finger plays) (passive). Samples: *Row, Row, Row Your Boat, Old MacDonald, Wheels on the Bus, Open Shut Them, Itsy Bitsy Spider, Ring Around Rosie.*

10:15–10:30 Snack (juice and crackers) and bathroom.

10:30–10:55 Outside free play (active). Samples: rock collecting (each child has paper bag), beach balls, bikes, swing set, sandbox, paintbrushes and buckets of water.

10:55–11:10 Story time—outside stories about nature (passive).

11:10–11:25 Craft project—pasting leaves on paper.

11:25–11:50 Lunch-indoor or outdoor picnics. Background music helps everyone stay seated.

11:50–12:00 Clean-up and departure

RAINY DAY

9:30–10:00 Arrival and free play (active).

10:00–10:15 Circle time (see above) (passive).

10:15–10:30 Exercise and music time (active). Samples: marching band, Simon Says, dancing, pretending to be different kinds of animals.

10:30–10:45 Snack and bathroom.

10:45–10:55 String rigatoni noodles to make necklaces (passive).

10:55–11:15 Free play (active).

11:15–11:20 Clean-up time.

11:20–11:35 Stories.

11:35–12:00 Lunch and departure.

Four Rules for Fun

When deciding how to structure your playgroup day, the key words to remember are pre-planning and flexibility. Some activities will take much less time than anticipated, or the children will not be interested in the particular experience you have planned. Other times they will become totally involved, and you will find that you are lacking time for other things. Here are some basic guidelines:

1) Always overplan and set up in advance for any craft, play, reading, outdoor or snack/lunch time.

2) Be sure all supplies are out so you are not frantically searching for or cutting items while the children are creating havoc somewhere else in the house. At worst, you will have leftover ideas for your next playgroup session.

3) The children should remain together in the same room at any given time, and it is generally a good idea to alternate active and passive activities (for example, storytime followed by exercise).

4) Toddlers have short attention spans and need frequent activity changes. Nice weather and a safe enclosed outdoor play area are a wonderful combination in any season. Ask the other parents to send appropriate outdoor clothing—a romp in the snow can be loads of fun!

I, however, was so grateful to have three out of four playgroup mornings "off" that my having to set aside one morning every two weeks seemed like a small price to pay!

HOW TO BEGIN TO SET UP YOUR PLAYGROUP
If you have decided that you would like to form a playgroup for your toddlers but you do not know anyone else who is interested, try word-of-mouth advertising through your neighborhood. Talk to other parents at playgrounds and at the library, for example; and place notices on bulletin boards, in apartments, pediatrician offices, religious institutions, mailboxes, health clubs and supermarkets. Of course, it is preferable for all members to live within a short driving distance from each other.

When looking for members, keep in mind that nursery schools often fill their spaces quickly; therefore, parents often select a school 9 to 12 months prior to a September starting date. Also, joining a playgroup may be a unique idea in some areas and could require someone "selling" parents on the concept before it is accepted.

A crucial factor in the success of the playgroup is its number of members. When one parent will host the group, 4 to 5 toddlers are manageable; two parents or a parent plus a helper can comfortably guide a group of 6 to 7 children.

Once members have agreed to participate, an organizational meeting should be scheduled (see box). At that meeting, the topic of multiples and the special considerations they need (or don't need) should be discussed. For example, parents of singletons are often worried about twins causing "double trouble," so it is important to explain to other host parents your twins' special personalities and differences.

If your children are identical, it is helpful to explain to members of the group that you will dress them differently and/or tape masking tape with their names on it to their backs to avoid unnecessary confusion and to bolster each child's own individuality.

My children, Aliza and Yonatan, were one of two sets of twins in their 2-year-old playgroup; the other set was identical boys, and two additional singletons rounded out the playgroup. I found that all of the twins seemed to adjust to the playgroup situation more quickly than the singletons and were never treated as duos, but as separate children. ♥

Early Childhood Programs Can Be Exciting

How your very young twins can benefit from organized play/learning with Mom and Dad.

By Diane M. Sharon

My identical twins, Reena and Susannah were "late" walkers. They took their first steps alone within hours of each other at 15 months of age, just a day or two before the mother/child classes I had signed us up for were scheduled to begin. But, while Reena had toddled on and never looked back, Susannah had taken her first steps, walked around a little bit and had gone right back to crawling. I figured she'd be fully vertical when she was good and ready, but my husband was frantic.

The first morning of "school," Reena walked into the classroom, and I carried Susannah. Now we were in a room filled with toddling children and their mothers (or caretakers), waiting for the start of the "Music Dance and Storytime" session for walking-to-18-month-olds.

I put Susannah down on the floor where 10 other children about her size were toddling around and falling—bump!—onto their diapers. She took one look at all those vertical toddlers, including her sister, and stood right up.

She never went back to crawling after that, and my husband, who had been very skeptical of any formal program for children that young,

was sold on the value of peer group learning.

When I signed us all up for these parent/child sessions, my objective was to have a place to take the girls during the upcoming winter that was indoors, had a stimulating activity and was full of mothers with children my children's age. But most of all, I wanted a place where I could play with my twins in new ways—enriching my interaction with each of them

MYRIAD CHOICES

The range of choices for parents of young children looking for adult/child experiences is dizzying. There are gym classes, art classes, music, formal and informal playgroups, mother/child "parkbench" workshops to talk about mutual concerns and "drop-in" community groups through local churches or private agencies. Some are highly structured, with set curricular goals and strict rules; others are informal. Some are free, others are quite expensive. Some are scheduled so working parents can bring their children on evenings or weekends. Others are attended by babysitters and children, and still others prefer to have only mothers or dads with the children. Deciding whether to sign up for a group and what kind to choose, depends on your needs as a parent, and what you know about your children. (For some places to take children or things to look for, see box.)

One grandmother of twins, Bernice Weissbourd, founder and president of Family Focus, a Chicago-area agency that provides drop-in centers for parents of children up to age 3, cautions against too much rigid structure or pressure to learn "facts" in early childhood sessions.

"The key is excitement," according to Weissbourd. "Children learn colors, body parts, shapes or the alphabet because they're all around them and because people they care about think it's wonderful when they do it; this kind of learning helps children feel good about themselves. Pleasure should be part of learning. If the child is enjoying what you're doing with him, he'll learn.

"The value of early mother/child programs depends on how learning is done. Know where your child is developmentally, and add to that," she recommended.

My twins loved listening to records and tapes, and "danced" to the music before they could walk. Music and art were things I remembered most fondly from my own childhood.

REAPING THE REWARDS

I knew there were things I wasn't ready to let my 15 month olds play with in my house, but felt they ought to begin experiencing—like bright colors of runny paint, big thick paintbrushes and squishy clay. I also only half-remembered my own nursery songs, and didn't recognize lots of the stuff on children's records we had for the girls. And, of course, I wasn't about to build a toddler gym in my living room. My house is furnished in "early childhood" as it is. So I looked for mother/child sessions that included music, movement and art.

Jill is a working mother whose identical twin girls are a few months older than mine. She believed that her children seemed to need physically active time, and she wanted to find a program in which she and her husband could take the girls together. When her girls were 20 months old, she signed them up for Saturday

The Organizational Meeting

The following topics should be addressed when forming a playgroup. A roundtable discussion of philosophies on early childhood play/education is advisable to identify individual goals and biases. This will set the tone and direction of the group. Answers to the following questions should be discussed:

1) How many days per week will the group meet?

2) At what specified times will meetings begin and end?

3) What is the rotation schedule? Will the setting change daily or weekly?

4) How can younger siblings fit in or not fit the group?

5) Will lunch be included and if so, does the host parent prepare it or does each child bring his own lunch from home?

6) How much structure should the group have and what should be included in the daily schedule/framework (very important to group success)?

7) Should the setting always be at home or are field trips allowed occasionally (playgrounds, museums, parks)?

8) What are emergency numbers, including pediatricians? Any allergy information should be included here, as well as any medications the child may be taking.

9) Are there any activities that parents might not want their children involved in, or anything that is "off-limits"?

10) Is every host parent aware of standard first-aid procedures, including CPR and the Heimlich Maneuver (used to dislodge an obstructing object that could choke a child)?

morning sessions at Gymboree, a franchised caretaker/child gym program with more than 300 centers across the United States, Canada and Australia.

"It was small and intimate—just 6 children," Jill reported. "Loved it. I decided on Gymboree because a parent of a singleton raved about it, and my twins were always active. I felt that they were the right age to explore gross motor skills."

Many mothers of young children aren't looking for specific kinds of activities as much as they are wanting to have a regularly scheduled place that their children—and they—can go for a change of pace.

Characteristics of an Ideal Parent/Toddler Program

According to many early childhood educators, a quality parent/child playgroup should include:

• Goals which stress fun and enjoyment and are appropriate for a specific age group.

• Nonachievement oriented play experiences.

• Parent/facilitator attitudes that reflect an understanding of child development.

• A warm and welcoming environment.

• Opportunities for parents to support one another in parenting issues and concerns.

In addition to the suggestions mentioned above, early childhood educators stress the need for safety in a parent/toddler program. These precautions include:

• Gym equipment which is placed a safe distance from walls.

• Sufficient space between pieces of play equipment.

• Organized and neatly arranged rooms.

• Equipment which is monitored and checked periodically.

• A program which stimulates your child and adds something to her day.

• Helps parents avoid putting too much pressure on children to conform or be part of the group.

Corinne, mother of 2-year-old twins, Seth and Mark, has been going to a mother/child program at a local community service agency for over a year. "Going to the 'Mommy and Me' program gives structure to the week," she remarked. "Meeting with other mothers of boys the same age as mine is an important part of the sessions," she explained.

Weissbourd agreed. "Mother/toddler groups can be of great value to the mother. They provide a place to go with new activities, new toys, new people and a new environment, so it's stimulating for both the mother and children. Meeting other mothers can help combat the loneliness and isolation mothers of young children often feel today. And seeing your children in relation to other children can be reassuring. Mothers become less anxious when they see their children behaving similarly to other youngsters."

SIGNING FOR TWIN-SPECIFIC REASONS

Many mothers of twins often sign their children up for parent/child programs because of reasons specific to the twinship. One mother of 8-month-old boy/girl twins, for example, started taking her children separately to Playorena, an infant/toddler gym program that operates in many states, including California, Texas, New Jersey, New York, Connecticut and Massachusetts. "I signed up for one series, and brought a different child each week," she explained. "I wanted to have an activity with each one alone, and meet other mothers of children who were my own children's ages. I believed that my children could benefit from an activity outside our home," she said.

Karen is the mother of 3-year-old fraternal twin boys, William and Edward, who attended nursery school. A former early childhood teacher, Karen wanted to see for herself how each of her children reacted in a classroom. "I realized that once they began nursery school, I would never again have a chance to be with them in the classroom, she said.

So Karen negotiated special permission to take her boys to alternate classes in a local music program for a few weeks during the summer. "The teacher and school were willing to cooperate with me and let my twins try splitting a single session.

"It's really amazing how different William and Edward are, and how differently they reacted to exactly the same children and the same teacher," she noted. "I really felt as though I could pay special attention to each child, and each had my undivided attention. They even made different friends!"

Many mothers of twins are relieved that the twinship lets their children have a built-in playgroup. But sometimes that very closeness can be cause for concern. One mother of identical twin girls now approaching 2 years of age recalled why she started her children in a parent/child program when they were 15 months old. "The girls had their interaction down to a science. That was part of what worried me. The movement of toys back and forth was practically choreographed—they sometimes took turns, sometimes tricked each other into dropping desired playthings and sometimes chased each other. But it was as though every move was completely synchronized with every other.

"I never even thought about how strange that was until we visited some friends with a young single child, who obviously didn't know their routines. My children were stopped cold—they couldn't understand why she kept breaking their rhythm by grabbing the toy she wanted. I made up my mind right there that it was time for them to learn to play with a lot of different children."

Other mothers of twins involve their children for the opposite reason—their kids are constantly at odds with each other and seem to need larger psychological and physical "turf." Linda, whose boy/girl twins are almost 2 years old, recalled, "At about 12 or 14 months of age, my twins seemed to be on top of each other all the time. I felt they needed the intensity of their relationship diluted."

So, Linda formed an informal playgroup with two mothers of singletons she had met when she took her children to an infant gym program. Three mothers and four children met in alternate homes once a week for two hours. There was no formal program or curriculum. The mothers chatted with each other and mediated disputes over toys among the kids.

BEING PATIENT IN A PLAY GROUP

Weissbourd is a great fan of unstructured mother/toddler groups like Linda's. "Neighborhood playgroups can work wonders," she said. "They don't have to be expensive. They can be in parents' homes on a rotating basis. A group of 4 or 5 kids is plenty for this age group. Each mother provides a planned activity and group songs; the atmosphere is casual and relaxed. It can be informal, but it does have to be organized, planned and not too overwhelming in terms of numbers of children."

Linda's participation with her twins in the informal mothers' playgroup made a real difference in their emerging relationship. "I wanted my twins to have experiences with children who weren't twins," she remarked. "Maybe it's something to do with trying to foster each child's individuality. I noticed right away that my twins never got in each other's way. In the playgroup, they almost ignored each other, yet the presence of the other was crucial. That was exactly what I wanted to achieve."

When Linda decided she needed this playgroup experience more than once a week, she looked for a program that had the same feeling as a playgroup, where she could be present and where the twinship was diluted. She found a group where the mothers play with the children, and where 1 year olds and 2 year olds play together. "It was an opportunity to get involved on the ground level of their education, to learn firsthand what early childhood specialists do with kids that age and apply this information at home," she commented.

At 17 months, Linda's son and daughter were the youngest in her second playgroup, and the older children served as models for the younger ones. At first, she found it hard being one mother with two young toddlers in the program. "The other mothers (of singletons) looked at me with awe as they wiped just one nose and diapered just one bottom," she admitted. "The kids needed their diapers changed; they drank from bottles; and they needed Mom to help them with the transition. It was very, very tiring."

Linda advises other parents to have patience with their youngsters when starting out in a program like this one. "As the kids got the routine, Linda recalled, "they developed skills and began to really love it. That took about three months."

HOW TO QUALIFY PROGRAMS

The important thing to look for in any program, according to Weissbourd, is that it adds to your child's day and is in tune with your child's needs. She is very negative on formal, pressurized learning programs, techniques like flash cards or very early "learn to read" programs, or teaching a child any facts in a routine "now you will learn this" fashion.

"Learning must be part of the child's activity," she emphasized, "not a formal, pressured situation. Any structured pressure to learn a fact—colors, shapes, numbers—in reality stifles a child's own energy and instead of building on what the child already wants to do, it discourages the child. There is a world of difference between creating a stimulating environment and pushing a child to learn."

Directors of some caretaker/toddler programs agree, and have designed their programs, whose content often differs broadly, with a similar concern for early childhood development.

Susan Astor is founder and director of Playorena, which has programs for children and accompanying adults from 3 months up to 4 years of age. The groups are divided into three levels. "The main goal of our program is fun and enjoyment," said Astor, whose background is in early childhood and special education.

"For kids, there's an environment to explore and practice developing skills. We have over 50 pieces of play equipment: soft shells, inclines, tunnels, things to bounce and balance on—the larger equipment you won't necessarily have at home."

Astor hopes though, that the exploration process is carried on at home. "Ideally, the child is given an opportunity to explore in a safe environment. For example, a gate might be put up on the third step of a stairway, and a child can practice stair climbing. 'Under the coffee table' is allowed to be experienced, if it's not glass."

Astor, like Weissbourd, is an advocate of activities that are appropriate for the individual child. "All kids don't have to touch their toes at the same time," she noted. "Kids can observe if

How to Find a Parent/Toddler Program Near You

Most communities do not publish a single list of all the parent/child activities available in their area, so you may have to do your own investigating in these ways:

• Ask mothers in your local mothers of twins club. The members may have already identified local programs for their club handbook, for example.

• A parent's league, or other parents association that makes school information available may have information on programs for very young children.

• Your local YMCAs or YWCAs, churches and synagogues often sponsor parent/child workshops or other activities.

• Check your telephone book to see if there's a franchised gym program near you, like Gymboree or Playorena.

• Your pediatrician may keep a bulletin board of neighborhood association meetings and other events that might include parent/toddler programs.

• Private schools in your area may sponsor parent/toddler sessions for young children, or may lease space after their regular school day to organizations who sponsor these sessions.

• Colleges and universities, especially if they have childcare facilities for faculty and staff, or an early childhood education department, may sponsor parent/child programs open to the local community.

• Start your own informal mother's group with other mothers of children the age of yours. Your mothers of twins club, local church or even a local playground may be appropriate place to hold your meetings.

Equipment Suggestions:

• An old mattress to jump and crawl on;

• Couch cushions or pillows to crawl over;

• Large cardboard boxes (from appliances) to draw on, cut out windows and doors, crawl through, or squish;

• Stairs or steps;

• Soap bubbles.

Ideas for Play:

• Start out with body parts: what they are called, where they are, how they move. Wiggle them. Tap them. Clap them. Listen to them. Look at them in a mirror. Put things on them, under them, over them.

• Move on to directions: Up/down, over/under, high/low.

• Go on to other opposites you can feel or act out: Loud/soft, fast/slow, wet/dry, big/little.

• Identify colors and shapes around you.

• Use props that move: balls, hoops, scarves, blocks.

• Move around to music or rhythm pounded out on a pot with a spoon, or to recorded music.

• Listen for sounds around you—sirens, birds, children, cars, splashing etc., and try to say what they are, and imitate them.

by Diane Sharon

they don't want to play. They can explore on their own."

Jan Brecht, director of the Toddler Discovery Program at the private Walden School in New York City, says that especially among children between 12 and 24 months, the children often just watch the activities in the classroom "circle" and then actively repeat what they've heard and seen when they get home. "Children don't actually have to be in the circle," she emphasized. "The energy of the song can reach them even if they're not participating in the circle."

Walden's discovery program differs from the Playorena or Gymboree type of offering in the broader scope of its classes. There is art and music in addition to gym. Brecht's background is dance, and the Walden program reflects her strong belief in music and movement. "Our goal is providing an environment that is creative and open, with a lot of stimulation," Brecht said.

Walden Discovery also encourages follow-up at home with songs, finger plays and music. The school makes songsheets of its most popular "hits" available to participating parents and caregivers. "At Walden, our goal is to come in and have a good time, make it enjoyable more than following instructions," Brecht stated.

"As parents," commented Astor, "we have preconceived ideas of what's good, which doesn't always coincide with the child's idea, especially when children are around age 2."

According to Astor's experience, kids know what they need. "Kids walk in; they know what to do. Especially in the city, for example, when kids see foam steps, or steps on the slide, they can't wait to get involved," she said.

But parents should get to know their own children, advised Astor. "With twins, the instructor can help the parent with the second child if they go in opposite directions. But then you're at the mercy of the instructor, depending on the size of the class and how much extra time the teacher can spare."

Astor says that ideally, one child per adult works best. "If you have childcare help at home, alternate bringing the children,"Astor recommended. "With one set of triplets, the mother brought the grandmother and the grandmother's friend to help."

Brecht agrees that the issue of separation of twin children needs to be an individual decision. Some siblings work well together and some don't, twins or not. "We had one set of twins in the walking to 18-month-old group with contrasting personalities," she explained. "One was outgoing, and one cried a lot. They came with the babysitter and the mother, but the mother was the central person. In art class, they ate all the materials. The mother seemed frazzled. When her twins were ready for a circle game, for example, the mother just began whether the rest of the class was ready or not, she was so relieved that hers were all in one place. She probably would have benefitted from taking them separately."

If her family doesn't have another adult available, and can't afford extra help, then Astor believes a mother should just bring both kids and give both an opportunity to experience new things.

Mothers of twins who have enrolled their children in parent/child programs cite specific, new skills their children developed from their practice at the program. "The classes gave my kids confidence in climbing," commented Jill, whose 2-year-olds have been to both Gymboree and Playorena. "One especially, has gotten very good—she learned how to climb over, which hand to use, and which way to face."

In my own experience, it's hard to separate what results from classes and what is just normal growth during a certain stage of development. There is one behavior change, though, that I believe never would have happened without my twins attending their classes, and that I never would have believed possible if I hadn't seen it with my own eyes.

At 14 or 15 months, I never expected my kids to pick up after themselves. I would do a couple of sweeps through the house while they were napping to clean up the debris for the next onslaught, which I thought was what you did when your twins were that age.

In class, though, the teacher would bring out an activity—a bag of scarves, brightly colored hoops, jingling bells, drums, tambourines, finger puppets, rubber balls-and when the class was through with the activity, she would sing,

"It's time to put the toys away, the toys away, the toys away. . ." and all these little children, including my own, would collect all the balls, hoops, or bells they could find and put them back in the basket or bag held by the teacher. I was amazed! If they could do that in class, they could certainly do that at home.

Now, my children think it's part of the activity to put things back where they belong, and will cheerfully drop even a most precious bath toy into the net bag when I sing the jingle. They'll even wave and say, "Bye-bye, toy." They were doing this at 15 months!

For Linda, the big dividend was seeing her children in another context outside the home. "My two kids went straight to different things. Dana bathes the dollies in the water. Philip is really blocks-oriented. They both love puzzles. They were both frightened by the same child, an overpowering kid, and they were attracted to different children. Philip loves movement and music class, playing with his toy piano right alongside the teacher who plays the big piano. Dana dances with her thumb in her mouth.

"I think all mothers, and mothers of twins especially, need an opportunity to see their children from a distance," Linda, the mother of boy/girl twins, reflected. "Mother/child programs give you an opportunity to suspend all those activities like washing bottles, putting the clothes in the dryer and making the beds, and let you stand back and really get a perspective and concentrate on getting to know each of your children."

Fathers need a similar perspective, says Jill's husband, Peter. Steve, a father of boy/girl 2 year olds, agreed. "It's a lot of work stimulating twins," he said. "For people to be fresh, they really need a lot of people on the crew. School programs are a good way to do that." ♥

What You Can do At Home

If a parent/toddler group is not available to you, or if you just want to bring some of the play-group "magic" home, here are some of the tools and tips used by early childhood professionals:

Music:
- Raffi records/tapes
- *We All Live Together* records/tapes (volumes I-IV)
- Sesame Street record albums/tapes
- Disney records/tapes
- *Wee Sing* cassettes and songbooks
- Classical or contemporary music the parent enjoys
- Made-up songs sung to familiar tunes (put your children's names into these jingles)

Finger play and hand and body games:
You may remember some of these from your own childhood:
- This Little Piggy (went to market)
- *Where is Thumbkin?*
- *Open, Shut Them*
- *If You're Happy and You Know It* . . . (clap your hands, etc.)
- *Head, Shoulders, Knees, and Toes*
- *This Old Man, He Played One* . . .
- *The Itsy Bitsy* (or Eentsy Beentsy) *Spider*
- *I'm A Little Teapot (short and stout . . .)*
- Hand, Hand, Fingers, Thumb How "Play" Becomes "Learning"

When Play Becomes Learning

By Janet Gonzalez-Mena

Toddlers play all the time. However, identifying what they do as play rather than as something else, and then seeing the benefits in those activities can be a difficult task. For example, finger painting is creative expression, but does smearing mashed potatoes on one's high chair hold the same definition? Beating a drum may be music, but is banging a pot lid defined the same way?

The problem with discussing play and learning with toddlers is that parents don't have a vocabulary to talk about children this young. The terms used for the older child, dramatic play (playing house), construction (block building), or creative expression (art or music), are not as easy to label when seen in the toddler.

Most toddlers play by using their bodies and senses to explore the world. They constantly conduct little scientific experiments to discover such things as what will happen if they unroll a whole roll of toilet paper or what kind of reaction they will get if they stuff that roll down the toilet. Sometimes the pure sensory pleasure of a play activity (like rubbing oatmeal in one's hair) takes precedence over its "scientific investigation" quality.

Naturally, this sort of play is not acceptable (under most circumstances) even if the children are learning something from it. When parents stop these kinds of activities it is helpful if they are able to recognize the playful, experimental, and sensory motives behind the behaviors. When parents see their toddler twins as childish rather than malicious it sometimes eases the adults' angry feelings.

The following story about 2-year-old identical twins Becky and Shelly, will highlight the concepts these children might be incorporating into their mental framework as they learn through play. Notice both girls' role-playing as they practice the nurturing and caring they have received.

The scene is a college day care center where Becky and Shelly are spending the morning in a group of other 2 year olds while their parents attend classes.

Becky comes into a carpeted area where large plastic blocks are arranged in a small enclosure. There is just room for her to crawl inside. Shelly follows Becky, watching as she disappears into the block "house." Shelly then toddles across the rug to where a doll bed is arranged with doll babies and blankets. She grabs a doll and blanket and returns to Becky who is remodeling the house by knocking several blocks down.

Shelly carefully arranges the doll on one of the horizontal blocks, turning it into a bed, then goes off for another blanket. As she returns, Becky comes out of the house, knocking over another block. Shelly's attention turns from the doll to the ease with which the blocks topple. She tips one, lets it go and enjoys the sound it makes as it hits the rug. Becky joins the fun, tipping over another block. In a short time, the two of them have demolished the enclosure, leaving blocks strewn all over the rug. The doll is abandoned under what was once a wall.

Becky climbs up on one of the blocks, balancing carefully, then steps across a two-inch gap to another block. Shelly follows her lead climbing around on the blocks. She jumps off a block onto the floor. Then her attention goes to a small set of stairs near the scattered blocks. Over and over, she climbs up and down these stairs, jumping off the bottom one each time, spinning around and climbing again. It is as though she is perfecting a skill by practicing it over and over again.

In the meantime, Shelly has stopped stepping around on the blocks and has started building some sort of new structure. She carefully selects a block, drags it off the rug and places it carefully on the floor. She goes back for another, placing it next to the first. Soon it is obvious that she has something in mind as she selects only blue blocks, leaving the red and yellow ones on the rug. Before long she has built a triangular shape out of the blue blocks lying on their sides—another enclosure but lower and a different shape from the original "house." When finished, she wanders away from the blocks, heading for Becky who is once again walking on the blocks still on the rug.

At that moment, an adult announces from across the room, "It's time to pick up for lunch now." Neither girl pays attention to this announcement. But when the adult arrives in the block area with a trail of children behind her, both girls suddenly get interested. They watch as children carry the blocks over and arrange them against the wall.

"The doll needs to go back in her bed," says the adult. Becky rushes to where the doll has been exposed from under her block cover. Shelly joins her. Becky picks up the doll, and Shelly grabs the blanket, and they return them to where they came from. Becky gets in the doll bed alongside the doll and Shelly covers her with the blanket. As the scene ends, Shelly is sitting on the floor by the doll bed singing a lullaby to her sister who has her eyes closed.

What were these two girls getting out of their play? What were they learning? They were obviously enjoying using their senses, listening to blocks fall, feeling textures of dolls and blankets. They also were enjoying trying some physical skills that may have been new, such as balancing, climbing and jumping. Shelly practiced visual discrimination as she chose blue blocks from a variety of other colors. She also experimented with shapes. Both girls practiced gentleness, with the doll and with each other and used their imaginations. "Pretending" involved holding mental images, which is the basis for eventually being able to use symbols.

Though this scenario occurred in a childcare center, many of the same principles listed below that applied there also can help toddlers learn through playing at home.

1) Provide things to do. Toddlers with a variety of objects to explore and play with may find alternatives to toilet paper unrolling and oatmeal smearing. They need things to experience with their senses, manipulate with their hands, crawl and climb on with their arms and legs. A household can't supply the same kinds of toys, equipment and materials that a school or center can, but with some imagination and ingenuity, parents can come up with plenty for toddlers to do.

2) Be available, but don't interrupt play unless necessary. Toddlers are reported to have short attention spans, yet when truly absorbed in play they can keep at something for a surprisingly long time. A toddler with a sponge, some soap suds and a table to clean may be occupied for as long as 15 minutes if he doesn't get distracted.

3) Be responsive. When one of your toddlers comes to you, try to respond. Put language into the situation by remarking about what you see, or helping the child word a question or an insight.

4) Provide help when necessary, but provide the minimum amount possible. Toddlers are bound to find plenty of problem-solving opportunities while playing. Practicing problem solving is the most valuable learning experience of all because it helps children come to see themselves as effective problem-solvers when they are adults. Rather than rescuing them from the problem, provide a small bit of help, like saying for example, "You need me to get the zipper started for you, but now you can zip it up yourself."

5) Provide protection. To feel free to play, toddlers need to feel secure that a powerful adult is nearby to keep them from harm. Toddlers must be kept safe from themselves, from each other, and from the objects around them. Knowing they will be protected allows them to explore beyond the limits of safety; it allows them the freedom to play. Knowing that they will be protected from the fury of another child gives them a kind of psychological security prerequisite to the healthy "give and take" of social play.

6) Provide limits. Toddlers need clear messages about what they can and cannot do. They will continually test to see if the limits change, but that doesn't mean that they don't need them. Limits, like protection, provide freedom because the children are then able to explore, play, mess around and do what they know is acceptable without constantly wondering when they will get in trouble.

7) Appreciate true play for what it is. A problem occurs when adults know that children learn from playing, so they take over the play and make it into "educational activities." Of course, it is fine to teach your twins and do things with them that are "educational activities" with learning objectives. But true play is different from adult-directed activities. True play, child-initiated and directed, is the way toddlers should be spending most of their time. ❦

Do They Need to be Around Other Kids?

By Janet Gonzalez-Mena

All children need playmates outside the family. The question is, how soon? Since toddler twins have a built-in play group, why is it important to expand beyond that?

Eventually, multiples need to open their relationships to include other age-mates. It doesn't hurt to start right from the beginning, rather than waiting until preschool or kindergarten to get them used to the idea that there are other children in the world. Of course, if twins are in child care, they're already meeting other children. Or if they were born into a large family, they may have less need for outside relationships. But what about twins who don't meet other children on a regular basis? What can parents do?

Parents can set up situations where their twins have a chance to naturally gravitate to other children while still in the company of each other if they join a play group, invite other children over, or meet parents and their children at a park, for example. It's easier for children to adjust to this new situation while a parent is present. This early beginning is especially important if twins are to face separation from each other when they enter preschool or kindergarten. Knowing how to relate to other children can take some of the edge off the pains of being apart.

BECOMING PART OF A GROUP

Children in a group who are allowed to play freely, move through the following succession of steps as they form relationships with peers. It may be helpful for parents to understand how children form friendships and eventually become group members in order for parents to have reasonable expectations about children's social behavior.

- **Playing around the edges.** When first introduced to a group of children in a free-play situation, newcomers often stick to the sidelines. They may seem to be ignoring what the others are doing or even be negatively affected by the group. However, this period is of benefit because the newcomers are getting used to the sounds and experience of being around their peers. Even though they don't look involved, they are.

This is a little like sticking one's toes in the water as "step one" when learning to swim or splashing around on the edge of a lake. One may not learn to swim that day, but it's a good introduction to the water.

- **Parallel play.** If children continue to be exposed to a group and feel more comfortable, they often begin to gravitate toward the center of the action to be close to others who are playing. They don't actually play with them, but repeat each other's words and pick up on play themes. They find pleasure in the company of others, even if they don't interact. Parents may or may not find that their twins stick close together while moving into the center of things.

- **Pairing.** Eventually, children start pairing up. One child will follow another around or two will begin paying attention to each other. You can see that this is happening when they stop talking so much to themselves and start talking to the other. At first, they talk at each other, but eventually they begin to talk to each other and to listen as well.

- **Shifting pairs.** It may be harder for twins

to form twosomes outside their own relationship. But as they watch other pairs come together, then shift and change, they may begin to get the idea of how "shifting pairs" works. If they can form temporary pairs with other children, they are on their way to expanding their ability to create and maintain further relationships an important life-long skill.

• **Expanded relationships.** It would be ideal if two pairs could play together and no one ever felt left out. Then parents could invite two children over and things would work well. Sometimes that happens, but more likely, triangles form.

Triangles can be very hard on toddlers, especially if they are twins. If two members of the triangle relate closely to one another, the third member feels left out. This situation creates plenty of squabbles and unhappiness. Because of triangles, some parents avoid playmates altogether, thinking that it's a peaceful solution to an unnecessary problem.

But there's another way to look at triangles: If children experience enough of them, they become tolerable. Twins come to see other children as friends instead of competitors. Eventually, the triangle becomes comfortable, and when it does, exciting new play unfolds.

Although the squabbles, hurt feelings and tears make life difficult when children form triangles, three important lessons emerge from the conflicts:

1. Children learn that it's worth trying to get along in order to maintain a friendship.

2. Children gain experience in discovering perspectives that are different from their own.

3. Children learn problem solving skills and conflict management outside the twinship.

The skills children learn when triangles are formed help them become valuable friends and eventually good group members who feel secure about who they are. Secure people feel free to make their own unique contributions to the friendship or to a group.

What can parents do to support the triangles that form when playmates are introduced to their twins? How can parents respond when twins feel miserable about a new relationship that seems to threaten their twinship? It's important for parents to model qualities that build solid friendships when responding to problems between their multiples and playmates—qualities such as sensitivity to the feelings and perspectives of others.

In order to model these qualities, parents need to listen respectfully and not rush in and solve the problem for the children in a heavy-handed way. Just taking a disputed toy away, or sending a complaining child to time-out, won't do it. Parents need to listen to the squabbling parties, get them to listen to each other and support creative solutions. In this way, they teach their children how to manage quarrels in order to promote relationships instead of destroying them.

As you can see, it's important for the social development of toddler twins that they have ongoing opportunities to interact with other children outside the twinship. These interactions also support intellectual development. Until twins experience other points of view, they can get stuck in their own. Having a co-twin helps, of course, but a little bigger variety adds richness. Seeing beyond one's own perspective is the kind of mind-stretch that pays off later.

Rx for Stay-at-Home Moms: Start a Play Group

By Michelle Krupp Leow

The sound of wailing toddlers awakens you. It's the only alarm clock you've known since you quit working. After you feed and change them, you do the breakfast dishes, laundry and . . . welcome to the life of a stay-at-home parent—a life of solid-food wishes and diaper-free dreams.

Being a stay-at-home mom can be a lonely profession. When you have multiples, you can feel especially isolated. I know. I've been at home for four and a half years with my twin boys and their older sister. I spend too much time talking to the television, hoping it will answer back. Even when good old Barney, the purple dinosaur, responds, he isn't exactly meeting my requirements for stimulating adult conversation. I long for the companionship of people who could relate to me and my situation. Fortunately, a mom down the street was able to take some time off from her job and invited us to join a play group.

STARTING A PLAY GROUP

The first step is finding others who stay at home. If you belong to a religious organization, this is a good place to start. Ask the secretary if you can publish an ad in the upcoming bulletin. It could read something like this: "Attention stay-at-home moms wanting conversation, companionship and a needed break from the laundry. I am starting a play group. Call for details."

Make sure to include name, address and a phone number in the ad.

Another place you might try is the local library. Many libraries provide story times. If you can attend a morning session, chances are you will find other parents who are home during the day.

If you're like me and have been devoid of social interaction for quite some time, try placing an ad in the neighborhood newspaper or neighbor section of the local paper. Contact your mothers of multiples clubs and ask to place an ad in their upcoming newsletters. Be sure to put in your general location so those who respond live in close proximity. The less time spent traveling the easier it will be on your play group members.

PLANNING THE PLAY GROUP

Keep your play group small so the number of children doesn't become too overwhelming. The group doesn't have to be limited to moms. Stay-at-home dads need conversation and companionship, too. When you've found about four other interested parents, schedule the play group's day and time. I've found that two hours is a good time limit.

Agree to be the host for the first session, but ask the others to open their homes on a rotating basis. Every member of the play group should organize and support activities. If someone is unable to be the host at their home, suggest a park or other inexpensive public place convenient to all of you.

The host or hostess provides refreshments for the group. Keep it simple. Offer juice for the children, coffee or tea for the adults and some cookies or fruit.

Don't feel pressured to spend hours baking cookies. Remember you are all parents of small children. This group is designed to relieve stress, not add to it. Ask parents to bring their own bottles and sipper cups.

AGE SPECIFIC ACTIVITIES

Consider the age of the participants to determine what types of toys the children will share and what should be stored away. You may find it helpful to set up a combination conversation and play place where parents can be close by to supervise their children. If the children are older, the adults may appreciate sitting at the dining room table while the children play in an adjacent room.

Relax and enjoy yourself. Don't forget to set up the next meeting before you leave.

MEETING NEW FRIENDS

It isn't necessary to have a group of friends to begin. I was only briefly acquainted with the mom who started our group, and the rest of us were strangers. It took only a few mornings sharing the ups and downs of parenting to become friends. Our children became good friends, as well. Because we all have similar schedules, we find time to get together outside of our play group.

Being alone with multiples can be a daunting task. Don't confine yourself to the house waiting for someone to call and invite you somewhere. Place that ad today. Start a play group. It's the best prescription I know for the lonely stay-at-home mom blues. ♥

Toying With Your Toddler' Minds
Choosing playthings that are more than just fun.

By Vera Caccioppoli

You can choose toys that not only bring smiles to your multiples' faces but teach them a thing or two. However, the overwhelming amount of choices can make you dizzy with indecision. Featured here are great toys that will make shopping easy. These toys are sure to keep your multiples entertained, as well as spark creativity and encourage learning and development.

No matter what educational benefits a toy boasts, if it doesn't hold the attention of your child, it's worthless. Deborah Barbara, a pediatric occupational therapist with Skill Builders, says the "most important thing is for a parent to know the child's likes and dislikes and the skills her child has already mastered."

Once they can walk, a new world opens for toddlers. They want to see, touch and taste everything. It's the way they learn about their world. For this reason, look for toys that resemble familiar everyday objects. Toys should have pieces that can be sorted, challenge eye and hand coordination, as well as enhance toddlers' visual and spatial relationships.

Push toys provide beginning walkers with something fun to lean on for needed support. Be sure to choose one that will serve your toddlers after they're steady on their feet. The T-Walker (The Natural Baby Company, $65) is a solid-wood wagon designed for long-term and multi-generational use. You can fix the handle in the up position to assist all your little wanna-be walkers.

After they master walking, set the handle at an angle to change the T-Walker into a doll carriage or toy wagon.

In her book, *Your Baby and Child*, Penelope Leach suggests buying fewer low-cost toys and spending your money on items with the most value. With toys, quantity is not better. Too many toys distract children. It's best to seek stimulating toys with developmental versatility.

BLOCK PARTY

Building blocks are fun and interactive. Cardboard blocks (Lillian Vernon, $10 to $18) are an excellent choice for toddlers and are high on several mothers of multiples' lists. Because they're lightweight, cardboard blocks rarely hurt children if they're thrown.

Primetime Playthings First Blocks (International Playthings, Inc., $10) won the Oppenheim Best Toy Award. Easy for babies to grasp, these fun-shaped, brightly colored nesting blocks provide several levels of learning activities, including stacking, nesting and, later on, shape-matching. They are excellent for hand and eye coordination, concentration, problem solving, and, best of all, they're just plain fun. The smallest cube makes a surprising and fun sound when rattled. Parents of triplets suggest buying two sets, but one is probably enough for twins.

For the two-plus set, Dr. Stevanne Auerback, also known as Dr. Toy, highly recommends Duplo toys. One particular hit is the Duplo Aqua Zoo (Lego, $50). With more than 55 pieces, it satisfies multiples' fun factor, plus it teaches kids to identify penguins, whales and polar bears.

BOUNCING BALLS

Balls have great developmental value and are inexpensive. Kids love them and therapists say they help eye-hand coordination as well as motivate gross motor skills.

Karen Bralley, president of the Virginia Families With Greater Multiples, says that the big Fun Balls (Gymboree, $7) are a real hit with her triplets. They have holes that are easy for infants to grip. They're also lightweight, which makes them safe for multiples with good throwing arms.

PUZZLING PUZZLES

Fitting puzzle pieces into an irregularly shaped hole requires the smooth operation of many muscles in the hands and fingers. In addition to the fine motor skills, puzzles boost critical thinking skills and aid concentration. In her book, *Early Childhood Materials and Equipment*, Janice Schultz said "shape/design orientation is one of the most important pre-academic abilities."

She suggests providing several levels of puzzle difficulty. Small World Toys makes great first puzzles. They're wooden and have little knobs, making lifting and replacing pieces easy. The shape and color series is also a fun way for multiples to learn colors. Dr. Toy recommends Faces and Places Puzzles (Cultural Toys, $20). These hit number 2 on his annual list of 100 Top Toys for Kids.

When selecting a shape-sorter, make sure a block can't be forced into the wrong hole. In order for a shape sorter to be a learning device "it must be self-correcting," Schultz says. This means that each block must fit only into its corresponding hole and only when held in the proper position.

Avoid toys that require hammers to bang the shapes into the opening; it's too tempting to use the hammer as a weapon. The best type of shape sorters are the ones that promote contin-uous action. This is when the completion of the action is also the preparation for a repetition of the action. The child is tempted into continuing the activity and, in a subtle way, is being encouraged to lengthen her span of attention. A popular and versatile shape sorter is Gazoobo (First Learning, $14). For endless stacking possibilities try Stacking Clown (Brio, $20).

ENERGETIC PLAY

My toddlers loved practicing getting in and out of the Musical Activity Chair (Fisher Price, $30). Once seated, they can play a built-in drum, tambourine, xylophone or electronic musical notes. Not only are musical sounds enjoyable to toddlers but the chair requires physical coordination to make music and bop to the beat. We only bought one chair for our three, and occasionally there are fights over it.

The Country Kitchen (Little Tykes, $118) is also a great toy. It utilizes both gross and fine motor skills and promotes pretend play. Kids love that it resembles a real kitchen, complete with sink and cabinets to open. Heavier than other kitchen models, it isn't easily pushed around by multiples. And there are plenty of activities to keep all of your multiples busy.

STIMULATING THE SENSES

For the absolute ultimate in sensory stimulation, the Indoor/Outdoor Ruff 'n Tumble Ball Pit (Hedstrom, $49) provides romping fun and promotes interaction without the sharing problems. For more than two children, a better purchase is the larger Ball Pit Mountain (Hedstrom, $79).

A must for multiples is a climber and slide, which is great for interactive and energetic play. They provide endless hours of crawling, climbing, sliding and encourage gross motor and imaginative play. Be sure to choose one with adjustable heights so your toddlers won't quickly outgrow it. Two well-constructed and fun choices are the Wave Climber (Little Tikes, $139) and the Town House Climber (Step 2, $109). ♥

Making Toys Fit Multiples

By Lawrence J. Schweinhart, Ph.D.

As the holidays approach, parents of preschool-age twins think about how to influence and fulfill their children's wishes for toys and gifts and how to coordinate the buying for similar children of the same age.

Some of parents' most frequent questions include: Should we buy our twins two of everything? Should each child "own" a toy? Should children learn to share and take turns? The three following concepts of child development provide the framework for answering these questions.

INDIVIDUALIZATION

Nature has endowed twins with many similar characteristics, and parents have a natural impulse to do the same regarding gifts. But parents also need to recognize and draw attention to the unique characteristics of each twin when purchasing gifts, as increasing individualization is the direction of healthy child development. If you're going to buy two toys for a set of twins, therefore, it is probably better to buy two different toys rather than two of the same toy.

From a developmental perspective, toys can be viewed as opportunities for physical, intellectual, and social learning. A tricycle teaches a child how to use various muscles and makes the child more mobile. A doll gives children the opportunity for role play, helping them to understand social relationships better. Blocks teach children about space and gravity. The more ways a toy can be used, and the more kinds of toys children have access to, the greater the variety of learning opportunities they provide.

CHILDREN'S SELF-CENTEREDNESS

Young children are self-centered; they are not selfish. Selfishness, such as keeping something to yourself even though you know someone else wants it, is an adult trait that involves understanding and rejecting the perspectives of other people. Preschoolers keep some things to themselves because they do not fully understand the wishes of others.

This natural self-centeredness gives them an intuitive understanding of personal property. "This is mine," they say, "and you can't have it."

Asking children to share is a developmental challenge to this self-centeredness. Sharing can take many forms, including: 1) This is mine, but I give it to you. 2) This is mine, but I give it to you for awhile. 3) This is ours, and we can share it. 4) This is ours, and we can take turns using it.

The self-centeredness of preschoolers means that they naturally do not share and, in fact, are not likely to share for very long without close adult supervision. But movement from self-centeredness to coordination between their needs and those of others is the natural direction of development, so children should be given opportunities for sharing.

MATCHING ACTIVITIES TO CHILDREN

In considering toys and activities for children, it is important to select ones that are appropriate to their levels of development and interests.

One quality to analyze is the complexity of a toy or game. On the ability to master complexity, the difference between a 3-year-old and a 7-year-old is dramatic, and growth in a child from year to year is dramatic. Some parents like to think of their children as advanced beyond their years, viewing such precocity as a sign of their superior abilities and therefore, their parents, as well.

There's nothing wrong with a healthy achievement motivation for our children, but we must be careful not to overdo it. Children need challenges they can meet. They do not need challenges that are beyond their current capacities.

Some twins will not develop at the average rate for many reasons and the variation in rates of development between a twin and his co-twin may be considerable, too. The goal remains the same for each twin to match activities to his level of development and the level of challenges that can be met. This goal applies equally to handicapped children.

The best way to tell whether a child can master a toy or game is to observe him trying to do so. Generally, children rise to challenges they can meet and derive some enjoyment from the process. If your child does not appear interested in the activity, it may be because it is too difficult. Alternatively, children soon become bored with activities that are too easy and not challenging enough. ♥

Chapter 10

PARENTING GUIDELINES

Giving and Teaching Respect

By Janet Gonzalez-Mena

Teaching your two unreasonable, unruly toddlers to be respectful may seem like an impossible task like all normally developing children at that stage, your twins may seem to relate only to the world from their own perspectives.

But by modeling respect for your twins and taking their needs and feelings seriously (as well as your own), you can provide a powerful example for them to follow. Any way of teaching respect other than modeling is simply superficial. For example, by using some powerful training techniques, you may be able to get your twin toddlers to speak politely and act mannerly, but these behaviors have little to do with truly respecting others as people with needs and feelings.

Magda Gerber, a Los Angeles infant specialist, believes it is valuable for parents to be aware of the importance of treating their children with respect. Talking about children in front of them as though they were "pieces of furniture" is one way of not showing respect, according to Gerber.

On the other hand, Gerber points out that a way to show respect is by telling toddlers what is going to happen before it does. This kind of preparation ranges from simply stating, "I'm going to lift you into your car seat now," to a more complex announcement like, "Mommy and Daddy are leaving, Lisa will take care of you while we are gone."

Accepting children's feelings about what is happening also models respect, according to Gerber. Saying, "I see that you don't like being strapped into your car seat, but I have to do it to keep you safe," is one way of expressing that acceptance, as is commenting, "I know you don't want Mommy and Daddy to leave and you feel unhappy about it."

Disrespectful alternatives to the above situations include surprising children by popping them in their car seats, or sneaking out on them without saying good-bye to avoid having to deal with their feelings about being left. Further disrespect is shown by discounting children's feelings by saying things like, "Oh come on now, don't be silly. Don't cry. It's not so bad."

Gerber said another example of how parents treat children like objects is by dressing them up, parading them about, and showing them off. Twins are particularly susceptible to this kind of treatment because they command so much attention. It is easy for parents to capitalize on the "cuteness" of their children's twinship and ignore each twins' individuality.

Respecting individuality is an underlying concern of many parents of twins and usually is easier to talk about than to do. Sometimes it is simply a matter of recognizing each twin's individuality, and helping the world to do the same—such as calling each twin by his name instead of lumping them together and calling them "the twins."

At other times, it is a matter of valuing their differences rather than comparing one to the other. Since the children are the same age, it is tempting to look at the development of one in relation to the other. The most common example of this comparison is in the case of boy/girl twins who often develop at different rates.

This situation may be amplified in the case of twins born prematurely, as it was in one particular set of very premature twins. The boy had many severe problems as a newborn and was in intensive care for weeks; the girl was healthy, in spite of her small size, and went home as soon as she was big enough. Although the boy had no obvious disabilities as a result of his early health problems, he had some characteristics that are more common among prematures than among the general population. These characteristics included a high activity level, restlessness, difficulty in focusing or concentrating attention, low frustration level, and lack of coordination. These behaviors got him in constant trouble as he moved through his house like a tornado, creating general havoc.

It was difficult for the parents of this child not to compare him to his sister, who was nearly his opposite in every way. Since she was the same age, it was obvious when she reached a developmental milestone far earlier than her brother. The parents of these twins made a strong effort to respect the individual differences of their children, though it was not easy.

The examples so far have dealt with teaching respect by giving it. However, that is only half the story. The other half is your respecting yourself. You must not only give respect, but must also show that you are worthy of receiving it by being self-respecting.

As a parent of twins, you can easily get caught up in the trap of always putting yourself last. Raising a child demands a fair amount of self-sacrifice, and raising two at once demands even more. Toddler twins may seem to be so ever-needy that your own needs may get constantly put aside. However, it is important to remember that by always putting your own needs off, you are teaching disrespect.

Respecting needs—your children's and your own—is a balancing act that requires both sensitivity and awareness. You need to constantly be deciding what are the true needs of your family at a certain moment, and whose are most important. For example, you may feel you need an afternoon to yourself—away from your twins—yet your children may protest loudly at being left with a babysitter. If you respect yourself, you will be sensitive to your own needs and make a good decision about your priorities.

If, on the other hand, you have been out all day with your children, and you all arrived home exhausted, the situation may require you to prioritize taking care of your family's dinner instead of sitting down to rest.

Teaching your children to be respectful is no simple matter. Respect is more than superficial politeness; it has to do with treating people as people rather than objects, regardless of their age. Respect also deals with meeting needs and accepting feelings.

You can train your children to speak politely, to act mannerly, and to look as though they are being respectful, but you cannot train them to be respectful. The only way children learn true respect for others is by being treated with respect themselves, and by living with adults who have self-respect as well. ♥

They are Loved, but do They Feel Loved?

By Janet Gonzalez-Mena

At first glance, there's no comparison between a computer manual and an article about self-esteem. The manual is cold—full of technical words and diagrams. Self-esteem articles tend to be warm and fuzzy, full of friendly words and illustrated with cartoons. But dig down beneath the surface and you will find that both computer manuals and many self-esteem articles have programming at their core.

This self-esteem article is different. Children are not computers, and they can't be programmed. Someone sitting down at a computer knows that what they put in will determine what comes out. In computer talk, input determines output.

With children, neither the input nor the output can be controlled. Of course, parents strive to input positive messages and avoid negative ones. But no matter what messages they send, there is no guarantee how they will be received.

Take the simple message, "I love you." Self-esteem for most people depends to a varying degree on their perception of their own lovability—or, perhaps, "significance" is a better word.

With that in mind, parents tell their children that they love them. To add strength to the message, they couple the words with nonverbal gestures like hugs and kisses.

Since they also perform other ongoing, loving behaviors, such as feeding, clothing and nurturing the child, they think that they can sit back assured that their child is loved. Perhaps he is loved, but does he feel loved?

INDIVIDUAL DIFFERENCES

A family with preteen twin boys had one twin with extraordinary social skills who just naturally attracted people to him. People enjoyed how quick, lively and entertaining he was. He had numerous friends and was always making more; it was easy to send this child messages that he was loved.

His co-twin was quite different; slow to warm up to people, he often missed making social connections at all. His friends were few and far between.

The boys' mother reported, however, that it was the child who had so much going for him who thought of himself as unlovable. His less

Avoid These Top Five "Esteem-Busters"

Parents can't program children to have high self-esteem, but they can avoid practices which tend to lower it. Among those esteem-damaging parenting tactics to avoid at all costs are:

• **Comparisons.** Don't hold up one child as a model for his co-twin. Don't motivate by using competition. Appreciate the uniqueness of each child. Celebrate differences.

• **Criticism, labeling and name-calling.** Parents can't make children feel better about themselves by making them feel bad about themselves. Find ways to give children honest feedback without heavy negative judgments.

• **Discipline methods that make children feel powerless.** Empower rather than overpower. Don't tear down self-esteem with negative correction methods. Give children confidence in their abilities and in their goodness, even while correcting them.

• **Dishonesty and empty praise.** Give honest feedback and encouragement rather than trying to boost self-esteem through empty words and pretending to be excited about nonexistent successes. Praise is no cure for low self-esteem. Call attention to children's legitimate successes, but don't butter them up. Compare past performances to present ones, but not to a co-twin's. Praise with phrases like, "You picked up more blocks this time than last time," rather than, "You're the best block picker-upper I've ever seen."

• **Rescuing children when they face a problem.** Children learn from failure. When a child tries something and it doesn't work, that's clear feedback. Of course children need an array of positive experiences every day of their lives. However, in the name of success, parents sometimes go overboard in protecting children from failure, thus cutting them off from valuable learning experiences. It is important that adults be supportive rather than critical in the face of failure.

social brother, on the other hand, was quite contented and felt loved by all.

No guarantees come with children. Parents can input all they want, but, unlike computers which merely receive input, children perceive it—and they do so in a variety of unpredictable ways. Adults have no control over those perceptions. The point is, children who are loved don't necessarily feel loved. Children who are competent don't always feel competent, especially if they have a habit of comparing themselves to someone more competent than they are.

Programming for high self-esteem is a simplistic approach. If, in the name of promoting self-esteem, a parent tries to fool a child by painting her a false picture of herself, it won't work and if it did, it wouldn't be constructive. Take a child who is miserably aware of her lack of ability, who feels unattractive and unloved, who has little power to control anything in her life and is behaving in unacceptable ways. A parent can't raise her self-esteem by telling her that none of what she is experiencing is true: She simply won't believe it. If there is no reality to back up what a parent says, he is wasting his breath, and even if he points out her good traits, if the child is focused on what she perceives to be her bad ones, she won't pay attention.

It's harder to change someone's self-esteem than it seems. In fact, only when the person herself decides to change her perceptions will she allow someone else to be effective in helping her. Building self-esteem involves a collaboration—not a deception. The goal is to help children build a sense of self that is both valued and true.

That is not to say that parents shouldn't give their children all sorts of positive messages. Of course they should tell their children they love them and give them plenty of hugs and kisses; but positive messages alone won't ensure high self-esteem, even if those messages are 100 percent sincere and honest.

REALITY CHECK

Other areas besides significance are linked to self-esteem. To varying degrees, most people depend on their own perception of their compe-

tence, virtue and power to determine how they feel about themselves. For this to be a valid measure (rather than the product of a delusional mind), we must do some kind of reality check. My favorite definition of high self-esteem goes something like this: If an honest and realistic self-assessment of strengths and weaknesses results in more pluses than minuses, the individual enjoys high self-esteem.

This self-assessment is a lifelong process linked with the search for identity. It starts in infancy and continues, mostly on the unconscious level, throughout life as the individual asks himself who he is and proceeds to supply

Teaching Twins to Tell the Truth

1. Understand young children's fuzzy line between fantasy and reality. They don't perceive the world in the same way an adult does. Gently help them sort out the truth.

2. Be truthful yourself. Honesty is best taught through modeling. If you say there's no more dessert when the refrigerator is full of it, you're teaching lying. If you model that kind of behavior, you must expect your children to engage in it as well.

3. Don't back children into a corner when you know they've done wrong or made a mistake. Don't ask, "Who did this?" if you already know. Most children will try to save face or escape a consequence by going off into fantasy land if invited to do so. The younger ones may not even understand that that is what they are doing.

himself with the answers. This is a process that involves choices both conscious and unconscious. It's the element of choice that makes people different from computers.

At this point in history, there is a lot more known about lowering self-esteem than about raising it. Psychologists tell parents what not to do. That's where the programming idea comes in. Since negative input tears down self-esteem, it seems logical that reversing the process would build it up. But it isn't that simple. If it were, parenting would be a cinch!

So what are parents to do? While continuing to give their children positive input, parents should at the same time concentrate on raising their own self-esteem. Even without research, it's pretty easy to see that children's self-esteem is linked to that of their parents. And although parents can't control their children's choices or perceptions, they can control their own.

Parents should examine their own sense of self-worth by examining their self-image in each of four areas—significance, competence, virtue and power, concentrating on the area most important to them. (Priority areas differ with individuals.)

For example, many women score high in the category of significance; they feel loved, and they know that they are important to somebody. But if those same women regard power as important, their self-esteem may suffer because of a sense of powerlessness. They need to work on expanding their sense of power.

Although self-esteem eventually becomes established and relatively stable over time, it's not forever fixed and static. Creating and maintaining self-esteem is a lifelong process; it gets shaped and reshaped. It changes as children develop and circumstances change. It can even change instantly. For example, if Taylor is happily putting a puzzle together and Lindsay, who is much faster, takes over for her, Taylor may not feel as good about her own abilities as she did before.

TRUE BELIEVERS

Self-esteem brings with it self-confidence, which is a vital trait for development. What a child believes he can or cannot do sometimes influences what he can or cannot do. Children who perceive that they lack competence, for instance, may not try something because they have had bad experiences in the past, or simply because they have no confidence in themselves.

Likewise, what adults believe influences their behavior greatly. Beliefs can create a self-fulfilling prophecy. What people expect can turn out to be what they get, for no other reason than that they expect it.

Parents need to give children many opportunities to experience success. They can start by creating manageable, yet challenging environments and situations, and providing whatever support their children need to meet the challenges. Experiencing personal success in the face of obstacles gives children strong messages about their abilities and, in the long run, about their self-worth. 💚

Using Feedback to Teach

By Janet Gonzalez-Mena

Jessica and Peter, 2 1/2-year-old twins, are playing with some soft foam blocks. Jessica stacks blocks of similar size on top of each other. When they balance, the feedback she receives is, "This works." She doesn't need to hear the words to know it's true; she can see that it is so with her own eyes.

A natural consequence such as the one Jessica experienced above, results when children are left alone to experience natural or social reality. A parent needs only to sit back and let the feedback provide the lesson. In order for her children to learn about how the world "works"—the laws of physics and nature—a parent needs to stifle her urge to rescue her children from disappointment when their blocks fall, for example.

Here's another example: Jessica is headed for the sand on a three-wheel toy. Instead of rushing forward to head off the problem, her mother momentarily disappears. The wheels stop abruptly when they hit the sand, and Jessica lets out a howl while looking around for help. When she sees that none is available, she gets off the toy, pulls it back on the path, gets on and starts riding in the opposite direction. By her mother not rescuing her from that predicament, Jessica learned a lesson about "wheels in sand" through nonverbal feedback. Because she wasn't rescued, she suffered a reasonable consequence of her own act.

Observing the Twin-to-Twin Connection

"I find that one twin learns from the feedback that I give to her co-twin," said Teresa Snowder of Napa, California, mother of 2 1/2-year-old twins, Kasey and Megan. If both are tilting their chairs and Megan's slips a little, Kasey immediately stops tilting, too. When one gets hurt or scared, her co-twin responds to the feedback as if she were the one receiving it."

Snowder continued, "I also find that the feedback I give to one twin indirectly affects her co-twin. For example, one time Kasey was 'crying her eyes out' and wouldn't pay any attention to my attempts to communicate with her. Megan asked me, 'What's wrong with Kasey?' I turned my attention to Megan and tried to explain Kasey's feelings; before I knew it, I saw Kasey responding and being comforted by what I was saying to Megan. She couldn't take the direct communication; she had a mental block. But she could listen when I wasn't talking directly to her."

However, parenting is not always a matter of disappearing or sitting back and letting a lesson happen. Sometimes verbal feedback augments nonverbal feedback. For example, as Jessica' co-twin, Peter, approaches the old trustworthy family cat, his father says, "Pet her gently, like this," and demonstrates petting the cat from head to tail.

Peter, however, chooses to pet the cat in his own way instead of following his father's suggestion.

He is gentle, but he pets her from tail to head, ruffling her fur.

"She doesn't like it that way," explains Peter's father as the cat gets up and leaves the room, thereby silently reinforcing what Peter's father had told him verbally.

Sometimes the natural consequences of events are so dangerous that children must be protected from them to avoid getting hurt. If the family cat had not already proven himself to be harmless in the past, for example, Peter's father should not have allowed the consequence of unskilled petting to occur. Or, if Jessica had been known to bite Peter in the past, her parents should not have sat back and let Jessica

and Peter learn from each other about the consequences of rough play.

What parents can do, however, is to set up some logical consequences of activities, from which children can receive safe feedback. If Peter threatens to run toward the street while in the front yard, his mother needs to watch his behavior to ensure his safety in the front yard while saying firmly, "When you have shown me that you can stay away from the street, we can stay in the front yard. If you don't show me that you can do this, then we will have to go play in the back yard. That's the rule. You decide where you want to play."

Sometimes the feedback a parent gives initially is verbal. If Jessica hits her mother, a strong, "Ouch, that hurt me!" is the kind of feedback needed. If Jessica enjoys the reaction and reaches out to strike again, her mother's stopping her behavior by literally holding onto her hand will show Jessica that her mother won't allow such action. In addition, her mother's saying, "I won't let you hurt me," gives Jessica further feedback about her mother's position on the matter.

Here are some other examples of situations in which logical consequences are given to children to provide them with feedback on their actions:

• "We're trying to read a story. If you want to listen, you'll have to settle down; otherwise, you will have to leave the room. It's your choice."

• "When you change your clothes, then you may go outside to play."

• "If you want to finish your dinner, you will have to stay at the table. If you don't want any more to eat, you may go onto the porch and play."

Of course, for any of the above examples to provide feedback, a parent must follow through after her child makes his choice. The more common pattern is for a parent to get mad when her child makes a choice other than what she wanted. When anger arises, the lesson taught to the child is, "If I keep doing what I'm doing, Mommy will get mad and yell at me."

Using anger to control a child is not the best use of feedback. Often, it actually sabotages efforts to encourage appropriate decision making and learning because when a child realizes he has the power to make his mother mad, he often uses that power to get attention, thereby sidetracking the whole lesson.

SIX REASONS TO WORRY ABOUT HOW MUCH TV TODDLERS ARE WATCHING

1. Television takes good, healthy appetites and twists them so that children crave things that aren't good for them. Without television, children who are offered a variety of healthy foods usually choose a balanced diet. When influenced by commercials, the odds of that happening change.

2. Television interferes with social life. Toddlers are in the midst of becoming social beings. They need to constantly practice social skills. Television eats into their practice time. Conversations among family members drop when a TV is on.

3. Television is passive. Toddlers need to be active. They need to explore their world and interact with objects and people. They are highly motivated to do just that, if they don't get hooked on the passive entertainment mode that TV provides. Most toddlers don't last all day in front of the TV. But TV-viewing toddlers grow into 3 and 4 year olds who can spend hours and hours in the hypnotic state that television induces.

4. Children see violence on television. Even the news can cause problems for young children. Imagine what it does to toddlers when all those ugly scenes bombard their brains. Furthermore, though adults distinguish fictional violence from non-fiction, toddlers often can't tell the difference.

5. Television is designed to keep the viewer stimulated. If you count how long the camera remains on any one person or scene, you'll find the picture changes rapidly. Television gives viewers no time to reflect on the meaning of what's been seen. The effect is to condition children to a quick pace, causing them to become bored when things slow down.

6. A heavy diet of television works against learning to read. Children don't increase their listening skills, important prerequisites to reading, by watching TV. Instead of meaningful dia-logue, which teaches them to listen, they get stirred up, excited, stimulated by visual images and noise. Real life isn't like that. Books aren't like that. Therefore, real life and books are boring to many TV-raised children.

The toddler years are when many mental habits are developed. A TV habit works against inclinations such as persistence, concentration and active involvement—inclinations necessary to eventually become a reader.

THE FLIP SIDE

So those are the arguments of the me who wants to ban TV. Now here's the story of the other me—mother of five. I have to first say that I've been without television for several periods of my life, including my first 10 years, so I'm not the average parent.

A Natural Turn-Off

I asked a friend, Cindy Butler, whose twin boys are now 7 years old, for her advice about twin toddlers and TV habits. She told me that she didn't think TV-watching was a problem in the toddler years—because children are too young at that age to be interested in TV. Her children never sat still long enough to watch for more than a few minutes, she said. Why?

Her theory was that they didn't need entertainment from the TV, because they had plenty to do in just playing with each other and their younger brother. They were bored with cartoons and Sesame Street, she said, but they enjoyed video tapes, especially sing-along baby song tapes.

Butler and I explored together why the TV habit never grabbed her children. It turned out that there were more factors working than just their age. The family lives in the country and there is always something to do, she says. Besides, in the house she has a "craft room"; when she and the children are not outside, they are often doing crafts. She sews and has taught her boys to sew, too. Butler is not a TV addict herself, so modeling not watching television has an impact on her children, too.

It wasn't until the end of our conversation that she mentioned a 2 year old she knows who can sit through a whole movie on TV. She realized then that the fact that her children didn't watch TV as toddlers was probably influenced as much by her attitude and behavior as their age.

I was planning to raise my first child without TV, but broke down before he went to kindergarten. We still weren't an average, TV-watching family until my middle three children came along. Then, we did our share in contributing to those statistics about how children put in more hours in front of the TV than in school. I monitored, but life was hectic then; they managed to watch more than I wanted them to. Today, as grown-ups, they still do.

The last child, Tim, was born into a TV family, but by then I had read the research. The rest of my family wouldn't let me throw out the TV, so I carefully selected Tim's programs and pre-recorded them. That way, I could fast-forward the commercials. I remember being a little too slow now and then, and he'd beg me, "Please, let me see just this one." But other than his desire to see commercials, he didn't complain. We only had one TV, and I refused to allow any daytime viewing, so I had things pretty well under control.

I made it a policy to always watch TV with Tim. That policy had several advantages. It made TV a limited activity, because I never had much time to sit in one place for very long. It also put me right on the spot so I could explain what he didn't understand, find out how he reacted to what he saw, and put my own spin on things when necessary.

So, now that I've been more honest about my own story, I'm forced to come down from my high horse about eliminating the scourge of TV altogether.

Reasonable amounts of television may be all right, but remember, no television program is a substitute for active play in a rich environment. Electronics can't take the place of a caring adult who helps children find meaning in their experiences.

I'm not saying you should give away your TV, but I urge you to try turning it off for a week. I bet you'll find some pleasant surprises for both you and your children. ♥

Sleeping Keeps Me Awake

By Bruce Littman, M.D.

Infant sleep research is still considered a young science. One of its pioneers, Dr. A. H. Parmelee of the University of California at Los Angeles, Division of Child Development, traveled to Europe to study the techniques of infant sleep and organized a laboratory that has delved deeply into the subject for the past 30 years. For his work, he enlisted the help of a large number of families of young infants and over long periods of time followed the development of sleeping and waking patterns in children.

Many of us have been raised on the notion that young infants spend most of their days and nights sleeping; and when they are not sleeping, they are feeding. This hypothesis was not borne out, however, when families in Parmelee's study were asked to record their babies' waking and sleeping patterns. During the first week of life, the average baby slept only slightly more than 16 hours while others slept as little as 14 1/2 hours. The maximum amount of sleep recorded for this age never exceeded 19 hours.

This means that the new parent of twins has anywhere from five to 10 hours a day to be with wakeful babies. Parmelee also discovered that, by 4 months of age, the average daily sleep time had decreased slightly to a little less than 15 hours. The conclusion is that 1 week olds and 4 month olds spend about the same amount of total time sleeping in a 24-hour period.

They do it a bit differently, however. Most 1 week olds sleep no longer than four hours at a stretch while 4 month olds have sleeping periods lasting nine hours in length and occurring almost always at night. Thus, the average older infant is usually sleeping through the night.

Yet another old myth was shattered by Parmelee's study. He found that the early introduction of solid food had no bearing upon a baby's sleeping pattern. Therefore, while many of us would hope for the opposite, foods such as cereal do not hasten the arrival of baby's first full nights of sleep.

It would appear, therefore, that sleep needs change over time and, for that reason, should be looked on as a part of normal child development. Although it is reasonable to ask parents if their infants are sleeping through the night-time hours, it is much more important to determine whether the babies are showing some of the more subtle changes characteristic of sleep maturation, such as day and night discrimination, with more waking during the day and more sleeping during the night.

Sleep is also a behavior that is greatly affected by environmental activity. That is a fact true not only for young infants, but older children, teenagers and adults as well.

Much of the difficulty any of us experience falling asleep is attributable to the stressful events that periodically trouble our lives. Deadlines we failed to meet, arguments with a fellow worker, that long freeway drive home, or that bill we forgot to pay may create an emotional turmoil that will prevent a rapid onset of sleep at night.

Babies are not immune to such phenomena. They can be stimulated and aroused by activities in their daily lives. Their day is filled with activities such as bathing, feeding, playing, visitors to the house, drives in the car, trips to the supermarket, examinations by the doctor, immunizations, illnesses, sitting up, lying down, an hour or two in the swing and many more.

Parents often inquire as to what they might do to promote their babies' proper sleeping patterns. Although parents cannot make their babies sleep, they can keep their day's activities under control by limiting visitors, spacing out trips in the car, making the doctor's visit one day and the trip to the supermarket another, and restricting rowdy or active play toward the end of the day. These experiences actually serve to arouse the babies, not tire them out. As the babies get older, such limitations on activity can be relaxed. But when the babies are barely a few months old, it helps to pay atten-

tion to these limitations.

What happens when young infants who have been sleeping through the night suddenly begin waking again at 6 months of age? It does not appear to be true that hunger is causing the problem. As Parmelee has shown, sleep is not encouraged by food. It is also rarely a result of illness; this is usually a very healthy time for babies. What appears to be the most likely answer is related to the appearance of another developmental milestone during this period—separation anxiety.

As the infant begins to appreciate who his parent is and how stressful it is to be separated from that person, he may cry out for her if he awakens during the night. Parents often report that merely going into their infant's room will usually satisfy their child and allow him to return to sleep.

The second major sleep problem during infancy involves the older child (the 2 year old, for example), who does not yet sleep through the night. Parents in such situations often believe this to be an uncommon problem and fear that it is abnormal. However, the facts show otherwise.

In a study of sleep behavior, Naomi Ragins, M.D., a child psychiatrist, showed that only 58 percent of the 2 year olds she studied slept through the night or went back to sleep without needing attention. It was Dr. Ragins' belief that behaviors in the home encouraged such waking patterns to continue.

Improving the sleeping patterns of a 2-year-old toddler involves a consistent approach from both parents and includes setting a specific time for going to bed, insisting that the child sleep in his own room, keeping any "going to bed" rituals simple and quiet, and understanding that the child may be experiencing some anxiety over the nighttime separation. Night lights are occasionally helpful, as are favorite objects in the child's bed which can provide a sense of security.

Waking episodes should be met with calm encouragement for the toddler to stay in his own bed. If the parent shows undue stress at such moments, the child will quickly exhibit it as well and a return to sleep will be difficult. At all times, mothers and fathers should remember that sleeping patterns mature and that time will alleviate most problems.

If parents will work together to resolve them, those middle-of-the-night waking problems will gradually resolve themselves. But if sleeping problems (including problems related to going to bed end staying in bed; bedwetting, sleep walking, sleep talking, nightmares and night terrors) persist to the point of being disruptive, they should consult their children's health care provider. ❤

Smooth Sailing to Sweet Dreams

By Patricia Edmister, Ph.D.

Many parents dread the coming of evening because it signals the commencement of nightly bedtime battles with their children. Arguments and manipulative games that start when children are young can go on and on, often resulting in serious power struggles with parents as their children grow older.

THE RIGHT ROUTINE

Perhaps the single most useful tool in achieving a smooth bedtime experience is the proper routine. It is important to establish bedtime routines that, as the evening progresses, alert children as to what is about to take place, while at the same time allow them time to "wind down" from their day.

A good routine is a set of calm, relaxing activities which are similar, though not exactly the same, from night to night. A routine is different from a ritual in that the latter always proceeds in exactly the same manner. Unfortunately, children can become highly dependent on these activities occurring in exactly the same way every night, making it impossible for a baby sitter to do something a little differently, or for a parent to alter or stray from the ritual when necessary.

In extreme cases, children may use a ritual to try to control their parents, sometimes insisting that they go back and start the whole ritual all over again after some minor element has been changed or overlooked. Unfortunately, some parents buy into this game, and bedtime becomes controlled by the children.

Another problem results when children are allowed to fall asleep on the couch or watching TV, then are carried to bed by their parents. Dr. Richard Ferber, in his book, *Solve Your Children's Sleep Problems*, points out that this, like falling asleep with parents in their bed and then being moved, or having a parent lie down with children in their bed until they fall asleep, creates association difficulties. By that, he means that children learn to associate falling asleep with certain situations such as watching television or having a parent present. When these associated conditions are not present—such as when the children awaken during the night—they will be unable to re-establish the conditions requisite for them to fall asleep. As a result, they will often get up and involve a parent in getting them back to sleep under their associated conditions.

A third problem may arise when families travel or when children are ill, but usually the effect is short-lived. Because the children's routine has been broken, it may take a while to get things back to normal once they are recovered or return home. The important thing is to get back into the routine as soon and consistently as possible so that bad habits don't have a chance to develop.

Parents' primary goal is to have their children learn to fall asleep in their own rooms without them there; that is, under conditions children can re-establish for themselves if they wake up during the night. To do this, parents need to establish a relaxed, flexible routine that suits their—and their children's schedule.

HOW TO WIN BEDTIME BATTLES

Before deciding what time to set as each child's bedtime (even co-twins could have different

Why Do Children Fight Going to Bed?

1) They may be overly tired. In early toddlerhood, the 18 to 24 month-old child begins to need less sleep and starts to skip naps. By evening, however, he might be overly tired, and lose his ability to control his emotions, acting cross and irritable about everything.

2) Many children refuse to go to sleep because they are afraid they might miss something going on with other family members.

3) Some children are truly afraid of scary things—perhaps from viewing television programs inappropriate for their level of maturity. They may believe that staying awake, or being near their parents, is all that will protect them from what they fear. (Many 3–4 year olds are afraid of large animals, violence from TV or real life and dark rooms.)

4) Some children don't think it's fair that older siblings get to stay up later than they do, and desire the same privilege for themselves.

5) Some children are over-stimulated prior to bedtime, and then physically unable to settle down to sleep at the hour prescribed. (This is often a problem in families where one or both parents working outside the home get home late, want to play with their children before bed, and then have trouble getting the children to separate from them.)

6) Many children play power games at bedtime. These children use the occasion as an opportunity to exercise control by insisting that their parents perform certain rituals before they'll go down for the night, and then acting inappropriately when they don't get their way.

bedtimes), parents should think about his age, health, daily activities and personality, then ask themselves several questions. Does he usually wake up tired? Does he seem listless in the morning? Does he get up earlier than everyone else? Parents must keep in mind that each child is an individual and may need more or less sleep than another child. It pays to watch the sleep behavior of each child; parents will learn a lot about what each child needs.

Once a bedtime is decided upon, parents must stick to it as much as possible, since children do best with consistency and routine. Being flexible on special occasions is okay, but that should be the exception, not the rule.

It's a good idea to plan quiet evening activities—a warm bath, a bedtime story, a calm, short children's video—to wind up the day. Parents may want to set aside a little time to visit with each child about the events of her day. Also, they'd be wise to give each child a "time check" as bedtime approaches so he doesn't get stuck in the middle of a project and use its completion as a reason to postpone going to bed.

Leaving a nightlight on (or the door open) for a child who is afraid of the dark is fine, and letting her take a favorite toy, stuffed animal or security blanket with her to ward off feeling lonesome may also help. (Permitting a child to take a whole zoo of animals to bed with him, however, could lead to trouble; one will inevitably turn up missing and he won't be able to sleep without it.)

Most importantly, parents must stay out of the child's bedroom once he has settled down for the night. They mustn't fall for the "I'm thirsty" or "I'm scared" routines if they know they're not true.

Finally, realistic expectations should be set. Very few children will go to sleep immediately, and some simply don't need much sleep. If a child has a stimulating day, he may be more difficult to settle down and may require a little extra attention. That's fine, as long as it doesn't become a habit. He can still be expected to stay in bed, or in his room playing quietly, and not disturb others in the family.

TWIN ISSUES

Having two or more pre-school-aged children the same age and, in many cases, sharing a room, has both advantages and disadvantages. An advantage to twins sharing a room is that, once bedtime routines have been established, both children will probably be more willing to go to their room and stay there, since they are neither alone nor as likely to feel that they are missing out on something.

One disadvantage, though, is that they may keep each other awake with play or conversation. This is especially problematic if one needs more sleep than the other. If so, there are several possible solutions to the problem.

One solution is to simply put one twin to bed earlier than his co-twin. This can sometimes be facilitated by starting the bedtime routine a little earlier, with time built in for each child to spend some moments alone with one or the other of his parents. The sleepier twin will get his bath and story first, then will go to bed while his co-twin follows with his bath, his story—read somewhere other than the bedroom—and his quiet entry into bed. Since the sleepier twin may be the earlier riser, this schedule might provide some individual time with his parents for him in the morning before his co-twin awakens.

Another option involves sending the children to their room together, where they can enjoy a story and then maybe some relaxing music. Parents can go ahead and dim the lights, but permit the less sleepy twin to play quietly in bed. Usually, the sleepier child will be able to fall asleep as long as his still-active twin knows not to disturb him.

If one twin is a significant disrupter of the bedtime routine and sleep of the other, a final option is to allow the more complacent child to fall asleep by himself in another room while the child disrupting the routine is conditioned to sleeping in their actual bedroom. By making it a privilege to sleep in another room, the noisy twin can be encouraged to calm himself with the hope of eventually earning that privilege, too.

As a final note, it is important to remember that if a child's inappropriate bedtime behavior is compounded by disturbed sleep or other evidence of unhappiness or fear, professional help may be necessary to determine how best to address the problem. ♥

To Nap or Not to Nap?

By Janet Gonzalez-Mena

Naptime can be vital to the health of parents of twins, if not to the twins themselves, who usually readjust their sleep habits to find ways of getting the sleep they need. Parents of toddlers can either help their children change their sleeping patterns to suit the adult in their lives or find another way to get the relief time most need desperately if they are at home with their children.

One father of twin girls now 3 years old said, "We encouraged the ritual of our children taking a nap by insisting they stay in their rooms during naptime until the level of destruction repeatedly brought us to their sides." Then he and his wife found individual quiet time by taking turns watching the children so one of them could rest for a period every day.

Molly Sullivan, a Berkeley, California, early childhood specialist offered this advice on napping: "At some point during toddlerhood, most children wake up soon after going to sleep. At that time, it is imperative that they learn they can put themselves back to sleep. They need to be told clearly, 'It's still nap time.' My experi-ence is that noise from one child doesn't wake the other—eye contact does. A simple solution is putting up a curtain or screen between the twins or using some other means to keep them from seeing each other." She emphasized that a parent must be firmly convinced his toddlers still need naps. They will go back to sleep if his message is clear, she said.

NAPS AS A NUISANCE

Not all parents find naps a blessing. One mother of four children says, "I thought naps were a hassle. We couldn't go anywhere with the older kids in the afternoon because the twins had to nap. I was glad when they gave up napping, even though for a short period of time, one or the other sometimes fell asleep in his dinner plate . . . literally laying his head down in his mashed potatoes. Even with this, the freedom was worth it!"

Another parent found naps a problem for this reason: "My twins gave up napping at about 2 1/2 years of age. Recently I went back to work and put them in day care, where they are required to nap. Now with all that sleep in the afternoon, I can't get them to sleep until 10 o'clock at night. I hate it! I never have any time to myself in the evening."

Parents of twins must be aware of their own needs and find ways to meet them. Getting regular relief from parenting is essential on a daily basis. Time off from the exhausting job of being with toddlers all day promotes parents' mental and physical health. They should recognize this need and not feel guilty about arranging for it. One way to accomplish this is by continuing naptime through the toddler years, according to some parents.

Others disagree with this suggestion, arguing that children should understand their own physical needs. This important lesson should be learned in early childhood, they say, and resting when needed rather than as a routine is the best way to promote this learning.

Although this idea may work for some people, one mother of very active twin toddler boys, says, "When my twins were newborns, my aunt, also a mother of twins, told me, 'I have just one piece of advice on how to keep your sanity. Put them on the same eating and sleeping schedule. I've followed that advice and found that it works very well. My boys are definitely individuals, and they have different sleep needs. I have put them on the same schedule, which means that they nap about the same amount of time, but one wakes up earlier than the other in the morning. This mother also sees a relationship between diet and rest, so she

tries to keep sugar out of her boys' diets so they can rest without being all "hyped up." She keeps her boys together when they nap, considering it a real advantage that they can hop in bed with each other because, in her opinion, the togetherness helps them sleep.

ENFORCING RULES

Another mother of twins who are 5 1/2 years old said her children don't nap, but she insists they have a quiet time every day. "I put them in separate rooms at an early age, making sure they got enough fresh air and exercise, and always are put to bed early at night so they are tired, but not over-tired. I have made naptime a routine and I'm kind of strict about it. I found, though, as they got older, I couldn't let them sleep all afternoon or they wouldn't go to sleep at night. By the time they were 3 years of age, I had to wake them up after an hour's nap," she reports, "to insure a workable bedtime."

Both of these mothers have no complaints about their toddlers' naps primarily because they were very clear about their beliefs in naps and firm about following through with enforcement—the key to getting toddlers to follow any parents' rules.

Ambiguous feelings, guilt pangs, and hesitation cause parents to be inconsistent in their directions to their children which leads to their inability to manage their toddlers' rest time. Parents need to explore some options until they find the napping solution that's comfortable for their children and themselves. ♥

GROWING STAGES—
Practical Parenting Tips

CHILD-SAFETY SIGN

Just because you live on a quiet residential street or at the end of a cul-de-sac doesn't mean your children are safe from cars. Some motorists drive too fast. Others may not be paying enough attention. As much as parents urge kids to look for cars before crossing, many often forget to check before jetting into the street to chase a ball or meet a friend. Leslie Saba, mother of four, including twins, created a sign that alerts drivers. It says, "Be Alert . . . Children," in large letters on a bright-lemon yellow sign. When your multiples are outside, place it at the end of the driveway or the edge of the lawn. "Display the sign only when your children are outside," Saba stresses. "If it's always out, it will blend into the environment and drivers will be less likely to notice it." The sign costs $13.95. For further information or to order, call (800) 709-SAFE.

CHOOSING A PRESCHOOL

What type of preschool program would work best for your children? Should you separate your twins or keep them in the same classroom? Parents who are beginning to think about preschools need to know how to evaluate programs, prepare the children and make important decisions, like how many days should the first-timers attend and is the morning, afternoon or all-day session best for your children. *Smart Start: The Parents' Guide to Preschool Education*, by Marian Edelman Borden is a step-by-step guide to assessing programs, teachers, facilities, health considerations and early education issues. The author briefly addresses multiples-oriented topics,

such as classroom separation. There are checklists and age-related activity/achievement schedules as well as suggestions for ways to supplement your children's education while working at home. The book also includes a list of helpful resources.

Chapter 11

A UNITED FRONT

Consistency is the key to good behavior. When parents disagree about how to discipline, it is better to discuss it, decide on the approach and stick with it. It is upsetting for parents to find themselves arguing about discipline issues and confusing for the children. Present a united front. When twins are involved, it is doubly important to stand firm. Children generally want to please their parents, but they are not above uniting against you if they think they can bend the rules or play mom against dad. No two people will always agree and as the children grow older, you will change your view of the way you discipline. One fact should remain unchanged—parents should always support each other.

CHOOSE YOUR WORDS CAREFULLY

You're folding laundry when you hear Samantha scream. She's hysterical and runs to you, holding her cheek with her hand. She says her twin, Bailey, hit her. You're so frustrated with his bad behavior that you want to tell him so. Should you? Experts say no. It's best to discipline in non-insulting ways, says Betty Rothbart, M.S.W., in her book, *Multiple Blessings*. Rather than insulting or labeling them, discourage negative behavior in "kind, but firm language." It is tempting to yell, "Won't you ever learn? Don't hit your sister! You're mean!" But, it is more productive for everyone concerned to tell him that hitting is wrong and that he must use words to tell people when he's mad. Rather than focus on the negativity involved, calm the child and correct the behavior. Look for opportunities to encourage positive conduct in the future.

HOW DO THEY LEARN?

Teachers and psychologists have long known that students master skills in different ways. As parents, it is important to identify how your child absorbs information so you can set up the most stimulating learning environment. Some children require lots of visual stimulation; others need to hear in detail how to work their way through a project. And then there are those who must touch, feel, jump, crawl and climb in order to experience learning. It is vital for parents to remember that even though their multiples arrived at the same time, they will not always learn in the same way and that each will often move at a different pace.

AN APPLE A DAY

As busy parents know, maintaining a well-balanced diet for your family is not easily achieved. Now you can call (800) 366-1655 and The American Dietetic Association will refer you to a registered dietician. Consumers can also call (900) 225-5267 to get specific answers to nutrition questions. The cost for the call is $1.95 for the first minute.

DEMYSTIFYING CABINETS

Multiple toddlers banging on locked kitchen cabinets is nerve-racking. Take the mystery out of what's inside by leaving one or two cabinets unlocked. Stock up on unbreakable, plastic containers to pile up inside the unlocked cabinet. Let the busybodies crawl inside to take a peek and discover lots of fun. Little drummers will love to grab wooden spoons and strike up the band. Tiny tots can take turns stacking tall towers and all of these unbreakables double as great bath toys.

LESSONS IN SHARING

Elizabeth Pantley, in her new book, *Perfect Parenting—The Dictionary of 1,000 Parenting Tips*, states that "When you're a little kid, nothing really belongs to you." That certainly seems true enough for twins or triplets who vie with same-age siblings for possession of the hottest toys in the playroom. She recommends that parents establish rules about sharing very early on. And, perhaps most importantly, she suggests that parents "allow children to have a few important things that they don't ever have to share so that they will be more willing to share other, less-valued possessions."

NOISE POLLUTION

Little toddler twins are not only a handful, they can certainly be an earful, too. At this stage, everything seems to shift into high gear, including the way they use their voices. Although they are experimenting with limited vocabulary, they often do it in loud, screeching outbursts. Even at this young age, it is important to set noise control rules. Using your "inside voice" is one way of communicating to them that they can control their responses. When the screaming and yelling reaches an unacceptable level, it is up to the parent to set the example. Don't shout at them from another room. Go to them. Bend down so you are at eye level with them. Show them a disapproving look, and then clearly state that they must use a quiet voice in the house. Be consistent. When things get out of control again, and they will, repeat your calming actions and remind them of the inside voice rule. Also provide plenty of opportunities for them to use their "outside voices" by taking walks, running in the yard or playing at the park.

RAGING RASH

If your toddlers are complaining about sore throats, they could have a very contagious condition called hand, foot, and mouth disease. This virus is named for the red rash that breaks out in the mouth and inside of the throat and then spreads to the hands and feet. The rash usually blisters in the mouth within one to two days, and carriers will probably run a fever.

According to Arlene Eisenberg, Heidi E. Murkoff, and Sandee E. Hathaway, B.S.N., the authors of *What to Expect The First Year*, the virus affects young children and is passed from feces to hand to mouth. Because multiples are in close physical contact with one another, it could be easily passed from one sibling to the other. For this reason, hand washing is extremely important. Don't be fooled if one child breaks out before the other because the virus has a three to six day incubation period. While it may be just as painful for parents to watch the virus run its course as it is for the children suffering, take comfort in the fact that the rash and blisters usually disappear within a week. In the meantime, soothe sore throats with increased fluids and a softer diet.

A CUTE SAFETY MEASURE

Sun screen is always a must. However, the latest research questions whether it's actually enough to protect skin from damage. If you're worried about exposing your multiples' sensitive skin to dangerous ultraviolet rays, double up on protection with bonnets. Big-brimmed hats can shade faces and eyes from the bright summer sun, as well as add an adorable fashion touch to your already adorable kids.

POISON PROTECTION

Gardening, painting the shutters and staining the picnic table bring hazardous materials into your summer world. Curious little ones are very susceptible to accidental poisoning. You should always store fertilizers, insecticides, gas and oil products, paint, varnish and all household chemicals in a cabinet that can be locked or secured with a safety latch. Products should be stored in the original containers.

The number of your local poison control center should be prominently listed with other emergency telephone numbers. If you have reason to believe your multiples have ingested a poisonous substance, call the poison control center. (If, however, your child loses consciousness or is experiencing breathing difficulties, call 911 immediately.)

Poison control center staff members are trained to talk you through the emergency sit-uation. Be prepared to provide the following information:

- The specific substance/product name (bring the package with you to the phone);
- The quantity you suspect your child swallowed;
- The age of your child;
- The child's approximate weight;
- A description of the symptoms;
- Existing health problems or considerations;
- The distance to the nearest emergency facility.

Remember, multiples share with their siblings. If one puts something in his mouth, chances are the other one will give it a try. Poisonings often occur when equipment and supplies are in use. Be vigilant. Don't use poisonous products near small children or leave containers open or unattended at any time. It is a good rule to reject the large, economy size in favor of a smaller quantity that meets your immediate needs. Always rinse out containers and properly discard them.

BUG BITES

Summer equals playtime outside. It also means itchy, ouchie bug bites! *In Caring For Your Baby and Young Child, Birth to Age 5* the American Academy of Pediatrics encourages parents to stock up on calamine lotion. It's skin-friendly and relieves the itchiness associated with the bites of mosquitoes, flies, fleas and bedbugs. "Apply calamine lotion freely onto any part of your child's body except areas around his eyes and genitals," say the book's authors. For bee stings, the AAP recommends soaking a cloth in cold water and pressing it onto the area of the sting. This should reduce the pain and swelling. If the stinger is visible, don't try to pull it out; you could end up squeezing more venom into your child's skin. Instead, the AAP says to gently scrape it out of the skin horizontally. If you suspect the sting is that of a honeybee, because its stinger is barbed, it's best to just wash the area well and let the stinger dissolve. For the summer, it's a good idea to keep your children's fingernails short and clean. This will minimize the chances of infection due to scratching.

PLAYFUL PARENTS

Child psychologists and play therapists agree that parents are usually their child's first and most important play companions. Research indicates that parents foster creativity in their children when they actively participate in the play rather than just supervising the activity. When twins, triplets or more are involved, the skill levels will most certainly vary. Sometimes "the more the merrier" should be the theme and everyone can join in. There should also be a significant amount of playtime when parents focus on each individual and gear the activity to that particular child's ability level. Playtime isn't the time to test your child, it is an opportunity to interact with your child in a playful setting. Be spontaneous and go where the child leads you. The great thing about play is that everyone can do it. Use it as an opportunity to have fun together.

SAYING GOOD-BYE

How can parents handle painful goodbyes when they must leave their twins in the care of someone else? "First they need to examine their own feelings," says Janet Gonzalez-Mena, professor of childhood education at Napa Valley Community College in Napa, California. "Unacknowledged adult feelings can get in the way of helping children cope with theirs." Without realizing it, parents can become desperate to make their children happy—all because their own childhood separation issues are unresolved. Rather than trying hard to make the feelings go away, it's better to accept the children's upset and help them cope. Parents should acknowledge whatever feelings are expressed—pain, fear or anger—and offer reassurance. If the parents feel that everything will be fine, the children pick up the feeling. In some situations, one twin can accept the separation while the other twin has a more difficult time. It is important to acknowledge the feelings of each twin. Coping resources can help too—an object such as a familiar snuggly toy or a particularly interesting activity can help. Parents should never sneak out to avoid a scene. A goodbye, no matter how painful, is a requirement for building trust.

OPEN WIDE

Pediatric dentists are recommending that parents bring little patients in for an initial evaluation sooner than previously suggested. Within six months after the first tooth comes in or about the time of the first birthday is a good starting point for in-office dental education. A "happy visit" introduces the child to the dentist and the staff before there are problems to address. This is a good time for dental professionals to provide parents with information about oral and dental development. Pediatric dentists use the term "anticipatory guidance" to describe discussions on prevention of decay, good oral hygiene, encouraging healthy habits and how to deal with accidents and injuries. The best way to find a good dental practice is by "word of mouth." Ask other parents which dentist they use and what their experiences have been.

INSTANT RECALL

If you find yourself in a medical emergency with one of your twins, could you quickly provide important information about your child? A personal health record for each child is very valuable when time is critical. Pediatricians suggest your health record include the following:

- Allergies to medication or foods;
- A list of medications and the dosages the child is currently taking;
- Any pre-existing health problems or chronic condition;
- Dates of any surgeries;
- Current immunization record and any reaction your child may have had;
- Height and weight;
- Name and telephone number of your pediatrician or family physician.

If one of your multiples requires emergency care, be very clear about which twin has the problem. Your doctor has each child's medical history on file, but until emergency personnel can access your physician you will be their source of vital information. Having a clearly written medical history to refer to for each child could prevent confusion and save time when it means the most.

TUBE NEWS

Congress and the Federal Communications Commission (FCC) have mandated that television must "serve the educational and informational needs of children." But what constitutes educational programming? *Building Blocks: A Guide for Creating Children's Educational Television* was developed by Mediascope and the Children's Action Network (CAN), two non-profit groups, to help television producers create shows for children that meet the FCC criteria. As children develop mentally and physically, their television viewing habits go from simple observation to levels of complex understanding. CAN research shows that 3-year-olds:

- Imitate what they see and hear on TV;
- Are drawn to "fast-paced action, loud music and effects of cartoons";
- Cannot tell the difference between fantasy and reality;
- Identify characters as good or bad, but cannot discern complexities such as "mean with some redeeming qualities."

Television has a strong impact on young children. The *Building Blocks* guidelines encourage "a constructive dialog among the television industry, child advocates, and health and education representatives." But, ultimately, parents are responsible for selecting appropriate programs for their young viewers.

WORTH A THOUSAND WORDS

Preschoolers are a curious bunch. When twins become part of a larger group at day care or in school, other children are fascinated by the "Look-alikes." Multiples who are identical garner the most attention, but a clear explanation of twinship, even when boy/girl twins are involved, goes a long way in helping the other kids understand. Make books that focus on twins available to the teacher or care provider. Reading books and telling stories that involve twins is a great lesson for all children. Providing the resource material is one way you can make an important contribution to your children's learning environment.

TELLING ALL

It can be bothersome and annoying when you have a child who assumes the position of guardian of right and wrong in the household. But it can also be a bid for parental approval. If one of your twins is a tattler, there are ways to deal with this behavior. When one says, "Tommy took my truck," listen to the complaint, tell the child that you are happy he is playing by the rules, and end the discussion. Eliminate cause and effect (tattling results in punishment for the offender) by taking the other child aside and explaining the rules about sharing. Encourage them to work things out on their own by giving them problem-solving suggestions. When the child inclined to tattle successfully resolves a misunderstanding, lots of praise will reinforce his capable handling of the situation. If all else fails, separate them for a period of time. They will usually be so happy to have their playmate back, you will see their behavior improve.

BROTHERS AND SISTERS

Boy/girl twins enter developmental stages at about the same time, but they progress through some stages at different rates. For example, girls are generally quicker to potty train. When twins are the same sex, parents can expect to train their sons or daughters at the same time. With boy/girl twins, training is usually accomplished a few months apart. Between the ages of 3 and 4, when children have more social contact outside the home, parents often note differences in language development. Research shows that language in males develops at a slower rate than in females. Therefore, if you have boy/girl twins, your son might not speak as clearly or as soon as his sister. According to Edward Goldson, M.D., FA A.B, professor of pediatrics at the University of Colorado Health Sciences Center in Denver, "It is important for parents to remember that there are certainly emotional and behavioral differences in boy/girl twins. But, their individual development trajectory has more to do with their personalities and inclinations and is independent of their twinship."

TV SAFETY ALERT

Three and 4 year olds are some of the fastest little movers around. Parents of twins and triplets can attest to how far, how fast and how high their kids can run, jump and climb. University of Alabama at Birmingham researchers recently conducted a retrospective study of injuries and deaths involving television sets falling on children. The Children's Hospital of Alabama searched files from 1995 to 1997 and the U.S. Consumer Product Safety Commission (CPSC) compiled files from 1990 to 1997. There were 78 reported incidents involving children under the age of 11. Of those cases, 29 resulted in death. It was determined that the mean age of all victims was 36 months and the mean age of those who died from their injuries was 31 months. The CPSC report stated that stands and dressers were used as bases to support televisions in 76 percent of all the cases where data was available. In over half of the incidents investigated, children were found to have been climbing on the furniture to operate the TV controls. They concluded that toddlers are especially vulnerable and that in-home safety plans should include television placement in a child-safe location.

SAFETY GAME

Getting more than one child settled safely in the car is no easy task. To guard against fingers getting slammed in the car doors, after you buckle your multiples in, say, "Hands on heads!" Your kids will think you are playing a game, but this simple action can help avert painful injuries.

IF YOUR CHILD STUTTERS

It is very common for 3 year olds to stutter or show signs of some hesitation or stammer when they speak. Children are such sensory creatures that they are often unable to express clearly all the thoughts, ideas and information that they are trying to process.

Changes in the usual routine or the introduction of something new like potty training, starting preschool or a new baby in the family can affect speech patterns. You can help your child by speaking carefully, using simple words and sentences, listening patiently and resisting the urge to tell the child to slow down. If you minimize the attention you place on the stuttering, it usually goes away. Speech pathologists agree that if physical exertion or blinking accompanies the stuttering, or speech is affected for more than six months, a speech therapist should be consulted. Early intervention is more successful than waiting until the child is of school age.

FINGER FROSTING

After you bake a batch of your family's favorite cookies, invite your multiples to do the decoration honors. Start with clean hands. Divide frosting into several small containers. Demonstrate how colors change (red and blue make purple, blue and yellow make green) by adding food color to the various bowls and allowing the kids to stir it in. When you've finalized your color palette, have the cookie artists use their fingers to frost the cookies. Encourage them to outline, add horizontal and vertical lines and squiggles. The kitchen is a wonderful classroom, and cookies are the perfect teaching aids. Delicious!

MORE ON WEANING

When to wean can be doubly difficult for mothers of twins who are breastfeeding, knowing that breast milk is the ideal nutrition for babies. The American Academy of Pediatrics (AAP) recommends that breastfeeding continue, if possible, for "at least 12 months and thereafter for as long as mutually desired." If you choose to stop breastfeeding before this time, remember, most experts agree that any amount of time you breastfeed your babies is better than not breastfeeding at all.

ASSESSING DEVELOPMENT

Multiples who arrive prematurely often play a catch-up game in the early years. If you have concerns, it is appropriate to discuss them with your pediatrician. And if your medical professional has concerns, sometimes a developmental assessment is in order. According to Zero to Three, the National Center for Infants, Toddlers and Families, "Properly done assessments often result in either putting minds at ease if no problems are found or putting the wheels in motion for appropriate interventions that are more effective the sooner they are begun and when they build on a child's strengths."

Having prior knowledge of what will take place is a key component of a successful assessment. New Visions: A Parent's Guide to Understanding Developmental Assessment, is now available at no charge by visiting Zero to Three's Web site at www.zerotothree.org. Parents learn what to expect, how to prepare and how to participate most effectively. A glossary of terms and a resource list provide guidance through the process.

DIFFERENT TEMPERAMENTS

Temperament studies done by Stella Chess and Alexander Thomas, psychiatrists who pioneered temperament studies in the 1950s, have important implications for parents of multiples today, says Janet Gonzalez-Mena, a professor of childhood education at Napa Valley College in Napa, California. The parent who is calm and quiet may find an active child challenging. If the activity level of the co-twin is more like the parent, it may lead to favoritism. An outgoing parent may not know how to handle a shy, cautious child.

When dealing with temperamental differences, the first step is to recognize them as such—just differences. Parents should always adjust to a child whose temperament differs from their own. Although parents must accept the child's inborn temperament as a given, environmental influences can make a difference. The shy child has a good model in a bold parent, for example. Outgoing parents can help a cautious child become more socially active. In any case, multiples need to be understood as individuals. When parents accept differences in temperament, they show respect for their children's individuality.

A WORD TO THE WISE

There is a saying my mother-in-law has embroidered and framed in her home: "Inch by inch life's a cinch; yard by yard life is hard." I think of it often, especially when I am overwhelmed. As the mother of 18-month-old boy/

girl twins and five other children (count them—seven!), I am frequently overwhelmed. So, when the pot of macaroni is boiling over, one of the twins has a stinky diaper, and my 3 year old is fighting with my 6 year old over which video to watch, I break down the problems one at a time and work on the solutions. First, I lower the heat on the pot of macaroni not wanting to burn the house down. Priorities are important here! Then I settle the video dispute, and since the baby smells bad but isn't really suffering, I save him for last. My days are filled with a lot of work, but the rewards are evident. Our house is filled with laughter and love mixed with an occasional crying spell. The real secret here is not to look at the whole picture because the whole picture is pretty staggering. Remember, "inch by inch."

WORKING TOGETHER

Cooperation is a skill. Like all skills, it has to be demonstrated in order for your little ones to understand that they can do it too. As early as 6 months of age, children can understand the concept of taking turns when you show them how. As they get older, they are capable of exhibiting some control in the exchange. When you sit on the floor across from your toddler and roll a car or ball toward her, she will usually imitate your action and roll the object back to you. As dexterity improves, you can take turns putting the pieces in a puzzle and play other games that require more concentration. Taking turns putting toys back on the shelf or in the toy basket teaches your children the give and take of cooperating with another person. It's an important skill and one that's never too early to learn.

WHOSE SHOES

Here's a great tip for parents of multiples. Lisa and Bob Jackson of Littleton, Colorado, have no trouble keeping everyone's shoes straight. Two of their 2-year-old triplets wear the same size. So when Ben, Grant and Will get new shoes, Lisa or Bob uses an indelible marker to jot the owner's initial on the underside of the tongue of each shoe. Because shoes mold uniquely to the feet of the one who is wearing them, it is important that the right shoes are on the right little feet. The ID system is invaluable when it's time to pull three pairs of shoes from the pile, match 'em up and start the day.

UNPROCESSED JUICE WARNING LABELS

The Food and Drug Administration has new labeling requirements for sellers of fresh apple juice and apple cider products that have not been processed to reduce or eliminate microbes that can cause illness. The warning will aid consumers in identifying untreated juice products. If your children are in a day care center that serves apple juice or cider, it is recommended that you verify that only pasteurized products are being offered to your children. For more information on food safety, call the FDA Food Information Hotline at (800) FDA 4010. The new label will read:

"Warning: This product has not been pasteurized and, therefore, may contain harmful bacteria that can cause serious illness in children, the elderly, and persons with weakened immune systems."

TAKE A CLOSER LOOK

The garden is a great place of discovery and adventure for children. Some sunny afternoon, rather than bringing your multiples to the park to play, lead them out into your own backyard to explore. If they look closely, they'll see that a miniature world exists on garden plants.

Watch your children marvel as bright red ladybugs crawl up the stems and as tiny winged creatures hover over flower petals or bask on the smooth green leaves. If they're lucky, they may even get a glimpse of an earthworm poking its head out of the dark, cool soil. If your kids are squeamish, assure them that there is no reason to be afraid—these little critters are friends of the plants and flowers and help them grow and flourish.

MOM, MY EAR HURTS!

If you hear this complaint in the summer, your multiples may have "swimmer's ear," a common summer condition. Swimmer's ear is an infection of the ear canal that thrives when the canal is moist. Moisture builds when the air is humid, when children perspire heavily or when they swim. It begins with itchiness and discomfort and is followed by pain, swelling and tenderness in the ear. Swimmer's ear can be treated with antibiotic drops and a brief respite from water activities. As a preventive measure, you can have children wear ear plugs. Be sure to carefully dry the insides of the ears with a soft towel after swimming or bathing.

A POSITIVE OUTLOOK

The next time you start blaming yourself for your multiples' bad behavior, reassure yourself with the following suggestions from authors James Varni and Donna Corwin in their book, *Time-Out for Toddlers*. They remind parents that bad behavior is common to all children—it means that your kids are "normal."

Try to remember you are not alone. Find comfort in knowing that most parents face the same behavioral concerns that you do. Misbehavior in children is a natural part of growing up. You are capable of managing your children's behavior. It's important to think first before jumping in to solve each and every problem.

AVOIDING CAR SICKNESS

It's traveling season. Time to pile the kids into the car and hit the road. Before you do, you may want to consider the following suggestions offered by *Traveling Healthy Newsletter*. These tips are sure to keep your multiples' tummies settled during summer road trips.

Offer your multiples plenty of water or juice to drink.

Don't let your kids ride on an empty stomach. However, avoid large meals before and during the trip.

Keep the car cool and ventilated.

Arrange the car seats so kids can look out the windows during the drive. They're less likely to feel ill if they are looking out into the distance.

Drive at night whenever possible so kids can sleep through the ride.

Got chocolate milk?

Believe it or not, chocolate milk is actually good for kids. Pediatricians and milk producers agree that it has just as much calcium and other nutrients as regular milk. There's no reason to worry about the chocolate. Doctors say the caffeine in it is negligible—especially when compared to the alternative: caffeine-saturated soda pop. And dentists say the sugar in the chocolate is low compared to the high content of good stuff: calcium and phosphorous, which protect against tooth decay.

GOOD TO EAT, GOOD FOR YOU

A balanced diet? How do busy moms or dads of multiples make sure their little ones are eating the right things in the right quantities? The American Academy of Pediatrics, in its reference book, *Caring for Your Baby and Young Child*, outlines a one-day menu for a 4 year old who weighs about 36 pounds.

Breakfast
1/2 cup 2% milk
1/2 cup cereal
1/2 cup citrus juice, tomato juice or 1/2 cup cantaloupe or strawberries

Snack
1/2 cup 2% milk
1/2 cup bananas
1 slice whole wheat bread
1 teaspoon margarine
1 teaspoon jelly

Lunch
3/4 cup 2% milk
1 sandwich: 2 slices whole wheat bread, 1 teaspoon margarine or 2 teaspoons salad dressing, and 1 ounce meat or cheese
1/4 cup dark yellow or dark green vegetables

Snack
1 teaspoon peanut butter
1 slice whole wheat bread or about 5 crackers
1/2 cup fruit juice

Dinner
3/4 cup 2% milk
2 ounces meat, fish or chicken
1/2 cup pasta, rice or potato
1/4 cup vegetable
1 teaspoon margarine or 2 teaspoons salad dressing

The AAP recommends consulting your pediatrician if your children refuse to eat a balanced diet. A vitamin supplement may be needed.

GOOD-BYE ANGER AND FRUSTRATION

When a "battle of the wills" begins, giving your young multiples time to emotionally shift gears from one activity to the next pays off. If it is time to leave the playground or finish a favorite activity, give the children fair warning. Put it in terms they can understand—three more trips down the slide, one more story. Ask the children to repeat what you said so you can be sure they understand. Praise them when they repeat the instructions clearly, and compliment them again when they move on to the next activity without fussing. The ability to listen and cooperate are important skills for your little ones to learn.

LABELS AND FAVORITISM

Favoritism can arise when one child is going through a difficult stage of development. According to Janet Gonzalez-Mena, who teaches early childhood education at Napa Valley College in Napa California, sometimes parents mistake a stage for a lasting personality trait. Toddlers can be defiant and rebellious. She describes this as the "stage of autonomy." If one twin starts into the stage of autonomy before the other, it is important not to label him the rebellious one.

If rebels turn you off, you may well begin to show favoritism to your more compliant child. When one of your children demands more attention, it may happen that the parents spend more time with that child and ignore the one who isn't so needy. Give both children attention even though only one is crying for it.

If one child lives in the shadow of the other, that child might experience feelings of resentment over what he or she perceives as the parents favoring the other twin.

It is important to pay close attention to what your toddlers tell you through both words and behavior. Behavior, including misbehavior, is a form of communication. This can be especially true when you are dealing with toddlers whose use of words is still limited. Parents have to learn to read their children. Awareness is the key to avoiding favoritism.

FLAVORFUL PRESCRIPTION MEDICINES

All parents of 3 and 4 year olds are familiar with what a struggle getting the kids to take their medicine can be. Now some prescription medications are available in delicious flavors. Kenneth Kramm, the founder and president of FLAVORx, developed the new products to make the seizure medicine his daughter required more palatable. There are 42 different FDA-approved flavors that pharmacists can use to disguise the unpleasant taste of many medicines. If your multiples are on a special medication, check with your pediatrician to see if FLAVORx is compatible with their prescriptions. The fancy flavor adds to the cost of the prescription, but it might be worth it to get the kids to take their medicine without a fuss and for parents to be sure their young children are swallowing the prescribed amount.

AN IRON-RICH DIET

Now that your multiples are beginning to feed themselves, it's difficult to make sure they consume the proper amount of nutrients. Toddlers can be fussy eaters and with their new feeding independence they often insist on eating only what they want to eat. According to The Institute of Pediatric Nutrition, toddlers need 10 milligrams of iron daily. Good sources of iron include red meat, eggs, dried fruits, spinach and other green-leaf vegetables. Iron fortified cereals and beverages are also available options. As long as your children's diet is rich with these items, iron supplements shouldn't be necessary. For more information on iron intake or to ask questions regarding children's nutritional requirements, contact the IPN at (800) 721-5222.

HAND AND FINGER MOVEMENTS

Toddlers learn new things everyday. If you look closely, you may see your multiples becoming more and more proficient at manipulating little objects and at putting things together and taking them apart. In the book *Caring for your Baby and Young Child*, the American Academy of Pediatrics urges parents to take note of developing hand and finger skills. During this stage children should start scribbling spontaneously, turning containers to pour out contents, building towers of four or more blocks and possibly using one hand more than the other. Don't be alarmed if your children don't follow this example exactly. All children develop at their own pace. If you have concerns, contact your pediatrician.

SAVE THAT TOOTH

If one of your multiples sustains an injury to the mouth resulting in a broken or loose tooth, would you know what to do? *A Parent's Guide to Medical Emergencies* by Janet Zand, O.M.D., Rachel Walton, R.N., and Bob Rountree, M.D., suggests that acting quickly and following up with your dentist are key. When an injury occurs, carefully clean your child's mouth checking that all teeth are skill intact and in alignment.

Examine the gums and tissue for lacerations. If a tooth has been knocked out, do not be excessively concerned about saving the tooth if it is a baby tooth. However, if it's a permanent tooth, follow these recommendations:

• Do not scrub the tooth.

• Rinse off debris with a prepared solution such as Save-A-Tooth, use saline solution, such as eyewash or the child's own saliva.

• After rinsing, position the tooth in the socket. Do not wait for the dentist to reposition the tooth as replacing it immediately will help prevent clotting in the socket.

If the tooth has been pushed into the socket, firmly take hold of the bone and palate above the tooth with your thumb and forefinger. Gently massage the area to encourage the tooth back into its normal position.

When a permanent tooth is fractured, the inner tooth is exposed. A shallow chip may require minimal cosmetic repair, but a deep fracture demands immediate treatment to prevent infection. Cover the area with plastic wrap and have your child bite down on a piece of folded gauze. As soon as you can, call your dentist and arrange for an emergency appointment.

TAKING CONTROL

As toddlers begin to discover their own will, power struggles start to occur between parents and children. To minimize your toddlers' resistance to your wishes, give them choices, says Janet Gonzalez-Mena, a professor of childhood education. "Choices divert the children's energy from trying to win to trying to decide." When giving medicine to your children, "instead of saying, 'Open your mouth now,' give your children the opportunity to choose. Ask them, 'Do you want the red spoon or the blue one?' or 'Do you want to hold the spoon yourself, or shall I put it in your mouth for you?'" Be sure to make clear that "no medicine" is not a choice. This way, you remain in charge, and your children feel good because they have some control within your limits.

MAKING DEMANDS

Alice Vollmar of Minneapolis, Minnesota, is the mother of six children, including fraternal twins. She is a frequent contributor to TWINS magazine. In a recent conversation with Dr. Lisa Miller, a clinical psychologist at Valley Children's Hospital in Fresno, California, they discussed the importance of meeting each twin's needs when one twin is more demanding. "If a child is particularly demanding, the first step is to rule out physical problems. Next drop the word 'demanding,'" says Dr. Miller. "Encourage parents to reframe their child's behavior positively. Is she more adventurous? More of a leader? More active?" Dr. Miller's strategies for dealing with a demanding twin include:

- Address the source of the demanding behavior. Is the child tired, hungry or bored?
- Set limits and stick to them.
- Respect your child's personality.
- Teach self-comforting techniques, such as cuddling up with a blanket.

- Talk about what he is doing.
- Comment on your twin's behavior when he is being patient.

To help a non-demanding twin feel included, she suggests:

- Tell her you appreciate her patience.
- Spend time each day alone with her.
- Ask her questions and initiate conversation with her.
- Arrange one-on-one outings without the other twin.

More extreme behavior most likely requires professional attention. Some characteristics to look out for include: If one twin inflicts pain on the parents or the other twin, parents notice developmental delays, the child exhibits hyperactivity, which interferes with sleep and learning, or if the child puts himself in danger when he is old enough to know better. If your child displays any of these signs, Dr. Miller recommends a professional evaluation.

FUN, FUN, FUN!

Between the ages of 1 and 2, your multiples will develop better hand-eye coordination as well as the fine motor skills needed to pick up small objects. During this period of growth, children begin to successfully use their thumbs and forefingers to grasp things. Toys that have great appeal and encourage the refinement of these newly developed abilities are board books, simple puzzles and connecting toys, like large stringing beads and large crayons. Many parents of multiples wonder whether they should buy two of everything. At this stage, a variety of books and toys will provide enough fun for everyone. Most parents agree it isn't necessary to duplicate all playthings at this stage, but that occasionally it is nice to select two items, such as special dolls, so that each twin will have a few things that are hers and hers alone.

DOUBLE DIPPING

"Of all the challenges I've encountered in raising young twins, I've found feeding them to be one of the most difficult tasks," says Katherine M. Carlman of Glastonbury, Connecticut, the mother of three daughters, including fraternal twin toddlers. When entertaining guests,

Carlman watched in amazement as her finicky twins dug into the dip with, in her words, "a ferocity unrivaled by wild beasts." She now serves dip at every meal. It's yummy and healthy, too. These are her personal recipes for delightful, delicious "double dipping":

Quick Morning Dip

1/2 cup frozen strawberries
1/2 cup apple juice
2 tablespoons orange juice

Add ingredients to a food processor or blend and whir until smooth. Serve with cut-up waffles or pancakes. (Using frozen waffles or pancakes speeds up preparation time for this fruity breakfast.)

Yummy Yogurt Fruit Dip

1 cup plain yogurt
2 tablespoons brown sugar (or more, depending on your taste)

In a bowl, stir both of the ingredients until smooth. Serve with cut-up fresh fruit, such as bananas, peaches or pears.

Veggie Dip

1 cup plain yogurt
1 tablespoon dry vegetable soup mix
1 package chopped frozen spinach

Defrost spinach and thoroughly drain it. Set aside. Stir the yogurt and soup mix together in a bowl. Add as much spinach as you can. (Reserve the remaining spinach for another batch of dip, or add it to scrambled eggs, soup or other foods.) Serve dip with steamed vegetables.

PLEASE NOTE: Raw vegetables are a choking hazard to small children. Be sure to never serve fresh, hard vegetables to children under the age of 3.

A SANITY SAVER

When Diane Rarick received the news that she was expecting twins, she knew life with three children under 2 was going to require some serious organizing. "When my husband went back to work, I panicked at the thought of being home alone with a toddler and infant twins," said Rarick. What saved her sanity for the next

six months was a set of teenage twins she affectionately called her job-sharing mother's helpers. For a few hours after school each day they did myriad tasks such as folding 150 cloth diapers a week, playing with Nathan while Rarick nursed Katie, taking older brother, Jonathan, outdoors or watching all three kids while she took a nap or shower. "Once in awhile I asked my helpers to load the dishwasher or run the vacuum cleaner. I paid each girl a very reasonable wage which was a small price for preserving my sanity," Rarick recalls. If you are lucky enough to have teenagers you trust, it is a wonderful way to get the extra help you need and a well-deserved break from having the full responsibility for all the kids, everyday, all day.

SHARE AND SHARE ALIKE

Don't be discouraged if your toddler twins have a hard time sharing. It isn't because they're selfish. They're simply too little to understand the concept. Children can't comprehend giving and receiving. They believe what is theirs is only theirs. One way to encourage sharing at this young age is to use words of reason. Ask one twin if it would be OK to let her sister play with the toy when she is finished. If she still says no, don't persist. Try again another time. Eventually your twins will understand how to share, and it will become second nature.

IN THE EARLY YEARS

Research on the human brain continues to show that the first years are the most important, says Janet Gonzalez-Mena, a professor of childhood education at Napa Valley College in Napa, California. What happens early on determines how the brain develops. Children need to "make connections," say the brain experts. "As a long-time professor, I've seen information like this grab parents up and spin them around," Mena says. "Each time new scientific information comes out, a flurry of products hits the market—products to stimulate babies and make them smarter.

"However, the implications of the new brain research are very simple: Pay attention to your children. Talk to them. What they need is not more stuff, but connections to adults. Multiples have the advantage of each other to connect to, but that is not enough by itself. They need interactions with adults they are attached to—adults who touch, hold, talk to them and help them explore and understand their world."

COPING STRATEGIES

In her master's research project, "The Stress Level of Parents of Multiples As Measured by the Parenting Stress Index," Lisa Cantwell-Bruce, a nurse and mother of four, including twins, found that many parents of multiples have difficulty adjusting to the stresses of parenting in two areas: They find that parenting multiples takes over their identity, and they see their partners as less helpful and supportive than they had envisioned. After interviewing several moms and analyzing her own experiences, she found simple strategies to help parents maintain their identities, as well as improve their parenting partnerships:

Get out of the house—Take a walk with your multiples. It's affordable, healthy and a great way to meet other parents in your neighborhood.

Join clubs—Be sure to enroll in your local parents of multiples club to lessen the isolation you may feel.

Talk with your partner—Make time to talk face to face with no interruptions, even if it's only for a few minutes each day. This keeps the lines of communication open. ♥

- **Allison Berryhill**, of Atlantic, Iowa, is a freelance writer and the mother of six, including twin boys born in September 1994.
- **Linda Baraban**, of Topeka, Kansas, is a registered nurse and the founder of a Kansas City-area group for the parents of higher multiples. She is the mother of triplets.
- **R.C. Barajas**, of Arlington, Virginia, is a freelance writer and the mother of three, including twin boys born in December 1994.
- **Vera Caccioppoli**, of Falls Church, Virginia, is a freelance writer and the mother of triplet boys.
- **Jill Case, M.A., L.P.C., N.C.C.**, of Colorado Springs, Colorado, is a professional counselor specializing in play therapy. She is the mother of four, including boy/girl twins born in Oct.1996.
- **Patricia Edmister, Ph.D.**, of Sherman Oaks, California, is the director of developmental psychology and children's study at the California Family Study Center. She is the mother of boy/girl twins.
- **Pat Fasanella**, of Menominee, Michigan, is a freelance writer and the mother of identical twin boys.
- **Joanne M. Gonsalves**, of Denver, Colorado, is a registered nurse, freelance writer and the mother of four.
- **Janet Gonzalez-Mena**, of Napa, California, teaches early childhood education at Napa Valley College. She is the author of the book, *Dragon Mom*, and the mother of five children.
- **Elizabeth Hyde**, of Boulder, Colorado, is an attorney and a freelance writer, and the mother of three, including twin girls.
- **Kay Lynn Isca**, of Fort Wayne, Indiana, is the publisher of the newsletter, *Japan Notebook*, and the mother of four, including identical twins.
- **Michelle Krupp Leow**, of Toledo, Ohio, is a freelance writer and the mother of three, including fraternal twins.
- **Cheryle Levitt** is a pediatric nurse and mother of three children, including fraternal twins.
- **Bruce Littman, M.D.**, is a practicing general pediatrician in Canoga Park, California. He is an assistant clinical professor of pediatrics at the UCLA School of Medicine and the father of two children.
- **Adam P. Matheny, Jr., Ph.D.**, is a professor of pediatrics at the University of Louisville School of Medicine and the director of the Louisville Twin Study.

- **Michael K. Meyerhoff, EdD.**, has been the Administrative Director of the Center for Parent Education in Newton, Massachusetts. He has conducted workshops on "Educating the Infant and Toddler" throughout the United States and Canada, and has developed many parent-education programs.
- **Eileen M. Pearlman**, of Santa Monica, California, is a psychotherapist and the director of TwInsight. She is an identical twin, is married to a fraternal twin, and has two daughters.
- **Bethany Reid**, of Bothell, Washington, teaches literature and English composition at the University of Washington and is the mother of fraternal twins.
- **Colline Schibig**, of Bethpage, Tennessee, is a freelance writer and the mother of boy/girl twins.
- **Diane M. Sharon**, of New York City, is the acquisitions editor at Boardroom, Inc. and has identical twin girls.
- **Celeste N. Schroeder**, of Port Moody, British Columbia, is a freelance writer and the mother of three boys, including twins born in 1994.
- **Lawrence J. Schweinhart, Ph.D.**, is co-director of the Center for the Study of Public Policies for Young Children at the High/Scope Educational Research Foundation in Ypsilanti, Michigan, and is co-author of the book, *Young Children Growing Up: The Effects of the Perry Preschool Program on Youths Through Age 15*.
- **Harriet F. Simons, LICSW, Ph.D.**, is an adjunct member of the faculty of South College of Social Work and has a private practice in Wellesley, Massachusetts. She is the mother of a daughter and boy/girl twins, all of whom are now toilet trained.
- **Patricia M. Stein, R.D.**, is co-author of *Anorexia Nervosa: Finding the Lifeline*. She has more than 20 years experience in the field of nutrition counseling and a private nutrition counseling practice.
- **J. Cameron Tew**, of Wendell, North Carolina, is editor of the *Raleigh Extra* and the father of triplet boys.
- **Alice M. Vollmar**, of Minneapolis, Minnesota, is a freelance writer and the mother of grown male/female twins.
- **Tina W. Zimmerman**, of Augusta, Georgia, is a speech pathologist, freelance writer and the mother of twin girls born in August 1992.

More Parenting Resources
From the Publishers of TWINS

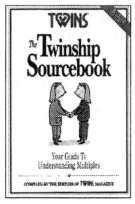

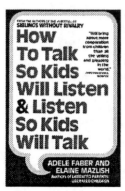

TWINS Magazine

CHILDREN'S BOOKS

A selection of simple, delightful stories and rhyming books featuring multiples.
These are some of the finalists from the TWINS Magazine Fiction Contest.

Many more children's books available, including more than 15 EXCLUSIVE
TWINS Books! Check out the GREAT SELECTION at www.TWINSmagazine.com

---

TWINS® BOOKSHELF ORDER FORM

Please send me the following books:

LIST BOOKS

	PRICE x QUANTITY	AMOUNT DUE
_____	x _____	_____
_____	x _____	_____
_____	x _____	_____
_____	x _____	_____
_____	x _____	_____
_____	x _____	_____

SUBTOTAL _____

Sales Tax (Colorado residents only, add 3.8%) _____

Shipping & Handling (see chart on right) _____

TOTAL AMOUNT DUE _____

SHIPPING & HANDLING

$ 0 to $25.00	$3.00
$25.01 to $35.00	$4.00
$35.01 to $45.00	$5.00
$45.01 to $55.00	$6.00
$55.01 to $90.00	$7.00
$90.00 +	Please call

EXPRESS SHIPPING
(3 to 4 day delivery)
Add $1.00 per book (children's books)
Add $3.00 per book (adult books)

INTERNATIONAL SHIPPING
Surface delivery -
Add $1.00 per book to Regular S&H

Airmail delivery -
Add $25.00 to Regular S&H

PAYMENT MUST ACCOMPANY ORDER
Payment enclosed (Payable to TWINS Magazine)   Bill my: ☐ MasterCard   ☐ VISA ☐ AMEX   ☐ Discover

CARD NUMBER _____   EXPIRATION DATE _____

NAME ON CREDIT CARD _____   SIGNATURE _____

NAME OF RECIPIENT _____   PHONE _____

ADDRESS _____

CITY _____   STATE _____   ZIP _____

Send your order to: TWINS Magazine • 5350 S. Roslyn Street, Ste. 400 • Englewood, CO 80111

Tel: 1-888-55-TWINS (toll-free) 1-888-558-9467 Fax: 303-290-9025